Ghost Towns and Mining Camps of New Mexico

University of Oklahoma Press : Norman

GHOST TOWNS AND MINING CAMPS OF NEW MEXICO

James E. and Barbara H. Sherman

Maps by Jim Cooper

By James E. and Barbara H. Sherman

Ghost Towns of Arizona (Norman, 1969)
Ghost Towns and Mining Camps of New Mexico (Norman, 1974)

Library of Congress Cataloging in Publication Data

Sherman, James E.
    Ghost towns and mining camps of New Mexico.

    Bibliography: p. 259
    1. Cities and towns, Ruined, extinct, etc.—New Mexico. 2. New Mexico—History. I. Sherman, Barbara H., joint author. II. Title.
F796.S47   917.89   72–9525
ISBN 0–8061–1066–X (hardback); ISBN 0–8061–1106–2 (paper)

To our son David, a good trooper

Preface

This book is planned to serve as a pleasant diversion and fun guide into New Mexico's colorful past. Its purpose is to lure and fascinate the tourist as well as the New Mexican adventurer. New Mexico is a treasury of defunct mining camps, abandoned railroad towns, and deserted farming and lumbering communities. Since the list is endless, we have selected a cross section of ghost towns and mining camps throughout the state. In this book a ghost town is defined as a community that has lost the commercial impetus that gave it its original life. The communities may or may not be totally deserted, but all have retired from the rapid pace of modern-day living.

The accuracies of the town's vignettes are only as reliable as the sources. Included among the standard references are reports from newspapers, journals, and early records, all of which may well be partial and lacking in objectivity. We have employed the information as we found it. Glimpses of approximately 130 old towns are presented, along with many old and contemporary photographs, advertisements, and maps.

Aided by a grant from the American Association for State and Local History, we visited well over a hundred ghost towns or their sites, interviewed scores of people, collected over three thousand photographs and consulted the major libraries in the state during our research into New Mexico's legacy.

We express our deepest gratitude to the many libraries, research associations, and other persons who aided us in compiling this book. We extend our sincere thanks to the American Association for State and Local History for their much appreciated grant; to the Museum of New Mexico at Santa Fe and their competent staff, Dr. John Polich, Lucille Stacy, and Sally Wagner; to New Mexico State Library at Santa Fe and their efficient and courteous librarians Virginia Jennings and William Farrington; to New Mexico Record Center and Archives at Santa Fe and its highly proficient staff, Dr. Myra Ellen Jenkins and Richard Salazar; New Mexico Highlands University at Las Vegas and chief librarian, David Eshner; *New Mexico Magazine* and editor George Fitzpatrick; Zimmerman Library at the University of New Mexico in Albuquerque and librarian Phil Fangan; Albuquerque Public Library and Katherine McMahon; Gallup Public Library and Octavia Fellin; Socorro Public Library and Mrs. Charles Holmes; Old Lincoln County Courthouse and Belle Wilson; New Mexico State University Library at Las Cruces and Mrs. Buder; Black Range Museum at Hillsboro and Lydia Key; Silver City Public Library and Mrs. M. L. Lundwall; Western New Mexico University Library at Silver City; Library of Congress and Victor Margolin; National Archives; California Historical Society; Pinkerton's Inc.; Hoover Library, West Branch, Iowa; National Archives; Department of Postal Research; University of Arizona Special Collections, Tucson, Arizona; Pioneers' Historical Society, Tucson, and the U.S. Geological Survey, Denver, Colorado.

It is virtually impossible for us to list everyone who in some way contributed to the preparation of this book. During the two summers we spent traveling throughout New Mexico, we were greatly impressed by the warm hospitality and overwhelming friendliness shown to us by the many persons whom we encountered. Although we are unable to acknowledge each individual who helped us, we express special thanks to the following for interviews, photographs, and information: to Thomas Adlon and Mr. and Mrs. Mike Stead of Albuquerque; Earl Morgan, Alma; Jackie S. Silvers, Ancho; Cora Boone, Carrizozo; Mr. and Mrs. George Pendleton, Cloverdale; Louis Battisti and the Pancho Villa Museum at Columbus; Florentino Padilla, Cuba; Frank Ray of Gold Hill Ranch; Mr. and Mrs. Moises Mirabal, Grants; Babe Thorn, Hermosa; Ralph Lindsey, Hillsboro; William Tipton, Las Cruces; Audrey Simpson and the W. W. Walker Family of Las Vegas; Glen H. Dorsett, Lordsburg; Joe Huber and Edward Kissler of Madrid; Rev. E. Debaenst, Magdalena; James Giles, Mogollon; Bonnie Smith and Herman Wisner of Organ; Mr. and Mrs. Fred Dixon, Pena Blanca; F. Stanley, Pep, Texas; Bob Anderson, Mr. and Mrs. Frank Berry, V. A. Dogget, Ruth Hart, Joe Kastler, Dorothy Meng, Evelyn Shuler, John Southwell, Joe Taylor, Claude Vit, Louise Wright, and Joe Young of Raton; Mrs. Dean Fite and John Ramirez of San Antonio; Frank, Rita, and Janaloo Hill of Shakespeare; Lucien File, George Griswold, and Lena Meriwether of Socorro; Jack Boyer and the Kit Carson Museum at Taos; George Eckhart, Tucson, Arizona; and Bud Crenshaw, White Oaks.

Our personal thanks to our son, David, for his good nature during the rigors of research and traveling; Jim Cooper for his excellent maps; Jim McBain, of Scot Photo, for his fine service; Heinrichs Geoexploration Co., for the time off to finish the book, and to Joe and Bettie Gilliland for their tent. To the many other individuals throughout New Mexico who allowed us to trespass on their property and gave us directions, and to those authors whose previous works were invaluable, our thanks and appreciation. We are deeply indebted to all who helped make *Ghost Towns and Mining Camps of New Mexico*.

JAMES E. AND BARBARA H. SHERMAN
Tucson, Arizona

January 23, 1974

Contents

Preface	*vii*
Albemarle	2A
Allerton	2A
Allison	3A
Alma	3A
Amizette	7A
Ancho	8A
Andrews	10A
Baldy	10A
Black Hawk	12B
Bland	13B
Blossburg	16B
Bonanza City	19B
Bonito City	20B
Brice	21B
Brilliant	21B
Cabezon	24C
Carbonateville	26C
Carlisle	30C
Carthage	32C
Catskill	34C
Cerrillos	38C
Chance City	42C
Chloride	42C
Clairmont	48C
Clarkville	48C
Cloverdale	49C
Coalora	50C
Colfax	50C
Columbus	51C
Cooks Peak	56C
Coolidge	58C
Cooney	58C
Copper City	60C
Copperton	60C
Council Rock	61C
Dawson	63D
Diener	69D
Dolores	70D
Elizabethtown	73E
Engle	78E

Estey City	81E
Faywood Hot Springs	82F
Fleming	84F
Gamerco	86G
Gardiner	87G
Georgetown	91G
Gibson	94G
Glen-Woody	96G
Glorieta	96G
Gold Dust	99G
Golden	100G
Gold Hill	102G
Grafton	102G
Graham	104G
Hachita and Old Hachita	105H
Hagan and Coyote	107H
Hematite	109H
Hermanas	109H
Hermosa	110H
Hillsboro	112H
Jicarilla	116J
Johnson Mesa	117J
Kelly	120K
Kingston	124K
Koehler	129K
La Bajada	130L
La Belle	131L
Lake Valley	132L
La Ventana	136L
Leopold	137L
Lincoln	138L
Madrid	148M
Malone	152M
Mentmore	152M
Midnight and Anchor	153M
Mineral City	154M
Modoc	154M
Mogollon	155M
Navajo	162N
Nutt	162N
Oak Grove	163O
Organ	163O
Orogrande	166O
Otero	166O
Park City	167P
Parsons	168P
Paschal	169P
Perryville	169P
Pinos Altos	169P

Pyramid	170P	Telegraph	206T
Rabenton	172P	Tererro	206T
Red River	174R	Tierra Blanca	208T
Riley	175R	Tokay	208T
Robinson	177R	Trementina	208T
Rosedale	178R	Twining	210T
Sacramento City	179S	Tyrone	213T
San Antonio	180S	Valedon	217V
San Augustine	182S	Valmont	220V
San Geronimo	182S	Van Houten	220V
San Marcial	184S	Vera Cruz	222V
San Pedro	186S	Virginia City	222V
Santa Rita	188S	Waldo	223W
Sawyer	192S	White Oaks	224W
Senorito	193S	Winston	229W
Shakespeare	195S	Yankee	234Y
Shandon	198S		
Steins	198S	Maps	237
Sugarite	200S		
Swastika	202S	Selected Bibliography	259
Sylvanite	204S	Index	262

x |

To the Reader

The special format of Ghost Towns and Mining Camps of New Mexico *was designed for convenient reference. The towns appear in alphabetical order, from Albemarle to Yankee, and along with the page number is printed the alphabetical letter of the towns on that page.*

Directly under the name of each town is listed the county in which it is located, the direction and distance in miles from the nearest present-day town, the page number of the map upon which the ghost town is located, and the date when the first post office was established and when it was discontinued.

Albemarle

COUNTY: *Sandoval*
LOCATION: *about 30 mi. southwest of Los Alamos*
MAP: *page 243*
P.O. est. 1901; discont. 1903.

Thirteen mining claims known as the Albemarle group were located by Henry Woods, Norman Blotcher, and Chester Greenwood about January of 1894. The property passed into the hands of the Cochiti Gold Mining Company, which developed the mines and brought the mining camp to life.

The Albemarle group was situated in the steep, towering walls of Colla Canyon. Pockets had to be blasted out of the walls to provide room for the mine and mill buildings. The electrical power for the mine was transmitted from Madrid, a distance of thirty-five miles. Albemarle's Main Street stretched out below, in the bottom of the narrow canyon. Albemarle was often considered to be part of the Bland township, a larger mining camp three and a half miles away in Bland Canyon.

A road was built connecting Colla and Bland canyons. Although only a few miles in length, it was a remarkable engineering feat, blasted out of rock and costing fifty thousand dollars. A one-mile stretch of the road winding up the face of the cliff was forced to ascend fifteen hundred feet. Soon heavily laden freight wagons began rolling along the newly constructed road, their iron tires eventually wearing eight-inch ruts into the solid rock. A story is told of two freight drivers, experienced Old Man Morgan and the other a less experienced driver from Santa Fe. One day at Bland, Morgan had his team hitched up and ready for the tedious, heavy pull up the road to Albemarle, when the Santa Fe freighter, noticing the number of horses Morgan was using, commented that he could make the same haul with only two mules. The casual remark reached the ears of some passing miners, and the bets were on. Morgan, knowing what the outcome would be, refused to become involved as the Santa Fe man hitched up his mules and started for Albemarle. Moments later, on the most perilous section of the road, one of the mules slipped. Pandemonium broke loose, and the wagon and team toppled over the cliff. The freight was lost, one mule broke his neck, the other had to be shot, and the poor, disillusioned driver spent time in the hospital.

As the mines deepened, the ore decreased in value, a development which soon caused Albemarle's death. The large stamp mill completed only three years earlier, in 1899, closed indefinitely in 1902. The wooden buildings of the mining camp collapsed, and the mill equipment rusted as Nature began spreading her mantle of camouflage.

Allerton

COUNTY: *Sandoval*
LOCATION: *about 30 mi. southwest of Los Alamos*
MAP: *page 243*
P.O. est. 1894; discont. 1896. Re-est. as Woodbury, 1899; discont. 1903.

References to Allerton are scanty. It was probably the same place later known as Woodbury, or, if not, at least these two camps were very closely allied. Allerton was the older of the two, getting its start about 1894. On February 26 of that year a meeting was called by holders of mining claims in Pino Canyon, who elected officers and organized a townsite company known as the Allerton Town Company. In 1897 Allerton reported a population of fifty and the following businesses: Blain Bros., general merchandise; W. D. McCoy, groceries; P. Tinan, saloon; J. Chipman, meat market; and J. K. Sayles, saloon. The Allerton post office had been discontinued the year before. Mining was the principal resource which supported this apparently small and short-lived community.

In 1896 the Woodbury mill was built about seven miles below Bland, to reduce ore from the Iron King Mine. The plant was owned by the Cochiti Reduction and Improvement Company of Denver, of which R. W. Woodbury was president. In July, 1900, the mill at Woodbury was reported as having been totally destroyed by fire. Lightning started the blaze, which caused a loss of thirty thousand dollars, with no insurance. By November a new mill at Woodbury was under construction, with several six-horse teams engaged in hauling the mill machinery from Thornton. It was related that the cyanide process used at the mill extracted only 40 per cent of the ore values, leaving 60 per cent to flow down the creek in the mill tailings and pollute the water badly. Dead rodents, rabbits, and dogs were a common sight along this stretch of the stream. The mill was apparently never much of a success.

Allerton and Woodbury, presuming they were the same place, have vanished.

Allison

COUNTY: *McKinley*
LOCATION: *3 mi. northwest of Gallup*
MAP: *page 245*
P.O. est. 1913; discont. 1937.

Allison, located on a coal belt just northwest of Gallup, once flourished as a coal mining camp. Now, greatly reduced in size, the community claims a small cluster of homes and shade trees on a dirt road.

Before coming into the ownership of its namesake, Fletcher J. Allison, in 1897, the Allison Mine was opened by Gus Mulholland and later worked by Andrew Casna. After Casna was killed at the mine, presumably by Indians, his aggrieved widow fled to Germany, where she remained for a number of years. Her failure to keep up the development work necessary to retain her husband's claim resulted in a filing on the mine site by F. J. Allison and W. A. Patching. They worked the Allison Mine until 1917, when the Diamond Coal Company bought them out. Allison was a company-owned town. Employees lived in the three- and four-room houses, supplied with water and electricity, owned by the Diamond Coal Company. In addition to providing a livelihood for Allison residents, the company also furnished recreation for its employees in the form of tennis courts and a company-sponsored baseball team. The town reported a population of five hundred, a company store and meat market, post office, school, physician, and deputy sheriff.

Alma

COUNTY: *Catron*
LOCATION: *7 mi. north of Glenwood*
MAP: *page 253*
P.O. est. 1882; discont. 1896. Re-est. 1900; discont. 1931.

Alma has had a long life. The place still boasts a population of four or five families in the valley, but the business life of the town has long since disappeared. The old post office building is now a private residence, and another building, once a home, stands weathered and abandoned in a clump of trees. At one time the house was flanked on either side by a dance hall and a hotel, but both are gone.

Alma's history began in 1878 when a handful of settlers, John Keller, Robert Stubblefield, Maurice Coates, John Roberts, W. H. Beavers, and Morris Smith and his family, left Prescott, Arizona, and after a long journey by wagon arrived in the Frisco Valley at the place later known as Alma. Here they built cabins and settled down to an industrious life of ranching.

Precautions were taken against the Apaches, who chose not to disturb the newcomers until the spring of 1879. At that time a roving band of Apaches made a raid on the Frisco Valley, killing some of Keller's cattle. Obtaining the assistance of three other settlers, Keller and his party went after the Indians. Taking a detour, the party raced to Whitewater Canyon, where they tied a saddled horse to a tree to attract the Apaches. When the Indians arrived and took the bait, they were instantly fired upon by Keller and the other men. Three of the five Indians fell. The death of one of the Apaches was to cause much destruction and trouble for the settlers of Frisco Valley. He was Toribio, son-in-law of the chief, Victorio. Some people believe that it was revenge for Toribio's death that caused Victorio to go on the warpath. During April of 1880, Victorio and his band swept through the Frisco Valley and attacked the communities of Alma, Cooney, and Pleasanton. The attack on Alma lasted twenty-four hours and resulted in the death or injury of many settlers. One of the men killed was named Willcox. With his death was lost the secret of the location of a gold claim he had discovered a few days previously.

The Apache depredations continued to plague the valley. Five years later Victorio's successor, Geronimo, returned to the Alma area, raiding and killing. The constant menace of the Apaches caused many difficulties and hardships for the ranchers. During the eighties, mail coaches through the valley were forced to travel only at night for the daylight hours were deemed unsafe. Along the route coach drivers often saw small piles of stones with a broken twig or blade of grass across them. These were Apache signs, used to convey information unintelligible to white men. It became a habit among the coach drivers to rearrange or destroy the signs.

In spite of the Indian trouble, Alma continued to grow and prosper, reaching its height after 1880. The discovery of gold and silver ore at the nearby Cooney Mine tremendously boosted Alma's economy. Alma soon became the base of supplies for the surrounding ranches and mining camps. The mid-1880's found Alma with a steam mill, a stamp mill, saloons, general stores, hotel, blacksmith, shoemaker, physician, justice of the peace, and a population of 150 persons.

One of the cattle spreads nearby was the WS Ranch. A preacher who lived near Alma often had his Sunday sermons attended by the ranch cowboys. When his lengthy sermon ended, the boys and the preacher generally adjourned to the saloon across the street for a thirst quencher. On one occasion, when the parson indulged too liberally and completely passed out, the WS boys bound his his hands and feet, lifted him into a wagon, and sent him home. The good preacher's dignity was so shattered that he refused to preach for them again.

During the late 1890's the WS Ranch became the headquarters for Butch Cassidy and some of the Wild Bunch. Unknowingly, the ranch manager, Captain William French, hired the notorious Cassidy and some of his gang to work on the ranch. The ranch had been suffering from cattle rustling, but after Cassidy and his men took over, the rustling stopped. The Wild Bunch proved to be good workers and for a time stayed at the ranch. They were known by aliases—Cassidy as Jim Lowe and one of the gang members, Elza Lay, as William H. McGinnis. In time, McGinnis quit his job at the ranch and shortly afterward was recognized as one of the bandits in a train holdup near Folsom, New Mexico. About that time, Cassidy alias Lowe was offered the job as French's foreman at the WS. Although French had discovered Lowe's true identity, he liked the fellow and figured Lowe intended to go straight. The outlaw declined the offer, realizing the ranch might suffer if it became known that it was headquarters for the Wild Bunch. Shortly thereafter, Cassidy left the ranch.

McGinnis spent time in the penitentiary for his part in the Folsom robbery, but when released returned to Alma and lived there for two years. He stayed with Louis and Walter Jones, who in 1904 had built a large merchandise store at Alma. An addition on one side of the store contained a bar and, behind that, a utility room where saddles, ropes, and other cattlemen's equipment were stored. McGinnis claimed he knew where some money had been buried under a juniper tree on the Mexican border. One day he saddled his horse and told the Jones brothers that he would be gone two weeks. Thirteen days later he arrived back in Alma with fifty-eight thousand dollars. He dumped the money in a corner of the utility room, where it remained untouched until McGinnis left for Wyoming several months later. He reportedly went straight after he invested the money in a cattle ranch.

In 1913, Alma was reported to be a thriving and thrifty community, with a population of four hundred persons. A liberal populace estimate in 1936 was a hundred residents. By that time the post office had already been closed five years, so it is assumed that Alma's halcyon days were over.

Elton A. Cunningham, owner of the Cunningham Store in Alma.—*Courtesy Blachly Collection, University of Arizona, Special Collection.*

Alma, *circa* 1895: (1) Cunningham Store, (2) Jones-McKeen Merchantile Co.—*Courtesy James Giles.*

Above—The Wild Bunch. Left to right, standing, Bill Carver, Harvy Logan; sitting, Harry Longabaugh (Sundance Kid), Ben Kilpatrick, George L. Parker (Butch Cassidy).—*Courtesy Pinkerton's Inc.*

Right—Coupon book of the Oaks Company.—*Courtesy James Giles.*

Below—Alma, *circa* 1910. Jones-McKeen Merchantile Co.—*Courtesy James Giles.*

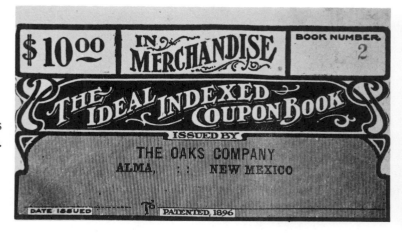

$10.00 IN MERCHANDISE BOOK NUMBER 2
THE IDEAL INDEXED COUPON BOOK
ISSUED BY
THE OAKS COMPANY
ALMA, :: NEW MEXICO
DATE ISSUED PATENTED, 1896

The
Jones-McKeen
Merc. Co.

Amizette, *circa* 1895. Main Street, looking northeast up Hondo Canyon.—*Courtesy Gusdorf Collection, Kit Carson Museum.*

Amizette

COUNTY: *Taos*
LOCATION: *14 mi. northeast of Taos*
MAP: *page 239*
P.O. est. 1893; discont. 1902.

Amizette, the once-acclaimed "Cripple Creek of New Mexico," has vanished. The log cabins were dismantled years ago, erasing the name of Amizette from the map. Although there is no ghost town to explore, a drive up Río Hondo Canyon offers rewarding mountain scenery.

The year was 1893 and the lure was gold when prospector Al Helphinstine and his wife, Amizette, moved up the canyon, refurbished an old cabin as a hotel, and ran a post office. As others followed, a town materialized and was named in honor of Mrs. Helphinstine. In addition to the eager Argonauts who rushed to Amizette there came the practical-minded Gerson Gusdorf, who saw money in merchandise. Well supplied with flour, shovels, some dynamite, and other commodities of necessity, he drove the first wagon up the densely aspen-wooded canyon, clearing a rough road as he went. Gerson set up shop in a tent until his wood-framed store was erected.

Saloons and dance halls, the inevitable twosome of mining camps, took root overnight as scores of people surged into the new town. Feverish excitement prevailed as gold pans scraped the Río Hondo and tunnels were burrowed into the mountains.

The gold was there. It was found and extracted, but there was no cheap means available of hauling it out of the canyon. Gerson Gusdorf and his brother, owners of the Shoshone Mine, were offered twenty thousand dollars for their property by Governor John L. Route of Colorado. They refused to sell and, as fate would have it, never made any money from the mine. The lack of cheap transportation shattered many a dream of the quick fortune. No one made any money except perhaps the Denver backers of the Rio Hondo Placer Company, who cashed in on the real estate potential of Amizette and sold lots. Gradually the 350 or so residents who formed Amizette drifted away, until the town was essentially depopulated. The boom had lasted one year.

Amizette revived for a time after 1895, when gold was found on nearby Gold Hill. In the year 1897 a population of two hundred was reported, as well as ten producing mines with an estimated daily output of six hundred tons of gold, silver, copper, and lead ore, plenty of good wood and water, and miners' wages of $4 a day.

Several years later, copper ore discoveries at the head of Río Hondo Canyon sounded a new cry, and the boom town of Twining superseded Amizette as the core of mining activity.

Above—Gerson Gusdorf (1869–1951), prominent merchant of Amizette.—*Courtesy Gusdorf Collection, Kit Carson Museum.*

Right—Amizette, 1895. Left to right, Aloysius Liebert's Saloon, Gusdorf's Store.—*Courtesy Weimer Collection, Kit Carson Museum.*

8
A

Ancho

COUNTY: *Lincoln*
LOCATION: *26 mi. northeast of Carrizozo*
MAP: *page 249*
P.O. est. 1902; discont. 1969.

In the summer of 1901 the railroad began pushing into the Ancho Valley. A year later a gypsum deposit was discovered which resulted in the building of gypsum testing plants, small sawmills used in connection with the plants, and finally the Gypsum Product Company plaster mill. This activity was followed by the discovery of fire clay and subsequent building of the Ancho Brick Plant, which developed into Ancho's major industry. The plaster mill, brick plant, lumbering, and railroad work supplied income for the prospering community of Ancho.

Ancho supplied several hundred tons of plaster to help rebuild San Francisco after the disastrous 1906 earthquake. Special blocks from the Ancho Brick Plant were used in the smelter stacks at Douglas, Arizona. Phelps Dodge bought the brick plant in 1917 and built a larger, more modern one consisting of sixteen kilns. The plant was in active production until 1921. In 1937 the Abileen Salvage Company purchased the property and dismantled the plant.

Today deserted company buildings and ruins dot both sides of the railroad tracks. Ancho's original one-room school burned down about 1930 and was replaced by the present school building, made of Ancho brick. The school closed in 1955, and the building is now used as a community hall. At one time 140 children attended school at Ancho, and two stores served the town. Now there are no stores. The town's combination store and gas station closed in September, 1963. The train depot built in 1902 closed for business in 1959 and was later moved to its present site north of the tracks where it now houses "My House of Old Things," an interesting museum. Today, only a few people live in Ancho.

Above—Ancho, 1918. Left building, company store. Right, first company houses built in Ancho.—*Courtesy Jackie S. Silvers.*

Abandoned homes of the plaster mill workers, looking northeast.

My House of Old Things Museum and Ancho post office, originally the Ancho depot.

Below—Ancho, 1918. New brick plant built by Phelps Dodge Corporation.—*Courtesy Jackie S. Silvers.*

Andrews

COUNTY: *Sierra*
LOCATION: *about 7 miles northeast of Hillsboro*
MAP: *page 251*
P.O. est. 1898; discont. 1907.

Located seven miles northeast of Hillsboro, Andrews was no doubt overshadowed by its more prosperous neighbor. Listed as its assets in 1905 were a population of a hundred inhabitants, a post office, two combination stores and saloons, and four mining companies. In the approximate vicinity of the one-time mining camp are some building ruins which may or may not have been Andrews.

Baldy

COUNTY: *Colfax*
LOCATION: *about 12 mi. northeast of Eagle Nest*
MAP: *page 239*
P.O. est. 1888; discont. 1926.

The strike that set off a boom and gave birth to the short-lived Virginia City, the long-lived Elizabethtown and the mountain burg of Baldy took place in the early 1860's. When a Ute Indian displayed a piece of rich copper float at Fort Union, W. H. Kroenig and William Moore paid the Indian to guide them to the outcrop from which the piece had come. The location was near the top of barren Baldy Mountain. Here, in 1866, the two men staked the Mystic Lode copper mine. Later that year Kroenig and Moore sent three men to do some assessment work at the mine. Camping at Willow Creek, one of the three began to idly pan for gold along the edge of the stream while waiting for his companions to cook supper. His first pan revealed color. Astonished and excited, the three began feverishly scraping gold from the stream, forgetting about the copper property and the assessment work. With winter near at hand, the men were forced to return to Fort Union. They were vowed to secrecy, but the news of their gold discovery inevitably leaked out. The next spring a wholesale stampede converged at Willow Creek and fanned out into every gulch and creek bed around Baldy Mountain. The Aztec Lode, discovered in 1868, was said to be the richest discovery in the west. High-grading was not above the men who worked the Aztec. It is said that they often slipped gold nuggets into their boots and trouser pockets. One high-grader was traced as far away as Chicago, where he had sold fifteen thousand dollars worth of gold.

As a result of all the mining activity several communities sprang up, and Baldy was one of them. High on the mountain, the camp had two boardinghouses large enough to house a hundred men. Supposedly, across the barroom wall inside Hotel Baldy was a painted line and the words "Altitude 10,000 feet—high, windy and lusty." Baldy lived for many years, but probably was at its peak in the early 1880's.

In 1897 Baldy claimed two hundred inhabitants, a public school, Methodist church services every Sunday, twelve producing mines, four stamp mills, a telephone line from Springer, a blacksmith, tailor, barber, launderer, justice of the peace, and the usual saloons, general stores, and livery stable.

When W. P. McIntyre arrived at Baldy in 1899, about three million dollars worth of gold had been mined from the area around the mountain. McIntyre was convinced that the mother lode rested somewhere in the hidden depths of Baldy Mountain, and so he generated the idea of a tunnel. He and his brother Alex devoted the rest of their lives to the tunnel project. The Gold and Copper Deep Tunnel Mining and Milling Company was incorporated in October, 1900, and the plan was to burrow into the mountain two thousand feet below the peak. For thirty-six years two tunnels in opposite directions ate into the mountainside. W. P. McIntyre died in 1930, with the project still unfinished. Six years later the tunnels met within an inch of each other in the heart of the mountain, but the mother lode was not there.

Baldy's life was finished. About 1941 the buildings of the town were razed. The site has been taken over by the Philmont Boy Scout Ranch, but a few relics of the mining camp are still visible, a smelter slag pile, the ruins of a stone building and chimney, mill foundations, and mine tailing dumps.

Above—Present ruins of rock building at Baldy.

Left—Foundations of gravity-fed mill. The site of Baldy is presently used by the Philmont Boy Scout Ranch.

Below—Baldy, coming of the telegraph, circa 1891.—*Courtesy Museum of New Mexico.*

Black Hawk

COUNTY: *Grant*
LOCATION: *about 16 mi. east of Silver City*
MAP: *page 255*
P.O. est. 1884; discont. 1887.

In 1881 a Negro named Bowman—but better known as "Cherokee Jim"—discovered a rich silver float in the Bullard's Peak district at the north end of the Burro Mountains. As a result of this discovery, John Black and his partner, Sloan, traced the float found by Bowman and discovered and located the source, the Blue Bell Mine, later known as the Alhambra. Shortly thereafter, the discovery of the Rose and Black Hawk mines produced the camp at Bullard's Peak. The end of the summer of 1883 saw about thirty steadily employed men at the camp, but by November the number had upped to 125, creating the necessity for an official townsite. Three of the camp pioneers, Twomey, Sullivan, and Lothian, appointed themselves the task. The townsite was laid out on a narrow mesa near the Black Hawk Mine. The new town reportedly was to be named "Carson" in honor of J. H. Carson, a resident of the community, but instead the name Black Hawk was adopted. Residential lots sold at a moderate price were soon dotted with substantial frame houses. Business lots varied in price from fifty to a hundred dollars, according to their location. Enterprise soon took hold, and business began to flourish. "Pap" Likes, the genial stage driver, put on the road a handsome coach christened the "Matt France" in honor of the manager of the mining company. The business place of Kerr and Sullivan, known as the Harp and Shamrock, celebrated a grand opening with the camp's first stag dance. It was the scene of much amusement, as four couples hoed down in hobnailed boots. Mrs. Nicolas opened a first-class eating house, a new lodging-house was constructed, and a bath parlor was erected next to Mr. Phillips' shaving establishment. Two Chinese arrived with their washing supplies, but quickly departed when told the place was unhealthy for them. Mr. Phillips had a monopoly of the laundry business. An attempt at cultural refinement was the organization of the camp singing society known as the Burro Glee Club.

Black Hawk witnessed its first death and funeral on Friday, April 18, 1884. The otherwise happy camp was clouded in gloom over the fatal shooting of John Huston by John Sullivan. Huston had spent a few days making the rounds of the saloons, heavily imbibing and in some instances engaging in quarrels with the men. One such victim of his contentious nature was Sullivan, a well known and popular prospector. Both were playing cards in the Miners Home when a quarrel arose between them. Hot, bitter words turned to action as Sullivan stepped behind the bar, grabbed a six-shooter, and fired. Huston fell, critically wounded, and died two days later. On Monday evening, Huston's remains, boxed in a rosewood coffin, were sadly conveyed about half a mile north of Black Hawk to the cemetery. Work stopped as every man followed in procession to the grave. Sullivan, the "good guy" turned bad, was whisked off to Silver City and placed in official hands.

Ore theft invariably transpired in most mining camps. One March day in 1886 a man named Miller informed the Black Hawk Mine superintendent, Platt McDonald, that he knew where some stolen ore had been cached. After being satisfied that he would not be indicted and would be paid for his trouble, Miller got himself deputized, took out a search warrant, and went to the Kerr brothers' house. He immediately tore up the floor boards and soon unearthed five packs of ore weighing over three hundred pounds. John and Barney Kerr, who had recently purchased the house from Henry Kinney, claimed no knowledge of the ore but stated that rightfully it was theirs, since it was on their premises. Despite their protests, the Kerr brothers were placed under arrest and taken to Silver City for a hearing.

Black Hawk boomed from 1885 to 1887. Some mining continued until 1893, but when production began to slack off the camp died. Today some mine dumps are all that links Black Hawk with New Mexico history.

Bland

COUNTY: *Sandoval*
LOCATION: *26 mi. southwest of Los Alamos*
MAP: *page 243*
P.O. est. 1894; discont. 1935.

Once a booming gold and silver mining town bustling with thousands, Bland is now deserted and closely guarded under lock and key. The town stands on private property which the owner has chosen to safeguard.

Bland's mining days were proud and generous, beginning in the early 1890's. After fabulous reports sparked the Denver *Rocky Mountain News* to proclaim the region as a "New Cripple Creek," a tide of humanity swept into the area, hastily set up clapboard buildings, and began extracting the wealth. The place soon became so crowded that miners took to sleeping in the streets, under a tree, or wherever they could find room. One resourceful individual pitched a tent, set up cots inside it, and charged $1 a night.

The new camp was named Bland in honor of Richard Parks Bland of Missouri, whose fight against the demonetization of silver had gained him national fame and even a nomination for the presidency of the United States.

The turn of the century saw Bland as a lusty, booming, hell-raising, hard-working metropolis. A full three thousand people had saturated Bland and the neighboring vicinity, including the town of Albemarle three and a half miles away but considered by Bland as part of its township. In March of 1900, fifteen hundred men were reported at work in the mines, mill, and sawmills. The continuous ring of the hammer and grate of the saw never stopped for Sunday, and over fifty buildings took shape within four months. Four sawmills were turning out lumber for the frenzied growth. Bland claimed two banks, the *Bland Herald* newspaper, a hotel, stock exchange, opera house, over a dozen saloons, a school, a church, and miscellaneous stores. Bland's most amazing feat was its location. The entire town was tucked along a narrow canyon aperture only sixty feet wide. When there was not sufficient room, the walls of the canyon were blasted to afford a pocket for a new building. In one instance, lack of space prompted a home owner to build his outhouse in front of his home on the main street.

The women of the town were the organizers and promoters of the town church and school. "Diamond Queen," well-known courtesan of Bland's red light district, contributed the altar and a Bible to the new Methodist Episcopal Church. Bland's educational system had a faulty beginning. The unruly students managed to drive away two teachers before the arrival of a strict schoolmaster, P. Carick Shannon, who shook the defiance out of the students and began to conduct class in an orderly manner.

Mrs. F. B. Bruce was one of Bland's most prodigious citizens. In spite of her total loss of eyesight, she could do just about anything. She was an immaculate housekeeper, a good cook, and a musician who played both the piano and the violin. She often played for school socials and dances. It is said that she always insisted upon carrying the lamp to the bedroom for a guest, fearful that the guest might trip and fall.

A singular and annoying predicament was reported from Bland in October of 1900. An immense swarm of grasshoppers had dropped into the creek from which Bland citizens obtained their water supply. The insects clogged up the stream and polluted the water and at one time were piled over a foot deep on the creek banks. The situation compelled the people to dig springs for drinking water. Fortunately, the problem was eliminated a few days later by a fresh rain that swept away the decaying matter and restored the creek to its original purity.

Mining production in the Cochiti district had started in 1894 and by the end of 1904 amounted to a little more than a million dollars. After this time the amount yielded swung downward, and in a few years activity ceased. Sporadic attempts were made to revive mining at Bland, but productive periods were short and not too profitable. Bland's boom had passed.

Bland, *circa* 1897. Miners House Saloon.—*Courtesy Museum of New Mexico.*

Bland Main Street, *circa* 1900.—*Courtesy New Mexico Magazine.*

Looking east down Bland's Main Street, *circa* 1880's.—*Courtesy Museum of New Mexico.*

Below—Homes along the steep canyon walls at Bland, *circa* 1890.—*Courtesy Museum of New Mexico.*

Above—Richard Parks Bland (1835–99), congressman who led the fight for free silver coinage with the Bland-Allison Act, after whom the gold and silver mining town was named.—*Courtesy Library of Congress.*

Dr. James Jackson Shuler (1858–1919), prominent physician at Blossburg during the 1890's.—*Courtesy Evelyn Shuler.*

Blossburg

COUNTY: *Colfax*
LOCATION: *5 mi. northwest of Raton*
MAP: *page 239*
P.O. est. 1881; discont. 1905.

A few miles up Dillon Canyon, the Blossburg coal mine opened in 1881. Promoters of the coal industry hailed the budding town as the Pittsburgh of the West. Jointly owned by the Raton Coal & Coking Company and the Santa Fe Railroad, Blossburg boomed for a dozen years. During its life Blossburg became seasoned to the usual gunplay and tragedies of a western mining camp. W. J. Cowan, while drinking heavily in a saloon, threatened the proprietor, Holland. The ensuing gunfight ended Cowan's life. During a drunken brawl in McArthur's Saloon, Jack Jones fatally stabbed George Wagstaff. There was a flood on April 20, 1886, and there were a few bad fires. An explosion in the Blossburg Mine on March 1, 1894, that killed five men and injured three, culminated the various tragic events.

In addition to the usual saloons and stores, as the population grew steadily Blossburg acquired a school, Catholic and Methodist churches, the Blossburg band, and the *Blossburg Pioneer* newspaper, first issued on January 21, 1882. The camp was quite self-contained except for the lack of a resident doctor. Every day Dr. James Shuler from Raton made the trip to Blossburg to minister to the sick. Nevertheless, emergencies often arose requiring the doctor's immediate attention when he was in Raton, hence the first telephone in Colfax County was installed at Dr. Shuler's home and office. Being quite a new innovation in those days, the insulated telephone wire was run along the fences. When a gate was encountered, poles were erected on either side of the gate and the wire elevated over the top. The termination point was Smith's Store in Blossburg, which served as an important convening place for the Blossburg people.

This is how Blossburg acquired direct communication with Raton.

One time a number of the Blossburg miners received threatening anonymous letters stating, in no uncertain terms, that they had better cease working at the mines. The angered recipients quietly sought to find out the originator of the letters and deal out an appropriate punishment—lynching. Greatly to the miners' embarrassment, the culprit was discovered to be none other than Ed Savage, the mine boss. Their well-made plans of revenge were quickly forgotten.

The turning point for Blossburg occurred in the summer of 1894, when a strike closed the Blossburg Mine. After much difficulty the labor troubles were settled, and work was resumed. It was not the same though; the damage had been done. Operations began to flounder and fold, and the mine closed permanently shortly thereafter. As new coal strikes shifted attention up the canyon to Brilliant, Blossburg, which once claimed over a thousand people, gradually became depopulated. By 1903 only a hundred persons remained, dwindling to twenty by 1939. Farming and ranching became the livelihood of these people.

No one lives in Blossburg today. A few stone and mortar walls are still visible in a cluster of trees, and there is a deserted two-story building with a balcony claimed by a local old-timer to have been once a store and home.

16
B

The coal mining camp of Blossburg from the northeast, *circa* 1900.—
Courtesy Evelyn Shuler.

The Raton band, which probably played at Blossburg, *circa* 1900.
—*Courtesy John Southwell*.

Bonanza City

COUNTY: *Santa Fe*
LOCATION: *about 13 mi. southwest of Santa Fe*
MAP: *page 243*
P.O. est. 1880; discont. 1883.

If you know where to look and you look hard enough, you can find scanty traces of Bonanza City. Faint foundation outlines, broken fragments of bottles and pottery, rusty scraps, and thick brick and rock ruins of a smelter encircled by black slag are located on a flat area southwest of Bonanza Hill on Bonanza Creek.

The discovery of silver, zinc, and lead in the Los Cerrillos Hills in 1879 triggered the organization of Los Cerrillos Mining District. John J. Mahoney, former United States consul to Algiers, located the townsite of Bonanza City the following year. By July, 1881, Bonanza City was host to a growing population, a fine water supply, a store, and a hotel and post office both run by Mr. and Mrs. Samuel Hull. However, the village lamented the need for another store dealing in general merchandise, a barber, and a shoemaker.

A social occasion reported at Bonanza City in August, 1882, was the gala seventy-fifth birthday party of Samuel Hull. After wagonloads of friends from Cerrillos and the camp arrived at the Hull house, the doors to their spacious dining room were flung open, exposing a table groaning with festive foods. Mr. Hull led the dinner conversation, reminiscing of the "good old days."

As the site of a smelter and reduction works, the town anticipated a big boom. There is mention that Bonanza City once reached a population of two thousand. It is not known whether this is actual fact. In 1884 the population is listed at two hundred. No doubt its peak was reached before this time, since the post office closed in 1883. In 1885 work in the area was still plentiful. Miner's wages ranged from $3 to $4 a day.

Bonanza City's brief history faded into obscurity shortly thereafter.

Charcoal sketch of the Marshall Bonanza ore concentrator where silver, zinc, and lead ores were reduced. The Marshall Bonanza Mine, located two miles from Bonanza City, was discovered by Hugh Marshall in the spring of 1880.—*Courtesy New Mexico Record Center and Archives.*

MARSHALL BONANZA ORE CONCENTRATOR,
BONANZA CITY.

"Struck it Rich," date unknown.—
Courtesy Museum of New Mexico.

Bonito City, 1904. Post office. Site now under Bonito Lake.—*Courtesy Museum of New Mexico.*

Bonito City

COUNTY: *Lincoln*
LOCATION: *about 11 mi. northwest of Ruidoso*
MAP: *page 249*
P.O. est. 1882; discont. 1911.

Log cabins appearing on either side of Bonito Canyon in 1882 emerged into the silver mining camp of Bonito City. As extensive mining attracted the inevitable merchants and men in other trades and professions, Bonito City quickly settled into a busy life. The town included three general stores, a hotel, school, saloon, post office, blacksmith, and a lawyer. Squire Charles Berry, justice of the peace, credited not a single killing within his precinct. This boast did not last long. Bonito City became the scene of a horrendous multiple murder which would be labeled as one of the worst crimes committed in New Mexico history.

On a May evening of 1885, friendly young Martin Nelson, a prospector and the town constable, went beserk. Entering the Mayberry Hotel he shot and killed seven victims: four members of the W. T. Mayberry family, a guest staying at the hotel, the saloonkeeper, and the grocer. All during the terror-stricken night the townspeople kept a close vigilance as the murderer was sought. Toward morning, Martin was tracked down and killed by Charles Berry. The slain were buried, but the never-forgotten tragic episode of that night haunted the life of Bonito City.

As years passed, miners left Bonito City to move on to more promising fields. The town post office, however, remained open a full decade into the twentieth century, although at one time only two persons were reported living in the town.

About twenty years after the closing of the post office, the canyon once again rang with activity as the buildings of Bonito City were stripped from their sites. The Southern Pacific Railroad, fulfilling its need for an adequate water supply, had chosen Bonito Canyon as the best place for constructing a dam. Bonito City, marked by the enormity of past crime, was blotted out forever by seventy-five feet of water. The last tragedy befell in 1945, when a raging fire swept the tree-studded slopes, marring the beauty that had once given Bonito Canyon its name.

Brice

COUNTY: *Otero*
LOCATION: *about 34 mi. south of Alamogordo*
MAP: *page 253*
P.O. est. as Jarilla in 1899; discont. 1904.
Changed to Brice 1904; discont. 1909. Re-est. 1919; discont. 1920.

S. M. Perkins, better known as "Ole Perk," prospected the Jarilla Mountains in 1879. Once he accidentally came upon an unfriendly Mescalero Apache camp. The Indians were about to kill him when they noticed that he was somewhat hunchbacked and decided to spare his life. He was given his freedom and allowed to prospect at will throughout the Jarilla district. "Ole Perk" discovered and located the valuable Nannie Baird Mine, which he later traded for two precious barrels of drinking water after his waterhole had gone dry. About twenty years later the district became famous as a gold, copper, and turquoise producer. The Nannie Baird was one of the principal properties.

The mining camp of Jarilla became known as Brice in 1904, after the El Paso and Northeastern Railroad ran a spur line from Jarilla Junction (Orogrande) up the canyon to the camp. In 1905 Brice reported a population of 150, a saloon, hotel, general store, and four mining companies. It also boasted the first schoolhouse in the area. Renewed activity in the camp in 1919 attracted a population of three hundred.

Today the road up the canyon is the old railroad grade, now stripped of its tracks. A brick powder house is the only building left at Brice. There are numerous mine dumps and hairpin roads that crisscross the workings.

Brilliant

COUNTY: *Colfax*
LOCATION: *about 7 mi. northwest of Raton*
MAP: *page 239*
P.O. est. 1906; discont. 1935.

The St. Louis, Rocky Mountain and Pacific Company organized in 1905 and opened the first Brilliant mine in January, 1906. The subsequent town of Brilliant, located in Dillon Canyon on the Atchison, Topeka and Santa Fe Railway, was company owned. Brilliant was a coal town, supplying this valuable commodity to the Santa Fe Railroad for locomotive use and for making coke at the Gardiner coke ovens five miles south of Brilliant. The population figures listed 350 in 1907 and claimed a telephone company, a school, the Japanese Hotel, the Brilliant Hotel, Brilliant Electric Company, Blossburg Merchantile Co., boarding house, recreation hall, Brilliant & Raton Stage Line, saloons, a sheriff, and a physician. There was no hospital or church. The sick were transported to either Gardiner or Raton, and the schoolhouse was used to hold church services. Substantial low-rent homes were built by the company for the employees and their families. The company sponsored a yearly Christmas party for the camp, and a Christmas tree was adorned with a present for every child in the school.

In early 1908 operations at the Brilliant mines were suspended due to the business depression of 1907. The camp reopened in September, 1912, and continued a lively existence well into the twenties. Ladies club meetings, baseball games between Brilliant and other local camps, dances, movies shown at the schoolhouse and the recreation hall, and an occasional mine accident were a part of the camp's life.

A killing was reported in September, 1919, involving Walter Fleming and Paul Sandoval, both of whom had been liberally imbibing homemade liquor. Fleming shot and killed Sandoval. Sheriff Hixenbaugh, arriving from Raton to investigate the crime, arrested a third party, Joe Kezele, for bootlegging.

In the early twenties the history of Brilliant began to merge into that of Swastika, another coal town owned by the St. Louis, Rocky Mountain and Pacific Company and founded a mile south of

21
B

Brilliant. For a while the two towns functioned side by side, until Brilliant closed its post office doors in 1935. During World War II the name Swastika was changed to Brilliant II, since the original Brilliant had ceased operating.

In 1939 a caretaker, his family, and a few other people comprised the ten inhabitants of Brilliant. Today no one lives there. The site is marked by dump piles, foundation outlines, and three or four roofed, partially intact buildings on the sloping hillside west of the Dillon Canyon road.

Motor and employees at the Brilliant coal mines, *circa* 1916.—*Courtesy Joe Young.*

Brilliant, *circa* 1925. Clubhouse and soft-drink parlor.—*Courtesy Evelyn Shuler.*

Below—Brilliant, looking northeast, *circa* 1916.— *Courtesy Joe Young.*

Above—Mr. George A. Honeyfield (standing), owner of first
mail and passenger service to
Blossburg and Brilliant, *circa*
1910.—*Courtesy Evelyn
Shuler*.

Present-day ruins at Brilliant.

Cabezon

COUNTY: *Sandoval*
LOCATION: *about 35 mi. south of Cuba*
MAP: *page 243*
P.O. est. 1891; discont. 1949.

Cabezon offers a beautiful, forsaken scene. It is truly a ghost town classic, composed of a dusty Main Street fringed by fifteen or twenty abandoned, weathered adobe and mudstone buildings, the pewless, unpeopled shell of the Catholic church, the derelict cemetery, the vacant stores, and the eerie silence of total desolation. Cabezon's once important life faded with the march of progress.

In the early 1870's several families of Spanish extraction settled along the Río Puerco a few miles from the base of majestic Cabezon Peak. They built adobe homes and settled down to a productive life of sheepherding and farming. Their community was called La Posta, and it functioned as a way station for travelers on the main route between Santa Fe and Fort Wingate. The town quickly adjusted to its status by acquiring saloons, stores, and a blacksmith shop. La Posta was located in the land of the Spanish and the Navaho,

but in the 1880's two enterprising Anglos also made it their home. Richard F. Heller and John Pflueger started a trading post in the town. Despite their alien nationality they were accepted and they prospered. Later Heller bought out his partner and the Heller general store, also serving as a post office, continued into the 1940's. At the time the post office was established La Posta became known as Cabezon.

Richard Heller became a leading and prominent citizen of Cabezon. Through his efforts and leadership the Catholic church was built. The Hellers also gained a reputation for their warm hospitality. Since there was no hotel in town, Mrs. Heller often put up weary travelers in their home, a beautiful eleven-room adobe opposite the store.

Heller owned a great deal of livestock. At one time he reportedly had ten thousand sheep and two thousand cattle. On several occasions it took as many as forty wagons to transport his wool to the market in Albuquerque. The Navaho Indians sent with the shipment took no credence in paper money, so the transaction was made with gold and silver coins. On the return trip to Cabezon one wagon would be loaded with money.

In 1897 Cabezon reported having a public school that functioned three months of the year,

24
c

Cabezon, looking south over the graveyard toward Cabezon Peak.

Catholic church services once a year, and a population of one hundred persons. The population of Cabezon and the neighboring vicinity in 1915 was placed at 375. There were also a couple of other stores in addition to Heller's, a sprinkling of saloons, and a justice of the peace.

For almost fifty years Cabezon served as a stop on the route westward from Santa Fe and Albuquerque, but gradually the circumstances that had gleaned prosperity for Cabezon began to change. The town's importance dwindled as new roads were built which greatly reduced travel through Cabezon. The Navahos who had served as vital contributors to the trade and prosperity gradually drifted away in their nomadic fashion. An object of erosion and drought, the Río Puerco's water table was lowered until it could no longer nurture the corn and wheat crops or the sheep and cattle. Richard Heller succumbed in March of 1947. The post office run by Heller's widow maintained a feeble existence for more than a year after his death; then it closed.

Today Cabezon is on private property and is posted against trespassers.

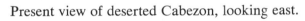

Present view of deserted Cabezon, looking east.

Prospectors on their way to the mines. Probably taken in Santa Fe, date unknown.— *Courtesy Museum of New Mexico.*

Carbonateville

COUNTY: *Santa Fe*
LOCATION: *about 17 mi. southwest of Santa Fe*
MAP: *page 243*
P.O. est. 1879; discont. 1880. Changed to Turquesa 1880; discont. 1899.

Three names seem to crop up together; Carbonateville, Turquoise City, and Turquesa. There appears to be a variance of opinion as to whether these were different places or the same. Probably these names all referred to the same townsite. The town was first named Carbonateville and functioned under the post office of this name for less than a year. Then the post office name was changed to Turquesa, and subsequently the town was sometimes referred to as Turquesa or Turquoise City; however, it more often retained its original name of Carbonateville in newspaper accounts.

The history of this area began long before Carbonateville sprang into existence. No historical date can be pinpointed, but it is believed that Indians were using crude methods to mine turquoise around Mount Chalchihuitl long before the discovery of America. Later on, during the 1600's the Spanish, with enslaved Indian labor, were involved in extensive mining operations. Two of the most interesting mines were the Mina-del-Tierra, which was worked for silver, and the old turquoise mine, Chalchihuitl. It was in the depths of the turquoise mine in 1680 that a cave-in occurred, burying alive twenty or so enslaved Indians. The furtive attempt by the Spanish to requisition more Indian workers to replace those buried sparked the rebellion that led to the Indian uprising of 1680. In the 1880's some fifty different Spanish workings were discovered in the vicinity of Carbonateville, but very few of the mines were open, because they had all been filled by either the Indians or the Spanish.

Mining interest in the area produced the town of Carbonateville, which was founded in January, 1879, and a year later sported about forty houses. The major drawback to the success of the camp was the scarcity of water, which had to be hauled from Bonanza City. Miners' wages were $2.50 a day. First class board ranged from $6 to $7 a week.

The most notorious figure in Carbonateville's life was E. M. Kelly, alias Choctaw Kelly, whose one serious affray captured national headlines. Kelly stood five feet eleven and was thin but strong, with a black mustache and goatee framing his face. He was a bitter loner who never made it lucky. After being grubstaked a couple of times without success, he eventually drifted into Carbonateville. His first winter there produced only a meager living and no rich strike. Kelly then opened a dance hall which failed, forcing him to go on the payroll as a miner to satisfy his creditors. One of the men working with him in the mine was Jack Reardon.

One Wednesday afternoon at Abbot's Saloon, Kelly started drinking heavily and soon became boisterous and offensive. His nasty temper soon led to a quarrel with a man named Sullivan, a small fellow who certainly was not physically equal to Kelly. As the dispute grew, and it appeared inevitable that Kelly would strike Sullivan, Jack Reardon intervened, trying to prevent a mishap. The interference so enraged Kelly that he drew a knife and rushed at Reardon. Another observer, Thompson, the camp constable, stepped in, siding with Kelly and warning Reardon to stay out of the fight. Several other bystanders quickly separated the men, whereupon Kelly rushed from the saloon and returned minutes later with a Winchester which he aimed at Reardon and fired.

Reardon was not killed immediately, but was mortally wounded. Kelly was promptly arrested. Reardon's popularity in Carbonateville triggered off great excitement in town. Many felt that Thompson was more guilty than Kelly, for it was his duty as a law officer to have put a stop to the quarrel instead of siding with Kelly. Crowds of irate men and cries of "Hang them!" issued above the noise of the court, causing Magistrate Maddix to place both Kelly and Thompson under heavy guard and order them taken to Santa Fe for protection. As was expected, Reardon died, and all Carbonateville turned out for his funeral.

Thompson eventually was cleared and released while Kelly was placed in the hands of Edgar Caypless, a lawyer. In spite of Caypless' valiant attempts, Kelly was sentenced to the gallows on February 17, 1882. Convinced that Kelly should not hang, Caypless appealed to the United States attorney general and the president of the United States, Chester Arthur. President Arthur granted Kelly a stay of execution, much to the disappointment of the Carbonateville miners, who were anticipating a well-deserved hanging. The execution date was rescheduled for April 17 and then May 19, but the hoped-for event never took place. Eventually Kelly's sentence was commuted to life imprisonment. The case was noteworthy because it tested whether or not the president of the United States had the right to commute a death sentence ruled by the Territorial Court.

In the year 1884 Carbonateville was reported to have a population of five hundred. However, by the next year mining in the district was on the decline. In 1897 only forty residents were listed at the once-promising mining camp.

An interesting sidelight is that Governor Lew Wallace read the proofs of his novel, *Ben Hur*, while staying at a hotel in Carbonateville. In 1905 some of the walls of the building where the historic event took place were still standing.

Nature has too well disguised the site of Carbonateville, if, indeed, there is anything left of it today.

Woodcut of Indians working in early Spanish mines with notched log ladders, from Wm. G. Ritch, *Aztlan, The History, Resources and Attractions of New Mexico*. D. Lothrop & Co. Boston, 1885.

Lew Wallace (1827–1905), Republican governor of New Mexico 1878–81. Wallace spent time in Carbonateville, where he held mining interests.—*Courtesy Museum of New Mexico*.

Below—Los Cerrillos prospectors, *circa* 1880.—*Courtesy Museum of New Mexico*.

Mule-operated winch at a shaft mine in the vicinity of Carbonateville, *circa* 1885.—*Courtesy Museum of New Mexico.*

Advertisement—Carbonateville was later called Turquoise City, *circa* 1885.—*Courtesy New Mexico Record Center and Archives.*

View of Carbonateville from the southeast, *circa* 1880.—*Courtesy Museum of New Mexico.*

Carlisle

COUNTY: *Grant*
LOCATION: *about 54 miles northwest of Lordsburg*
MAP: *page 255*
P.O. est. 1884; discont. 1896.

The few vestiges of Carlisle are ensconced in a rugged, isolated area of western Grant County four miles from the Arizona border. They consist of extensive mine dumps, ochre-colored mill pond stains, a rock chimney, a couple of adobe ruins, rock walls, and rubble. Numerous shafts and diggings pockmark the area.

The first prospecting in the Carlisle or Steeple Rock District took place in 1881, and in 1883 the Carlisle Mine was located. Prospective millionaires immediately began flocking to the opulent site forming the mining municipality of Carlisle. A few thousand persons made it their home, and it claimed the inevitable saloons and shops of a lusty mining camp.

The starting of a mill was always a good omen at any mining camp and rightfully a festive occasion. A five-stamp mill located three miles from Carlisle at a place known as East Camp received its formal initiation on December 17, 1886. A large number of men and women arrived from Carlisle by wagon, carriage, horseback, and on foot. Cigars, cider, wine, and hard liquor were freely dispensed to celebrate the affair. The signal for the momentous beginning of the mill machinery was proclaimed by blowing the steam boiler whistle, an honor given to one of the fair ladies at the gathering.

On a January day in 1898 a miner named Frank Griffin who worked at Carlisle met with a serious accident when he tried to thaw out some gunpowder on a stove. The ensuing explosion more or less wrecked the stove, the cabin, and Griffin, although the latter's injuries were not fatal.

Into the unlikely setting of a roaring boom town came young Herbert Hoover in 1898, just three years out of Stanford University. The future president of the United States was employed as assistant superintendent of the Steeple Rock mines. During his mining days at Carlisle, Hoover stayed with P. H. McDermott, the superintendent of the mines, who also served as the town's deputy sheriff. McDermott's kind and steadfast character was exemplified by the interesting story of Dong Fook.

The recipient of both good luck and a bad accident, Dong Fook became probably the only wealthy Chinese cripple around. During Carlisle's booming days, Dong Fook worked as a waiter in a Chinese chop house. Then because of a decision by a representative of the large English corporation operating at Carlisle, the mine and mill were closed. Left without a job and with only a small stock of supplies, Dong Fook and two compatriots, Dong Yue and Lee Shu, took to prospecting. A few weeks later Dong Fook returned to Carlisle, looked up McDermott, and explained that he had found a rich deposit. Being familiar, however, with the alien law preventing him from owning any land, Dong Fook begged McDermott to locate the mine, promising that he in turn would work it. An agreement was made, and shortly thereafter the Chinese went to work sinking a shaft. One day Dong Fook was carefully setting dynamite at the bottom of his twelve-foot shaft. He lit the fuse and started climbing up the ladder. Near the top a rung broke, and Dong Fook fell to the bottom and broke his ankle. Unable to extinguish the fuse and frantic with fear, the Chinese somehow managed to claw his way up the side of the shaft, clearing the top just as the dynamite exploded. Dong Fook probably would have died except for kind-hearted McDermott, who got him to a doctor in Lordsburg. Dr. Woods suggested that the only course of action would be to amputate Dong Fook's mutilated foot. Such a howl of protest followed that the doctor promised he would try to save the foot. Nursing himself with a concoction made from water and pieces of mineral from the mine, Dong Fook made a rapid recovery, but henceforth walked with a decided limp. With McDermott continuing to act as their superintendent and adviser, the Chinese went back to the mine to work with his partners and soon had sold enough ore to make a livelihood. After a while the mining property came to the attention of a San Francisco capitalist who negotiated with McDermott and bought the mine. True to his word, McDermott paid Dong Fook his full share, and with this wealth he and his two Chinese partners left for San Francisco and a trip across the Pacific to their Motherland.

Activity at Carlisle began to decline from the late 1890's on, and there was little productive mining. Then for a fifteen-year stretch beginning in 1932, Carlisle district experienced a second period of major mining production of gold, silver, and copper. However, the rip-roaring mining days of the 1880's and 1890's that had placed Carlisle on the map were never duplicated.

Herbert C. Hoover (1874–1964). One of Hoover's first mining positions was assistant superintendent at the Steeple Rock Mine at Carlisle.—*Courtesy Herbert Hoover Library.*

Below—Carlisle, present-day ruins.

Carthage

COUNTY: *Socorro*
LOCATION: *about 22 mi. southeast of Socorro*
MAP: *page 247*
P.O. est. 1883; discont. 1893. Re-est. 1906; discont. 1951.

The first coal mine worked in New Mexico was near Carthage and was called the Government Mine. It was worked by United States soldiers in the early 1860's in order to supply the smithing needs of Forts Selden, Bayard, and Stanton. In 1881, just before the completion of a bridge across the Río Grande at a point near Carthage, two United States Army six-mule teams returning from Carthage with loads of coal were somehow caught in the insidious sands of the river and lost. Fortunately, the government drivers managed to escape. Soon the Santa Fe Railroad constructed a bridge across the river and laid tracks to the Carthage coal fields to supply fuel for their locomotives. This venture nurtured Carthage into the busiest coal mining camp in New Mexico. In 1889 the town reported a population of three hundred persons, stage connections with White Oaks, water carried by rail from San Antonio, one school, and the Independent Order of Good Templers. Yet even in its halcyon days it still was described as being the most forlorn-looking place in the Territory. When Congress refused to issue a patent for the Montoya Grant, on which the coal mines were located, the Santa Fe Railroad tore up the tracks and moved Carthage lock, stock, and barrel to Madrid in Santa Fe County. On August 17, 1893, the *Old Abe Eagle* newspaper announced ". . . All the dwelling houses, coal chutes and machinery have already been moved. The place has practically been razed to the earth and the depot, adobe hotel and Gross, Blackwell & Co. store are about all that remain. . . ."

For the next ten years Carthage remained dormant. Then, in the early part of the century, resourceful citizens of San Antonio reopened the mines. The difficulty of economical transportation was solved when the New Mexico Midland Railway rebuilt tracks on the old Santa Fe grade from San Antonio, establishing Carthage as the railroad terminus. Carthage awoke with new vigor as the Carthage Fuel Company set the coal camp into action. The year 1907 reported the population at a thousand residents and also marked a tragedy for Carthage. A disastrous mine explosion occurred on December 31. About 1:00 P.M. a blast in the Dienal Mine took the lives of many miners and badly injured several others. The rescue party worked feverishly to extract the men from the wrecked mine, but poisonous gases made the task even more perilous. About fifty men were employed at the mine, and fortunately a large number of them were on the surface eating their noonday meal when the accident occurred.

Today what is left of Carthage is fast melting into oblivion. There is one fairly large adobe ruin once boasting three fireplaces and probably six rooms. It was the home of John Hart, the mine superintendent, who left Carthage about the mid-1940's. A rusted wood-burning stove, scattered debris, and hazardous holes left by bottle collectors litter the immediate area. A well-preserved cemetery is located about a mile north of the townsite.

Carthage cemetery.

Present view of mine superintendent John Hart's home at Carthage.

Below—John Hart's home with coal stripping dumps in the background.

Catskill

COUNTY: *Colfax*
LOCATION: *about 30 mi. northwest of Raton along the Canadian River*
MAP: *page 239*
P.O. est. 1890; discont. 1905.

The Maxwell Land Grant platted Catskill in the summer of 1890 and leased forest land for lumbering. Five major sawmills sprang up, a railroad branch line swung in from Trinidad, Colorado, two groups of brick beehive charcoal ovens were constructed, and board houses and business establishments mushroomed.

During the boom years thirty to fifty flatcar loads of lumber were shipped daily. The charcoal that was shipped was in such great demand that three thousand cords of wood were burned daily in the Catskill ovens.

As the town grew, Catskill citizens saw the necessity for a school. Finally Bill Wilder, Bill Cotton, and Bill Butler called a meeting at Butler's livery stable. During the meeting it was decided that the Blithen and Wilder mills would furnish lumber for a school, Butler's Livery would haul it, and Colonel Dick Cunn's store would supply the hardware. Soon the new frame schoolhouse graced the town and opened its doors to twenty pupils. By the following year the enrollment had tripled. Mr. Jones, the first Catskill teacher, found the students more than he could handle and fled after receiving his first month's pay. The job then went to Chip Chapman, who arrived at the school on his first day and found a pencil jammed into the keyhole of the front door. Undisturbed, he calmly grabbed an ax, knocked the door out, rang the hand bell, and, upon the arrival of the students, began teaching. School continued on schedule for the next eight months.

The Women's Christian Temperance Union was responsible for the Catskill church. They gave benefits to raise enough money to erect a church, and soon the whole town turned out for the laying of the cornerstone. The church was nondenominational and open to any sect that wished to hold services. The Reverend Lucas, a Seventh-day Adventist, came to Catskill and was so well liked that the townspeople asked him to preach to them every Sunday night. The parson consented, with the stipulation that there never be a collection taken. His popularity was so widespread that even the saloons closed for an hour so that the bartenders and gamblers might hear him preach.

At five o'clock on July 24, 1896, Catskill was terror-stricken by a huge wall of water that came rushing down the canyon. Fifteen miles of railroad were destroyed—seven miles being entirely washed away—twenty-five bridges were partially destroyed, the Newton Company sawmill was damaged, and large amounts of lumber were swept downstream. Fortunately no one drowned. Repairs were quickly made after the flood, putting Catskill back in the running.

By 1897, Catskill had settled into a prosperous well-equipped community. The school ran for nine months of the year, and church services were held for the Seventh-day Adventists, Presbyterians, and Christians. There was a Western Union telegraph, telephone connections to Raton, La Belle Stage Company, the usual stores, saloons, and hotels, a blacksmith, and a justice of the peace.

More noteworthy than the few unfortunate murders scattered throughout Catskill's history was the fact that Catskill was a happy and fun-loving town. Any occasion would launch a celebration. Catskill boasted a twenty-two-piece band, an eight-piece orchestra, a race course, a picnic ground, a dance pavilion and a ball park. Almost every weekend during the summer trainloads of excursion parties from Trinidad would arrive at Catskill for a good time. The Fourth of July never failed to draw large crowds.

On one such occasion the four hotels, the Brett, Gillum, Southern, and Fuller were quickly filled. One unfortunate visitor who failed to take time out from drinking found in the late afternoon that there were no vacancies, so he returned to Joe Fowler's pool hall. Eying the billiard table that rented for two bits an hour, the visitor got an idea. He reached into his pocket, dropped three dollars in silver into Fowler's hand, and climbed up on the table for a long nap.

At the turn of the century the timber around Catskill was becoming scarce. In January, 1902, the tracks of the Colorado and Southern Railway were pulled up, cutting off Catskill's life line. When the lumber people closed up and left, Catskill continued on a much smaller scale, substituting stock-raising for lumbering, but gradually, even the stockgrowers left.

On the fringes of a cattle-grazing meadow are the few surviving relics of Catskill; half a dozen wooden buildings, a cluster of red brick walls, scattered wood, and a couple of stone foundation outlines among the encircling trees. A small cemetery on the west slope of the hillside about three-fourths of a mile north of Catskill contains three rock-walled graves, one picket fence grave, and another five or six unidentifiable mounds. East of Catskill beside the Canadian River are a row of ten perfectly preserved red-brick charcoal ovens. Catskill, once so easily accessible by rail, now can only be reached with a four-wheel-drive vehicle.

Red brick ovens about one mile east of Catskill, where logs were converted to charcoal which was later shipped to smelters.

Above—Price of groceries at Catskill, August 10, 1893.—*Courtesy John Southwell.*

Advertisement—*Courtesy Museum of New Mexico.*

78   NEW MEXICO.

ALBERT LAWRENCE,   A. M. BLACKWELL,   H. W. KELLY,   H. G. FRANKENBURGER
President.   Vice President   Treasurer   Secretary.

THE

Maxwell Timber Co.,

General Merchandise and Lumber.

Sole Lessees of the Maxwell Land Grant Company for the manufacture of Railroad Ties, Piling, Mining Props, Telegraph Poles and Cord Wood.

The Largest Tract of Timber under one management in the United States.

Catskill,   **New Mexico.**

Catskill ladies' band, *circa* 1900.—*Courtesy F. Stanley.*

Above—Catskill ruins, looking northwest.

Above—Headstone in Catskill cemetery.

Grave fence in Catskill cemetery located about a mile north of Catskill.

Cerrillos, Palace Hotel today. Advertisement from *The Cerrillos Rustler*, October 24, 1890.—*Courtesy Highlands University Library*.

Cerrillos

COUNTY: *Santa Fe*
LOCATION: *25 mi. southwest of Santa Fe*
MAP: *page 243*
P.O. est. 1880 to present.

The Cerrillos Hills abound in legends of turquoise and silver, of ancient workings at Mount Chalchihuitl and Mina-del-Tierra, and of days when enslaved Indians mined the wealth for the greedy Spaniards. No doubt it was stories such as these that induced two empty-handed miners from Leadville, Colorado, to rediscover the Cerrillos wealth and produce a boom. In 1879 Frank Dimmitt and an Englishman named Robert Hart headed for the Cerrillos to try their luck. When they returned to Leadville with a collection of samples to be assayed, word spread rapidly of their high ore content, and the inevitable stampede resulted. The once unlucky miners from Leadville rushed to the Cerrillos and formed a quick tent town. This was the beginning of the village of Cerrillos or Los Cerrillos. The nearby communities of Carbonate-

ville and Bonanza City also resulted from this same strike.

By mid-summer of 1879, three hundred miners were at work gouging out the gold, silver, copper, lead, and zinc from the Cerrillos. Then coal was discovered along the Galisteo River, adding another important find to the rich treasures. The tent phase soon gave way to a modern, active town. By 1880 the railroad tracks of the Atchison, Topeka and Santa Fe Railway were being laid through Cerrillos. At this time the six men and the foreman working on the railroad had no place to eat or sleep. Mrs. Harkness, wife of D. D. Harkness, offered to put up the seven men in their home. When her husband returned from a prospecting trip he found that he and his wife were in the hotel business. The enterprise proved so successful that Harkness built an eighteen-room hotel called the Cerrillos House.

The unrulys of Cerrillos were not tolerated by the righteous and were quickly expelled from their midst. In January of 1882 a questionable character laying water pipes to the railroad station became bitterly offended at a slight affront from a fellow worker. Realizing his physical inability to lick the offender, he played on the fellow's one weakness— liquor. It was easy to get his victim drunk, and when he was in a complete state of stupified intoxication, the schemer knocked down the weakened inebriate and brutally pounded him nearly to death. His misconduct immediately brought about his arrest and stirred up threats of a lynching. The next day, while in custody, the prisoner was sitting in a saloon. In rushed an angry mob, overpowered the guards, grabbed the wrongdoer, and took charge. He was stripped, strung up to a slaughterhouse wall, and unmercifully flogged. Flesh tore loose and blood ran freely down his back before the punishment had been fully executed. The inflicted man was then cut down, given a blanket to cover his raw back, and told to get out of Cerrillos. This he did without any hesitation, and he was never seen again.

Throughout its mining days Cerrillos experienced ups and downs, but its all-time high population figure was claimed to be twenty-five hundred. In 1897 the town listed a flourishing report of its endowments: two churches, a Methodist and a Catholic; a public school with an enrollment of 130; three hotels; two livery stables; two blacksmith shops; several general stores; Wells Fargo Express; Western Union telegraph; and a population of eight hundred persons. Cerrillos also served as the supply and shipping point for the mining towns of Golden, San Pedro, and Dolores, and the coal camps of Madrid and Waldo.

Mining is no longer important to Cerrillos, and today the town functions as a tourist attraction. It is a charming place, claiming a few businesses, a Catholic church, and about fifty families. One of its more interesting attractions is the stately Palace Hotel built by Richard Green, who came from Jacksboro, Texas, in the 1880's with his wife and numerous children. The stone portion of the hotel was built first and contained a dozen rooms, including a bridal suite. Two years later the adobe section was added to serve as a dining room. At various times the hotel rooms were occupied by the tailor shop of Julius Muralter, the office of general practitioner Dr. F. Palmer, William Bishop's dentist office, and Masonic Lodge meetings. In 1906 Green died in his hotel, and after selling the property his widow moved to California. A later owner of the hotel, Mrs. Nellie Trigg, renamed it the Rock House Ranch.

Cerrillos' charm captivated Walt Disney, who used the main street as background for his Elfego Baca television series. Cerrillos was disguised as the town of Frisco, as is verified by signs still faintly visible on the buildings.

Cerrillos Main Street and the "Hotel Frisco," as it was called by Walt Disney for the television western based on the life of Elfego Baca.

Catholic church at Cerrillos.

Advertisement from *The Cerrillos Rustler*, May 15, 1891.—*Courtesy Highlands University Library.*

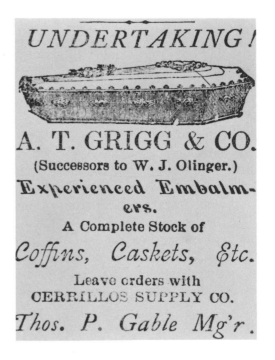

Cerrillos Main Street.

At Cerrillos quarters, engineers who surveyed the Santa Fe spur line from Waldo to Madrid in 1892.—*Courtesy Museum of New Mexico.*

Advertisements from *The Cerrillos Rustler*, December 7, 1888.—*Courtesy Highlands University Library.*

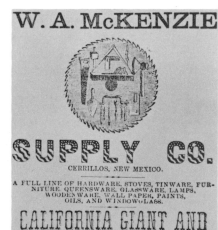

Chance City

COUNTY: *Grant*
LOCATION: *about 4 mi. south of Gage*
MAP: *page 257*
P.O. est. 1885; discont. 1886.

Chance City, also known as Victorio, was comfortably located in the Victorio Mountains three and a half miles southwest of the Southern Pacific Railroad station at Gage.

A trio of old experienced prospectors, William Kent, William Hyters, and J. L. Dougherty, struck argentiferous lead ores in the Victorio Mountains early in the 1880's. The Chance and Jessie claim groups on Carbonate Hill were purchased and developed by Randolph Hearst and two associates, Haggin and Head. Soon a townsite consisting of sixteen frame buildings and two adobes was laid out about six hundred yards from the mines. Water was the biggest problem, costing two and a half cents a gallon hauled in wagons from the Gage station. Mr. B. E. Lanagan was postmaster and kept a fine general stock of supplies in his store. The boardinghouse had accommodations for a hundred miners, and two saloons could quench their thirst.

Mining was discontinued for a time, with only small, intermittent production of gold, silver, copper, lead, and zinc ores valued at half a million dollars between the years of 1904 and 1937. Several rock and adobe ruins and scattered rubble mark the site of the former camp.

Chloride, office of Judge E. F. Holmes, date unknown.—*Courtesy Schmit Collection, University of New Mexico Library.*

Chloride

COUNTY: *Sierra*
LOCATION: *about 30 mi. northwest of Truth or Consequences*
MAP: *page 251*
P.O. est. 1881; discont. 1956.

One day in 1879 Harry Pye, a mule skinner and veteran prospector, was hauling freight to a military post when he picked up a piece of silver float in the canyon where Chloride now stands. The piece assayed high in silver, triggering Pye's enthusiasm. After completing his freighting contract, Pye returned to the canyon with a small party, prospected the area, found the mother lode, and made the first location, which was called the Pye lode. As a result Pye is credited with being the discoverer of the district. A few months later he was killed by Apaches.

Pye's lode sparked attention among other avid prospectors and induced them to explore the area. In January of 1881, eighteen prospectors camped at the mouth of Chloride Gulch and established headquarters. A band of thirty-five Apaches ruthlessly interrupted their mining venture by killing two members of the party and running off horses and mules. In the interest of self-preservation the prospectors left the area, but returned in March, laden with arms and ammunition. A store was erected, more miners filtered in, and the men realized a community was in the making and called a meeting to select a townsite.

The present site of Chloride was chosen, and lots twenty-five by a hundred feet were surveyed. In order to avoid future problems, lots were selected by lottery. Each lot was numbered to correspond with a ticket number which was put into a hat, shaken up, and drawn by one man. Lots were a valuable commodity and were used as bait to grace the all-male camp with the feminine gender. The men of Chloride offered a free lot to the first lady who made Chloride her home. Another incentive to populate the camp was the offer of a position on the city council to the father of the first newborn child "if it is known who he is." Fortunately virtue was not a deciding factor for the recipient.

The general threat of Indian raids did not hinder the influx of newcomers. Chloride grew in spite of

Chloride, looking west along Main Street.

the fact that the Apaches made occasional attacks as late as 1887. Within six months, Chloride metamorphosed from a tent, eighteen-man camp to a full-fledged town. By June, 1881, Chloride had eight saloons, three general merchandise stores, three restaurants, two butcher shops, a newsstand, lumber yard, assay office, boardinghouse, fruit and confectionary store, livery stable, post office, and the Pioneer Stage Line.

An episode that occurred in June, 1881, became the topic of conversation for many weeks and won for its performer unstinting praise as a bear fighter. Hugh C. Love stood six feet two inches tall and carried 210 pounds on his massive frame. One day he journeyed from Mineral Creek to Chloride Creek to examine his mine property. He had a pair of overalls which he was putting on before beginning work, when a huge cinnamon bear startled him from behind. Love was caught in a most helpless position, being hobbled by his overalls and out of reach of his rifle, which was leaning against a nearby tree. As the bear lunged at him, Love's only recourse was hand-to-paw combat, and a vicious fight ensued. The bear grabbed at Love's hand, tearing it to shreds, but Love used his free hand and struck the bear squarely on the nose. When the bear stood upright Love grabbed her around the middle and over and over they rolled. Sometime during the course of battle, Love managed to break the bear's grip, struggled to his feet and made a run for his rifle. His index finger was

too mangled to pull the trigger, but with his little finger Love fired the rifle, putting a bullet through the bear's brain. Although severely mauled, Love hiked two miles to his cabin to wash and dress his wounds, and the next day he walked to Chloride to the doctor.

Some of the citizens of Chloride began receiving letters scandalizing prominent local ladies and gentlemen. After a few months of receiving these letters the recipients became indignant and a few of them decided to form a committee to find out who was the sender. Through secret investigation the committee collected enough evidence to pinpoint the offender as Dr. James Reekie, a man of about sixty-five who had been practicing medicine in Chloride for five years. At eight o'clock on the evening of September 23, 1886, a party of thirty resolute residents quietly escorted Dr. Reekie to the upper end of town, doused him with a coat of tar and feathers, and ordered him out of Chloride.

During the 1880's Chloride steadily expanded, adding a church, school, *The Black Range* newspaper, a hotel, and five hundred inhabitants. This decade was Chloride's peak. Although population dwindled in succeeding years, the mines continued to produce. Today Chloride, a picturesque town, still claims a few citizens. The main dirt road is flanked by adobe ruins and fascinating old buildings ranging in variety from the peaked roof adobe with gingerbread decor to the wooden false front.

Above—"Bullfight," *circa* 1900.—*Courtesy Schmit Collection, University of New Mexico Library.*

Left—Fourth of July celebration at Chloride, from *The Black Range,* June 8, 1888.—*Courtesy Highlands University Library.*

Right—Advertisement from *The Black Range,* March 16, 1888.—*Courtesy Highlands University Library.*

Below—Chloride Masons, date unknown.—*Courtesy Schmit Collection, University of New Mexico Library.*

James Dalglish Groceries, Chloride, *circa* 1890.—*Courtesy Black Range Museum.*

Below—Chin Charley Hop Ke, Chloride laundryman, date unknown.—*Courtesy Schmit Collection, University of New Mexico Library.*

THE BANK!

Chloride, - - - New Mexico.

JOHN H. BEESON Proprietor.
WINES LIQUORS AND CIGARS
Always in stock.

THE
GEM SALOON,
Chloride, - - New Mex
H. E. PATRICK, - Proprietor.
Fresh Cigars and Liquors Constantly on Hand,
Call and Sample Them.

Above—Advertisements from *The Black Range,* October 21, 1887.— *Courtesy Highlands University Library.*

Below—Bear hunters, Chloride, *circa* 1890.— *Courtesy Schmit Collection, University of New Mexico Library.*

Wicklow House, Chloride, *circa 1890.—Courtesy Schmit Collection, University of New Mexico Library.*

Right—Wicklow House today.

46
c

Below—Chloride, looking east, *circa* 1890.—*Courtesy Schmit Collection, University of New Mexico Library.*

Chloride Main Street today. Pioneer Store, right foreground.

Log cabin at site of Clairmont.

A shooting skirmish was reported at Clairmont in 1884. One hot summer day pie-eyed Charley Shoemaker reeled into the restaurant owned by Louis Fay and, after a few hostile words, shot Fay in the stomach. Shoemaker immediately sought refuge in Kelly's saloon, while Fay stumbled out of the restaurant and into another saloon to find if anyone had a gun he could borrow. Mr. Sheridan quickly came to Fay's assistance by locating Shoemaker in Kelly's saloon. Soon James Gaddis, another friend of Fay, arrived with his revolver, entered the saloon, and covered Shoemaker. Still clutching his Winchester, Shoemaker refused to give up. Gaddis fired, Shoemaker returned the shot, and Gaddis fired again. Only one shot hit its mark, sending a ball through Shoemaker's right arm. A short while later, both Fay and Shoemaker were resting comfortably. That same evening, while practicing a fancy road agent's spin with his pistol, a driver from Cooney accidentally shot off the ends of three fingers and the thumb of John Kelly, a former deputy sheriff.

At the site of the one-time mining camp beside Copper Creek are two sturdy log cabins and a corral. Sparse debris can be found in the area.

48
c

Clairmont

COUNTY: *Catron*
LOCATION: *about 19 mi. northwest of Glenwood*
MAP: *page 253*
P.O. est. 1881; discont. 1883.

Clairmont, also spelled Clermont, was founded on Copper Creek shortly after James C. Cooney's ore discoveries on Mineral Creek. The camp eventually relinquished most of its population to Cooney camp when a road was built through Cooney Canyon in 1822, and the miners settled closer to the mine workings. For a short time, however, Clairmont was the center of population in the Mogollons, as well as a base of supply and headquarters for roving prospectors in the vicinity. In the spring of 1880, the Galveston Company spent twenty-five thousand dollars on several mining claims, which generated much excitement and hinted at great prosperity for Clairmont, but the anticipated boom failed to materialize. In a few months, Clairmont presented the appearance of a deserted community. However, in June of 1881 the camp reported making rapid strides toward prosperity, with daily additions to its population.

Clarkville

COUNTY: *McKinley*
LOCATION: *about 6 mi. west of Gallup*
MAP: *page 245*
P.O. est. 1898; discont. 1908.

Clarkville no longer exists but during its day it was an important lignite coal mining camp operated by the Clark Coal Company. The camp was founded about 1898 and was named for the owner of the property, W. A. Clark, a well-known mining magnate and millionaire.

Clarkville was reported to be a pretty little place with comfortably-built houses. Among the town's more noteworthy features were its two-storied brick commissary amply stocked with goods, its school building, the Clarkville Free Library, and the Clarkville Hospital. Clarkville claimed that it possessed so many favorable characteristics for the comfort, convenience, health, and moral standard of the miners that everyone working there seemed happy and contented. The fact that Clarkville had no saloons and a strict ruling against the sale of liquor on the premises supposedly elevated the town to a higher echelon of morality.

The mine was equipped with a complete electrical plant. A ten-ton electric locomotive of eighty horsepower propelled the coal cars from the underground mine workings to the surface. Telephone connections ran between the mine and town.

The population of Clarkville numbered four hundred in 1905 and two years later it had decreased to half that number. Shortly after that, the post office closed and the camp acquired ghost town status.

Cloverdale

COUNTY: *Hidalgo*
LOCATION: *42 mi. south of Animas*
MAP: *page 253*
P.O. est. 1913; discont. 1943.

The most southwestern place in New Mexico is Cloverdale. On some maps it is still labeled, but it can hardly be called a town. Located at the convergence of three dirt roads is an old deserted store built in 1918 and now padlocked and shuttered. This is Cloverdale. Farther along the westward road is the abandoned flagstone house of Henry Sanford, and still farther west is an old wooden outdoor dance pavilion, once a lively spot on Saturday nights. These seem to be Cloverdale's only remaining features.

Cloverdale's beginning is nebulous. At an unknown date either Bob Anderson or John Weames filed on a section of land and established the Cloverdale Ranch about a mile north of the vacant store building. In 1889 the land was sold to the Victor Land and Cattle Company. The area began to prosper in farming and ranching, and the community, which apparently was rather widespread, took on the name Cloverdale. During its existence it claimed population figures up to two hundred, a stage line to Animas, school, stores, blacksmith, and justice of the peace.

Cloverdale store built in 1918.

Coalora

COUNTY: *Lincoln*
LOCATION: *about 1 mi. northwest of Capitan*
MAP: *page 249*
P.O. est. 1903; discont. 1905.

In January, 1900, the El Paso and Northeastern Railroad began mining the coal fields one and a half miles north of Capitan, thereby giving birth to Coalora. The New Mexico Fuel Company established operations at Coalora and furnished employment to a large number of men by running three shifts at the coal mines. The inhabitants numbered a supposed two thousand in 1902, and of the camp's businesses the following were reported; the Southwestern Mercantile Company, Club Hotel, New Mexico Fuel Company Hospital, Wells Fargo Express, livery stable, and saloon. In 1905 the population was reported to be 350 persons. Coalora did not prosper for very long. When the railroad company built their line to the coal mine at Dawson, New Mexico, Coalora died. The camp has completely vanished.

50
c

Colfax

COUNTY: *Colfax*
LOCATION: *28 mi. southwest of Raton*
MAP: *page 239*
P.O. est. 1908; discont. 1921.

As a target of heavy promotion, Colfax should have succeeded, but it did not.

In early 1908, the New Mexico Sales Company surveyed and staked out town lots on a choice tract of land west of the Vermejo River at the junction of the St. Louis, Rocky Mountain and Pacific and the Dawson railways. The proposed town was named Colfax City, after the county. A full-scale promotional campaign augmented by the circulation of a thousand letters describing the advantages of buying lots in Colfax, went into effect. The company's pitch focused on luring farmers. The town was in the heart of rich farming land, it was situated on two railroads, nearby mountains abounded in wild game for the avid hunter, and it was close to other towns.

Colfax never fully blossomed, but it did manage to stay alive for some twenty-five years. A grade school attracted a small enrollment (never enough however, to compete in sports with neighboring schools), and the high school students commuted five miles to Dawson. A post office, a church, hotel, general merchandise stores, and a gasoline station accommodated the town.

Gradually the disadvantage of its location caused the various buildings and businesses of Colfax to fold. Surrounded by larger, more prosperous towns such as Dawson, Raton, Springer, and Cimmaron, which offered greater advantages, Colfax was doomed to fail. During the depression, when gasoline prices forced people to give up driving, they moved to one of the larger towns. Always at

Colfax Hotel today.

the mercy of outside interests and capital, Colfax could never successfully compete with its neighbors.

Today, Colfax presents a forlorn yet uniquely picturesque clustering of buildings. The two-story wooden building still visibly marking Colfax Hotel, a dried-up gasoline pump, a brick-front building once a combination store and bar and now housing Colfax's only residents, some deserted train coaches, the schoolhouse on the hill, and other assorted weather-beaten ruins remain.

Columbus

COUNTY: *Luna*
LOCATION: *32 mi. southeast of Deming*
MAP: *page 257*
P.O. est. 1891 to present.

Columbus, a little town quietly reposing on the Mexican border, has the potential to once again attract a sizable population. The reasons now are health and easy living, rather than the possibility of playing host to the military forces as it did in 1916.

The town began as a border station opposite Palomas, Chihuahua, about 1890, and a post office was established in 1891. Colonel Andrew O. Bailey, a Civil War veteran, and Louis Heller, promoter of colonies in Chihuahua, were two of the first settlers with an eye on Columbus as the gateway station on the proposed Northern Mexican and Pacific Railroad. The line was to cross the border at this point and extend as far north as Salt Lake City. These plans, however, never developed.

In 1903 the El Paso and Southwestern Railroad came through to connect El Paso with Douglas, Arizona. The Columbus and Western New Mexico Townsite Company was formed, and by 1905 Columbus was a solid little station with a population of a hundred residents, a general merchandise store, a saloon, and a customs inspector. As the community expanded, Perrow G. Mosely established the *Columbus News*, later called the *Columbus Courier*, and in 1910 a high school was built. In the next five years Columbus expanded to a reported seven hundred residents and advertised among its businesses the Columbus State Bank;

four hotels, the Commercial, Hoover, Columbus, and Luna; the Foxworth-Galbraith Lumber Co.; Columbus Garage; a Baptist church with the Rev. Joseph Laud as pastor; Crystal Theatre; T. H. Dabney, physician; three general merchandise stores; two barbers; three hardware and furniture stores; three restaurants; two billiard shops; five groceries; a jeweler; a drugstore; and an ice cream parlor. The town boasted of its proximity to rich silver, copper, lead, and zinc deposits; its fine marble and onyx quarries; and the inexpensive, fertile government land available for homesteading.

The everyday events that made news in Columbus have been overshadowed by the historical events that brought world-wide publicity to the town during the undeclared war with Pancho Villa.

In the winter of 1914 and the spring of 1915 the United States sent troops to Camp Furlong at Columbus and other border towns as a security measure. Pancho Villa and his command of several thousand Villistas had entangled the Constitutionalist army of Mexico's president, Venustiano Carranza. In addition to this revolutionary struggle, Mexican bandits increased the number of their raids across the border during 1915, stealing cattle and terrorizing the citizens of Texas, New Mexico, and Arizona.

On March 6, 1916, Camp Furlong, occupied by the Thirteenth Cavalry and commanded by Colonel Herbert J. Slocum, was manned by 7 officers and 341 men including noncombatants. The camp occupied the south side of Columbus opposite the E. P. & S. W. Railroad track from the business and residential district. Just before one o'clock in the morning on Thursday, March 9, Pancho Villa's raiders cut through the international fence some three miles west of the Palomas border gate and set forth on the last three miles to Columbus. About three o'clock and about a mile from their target the five hundred Villistas split into two forces. One detachment made its way silently along a drainage ditch to the north toward Camp Furlong. The other skirted west of the camp to hit Columbus from the southwest.

Gunfire first started in the camp as Private Fred Griffin, on guard at the west perimeter of the camp, shouted a challenge to the Mexicans. In return he received a slug in the belly but managed to kill

51
C

three bandits before he fell to the ground. The sound of the shots jolted the troopers from their sleep. In a state of complete confusion they grabbed their Springfields and clothes, if they could find them, and poured out of the barracks. The soldiers fired into the darkness at the faint shadows of the Mexicans. Twenty-six-year-old First Lieutenant John P. Lucas, who commanded the machine-gun troop, dashed barefooted past the barracks to a shack serving as an arsenal, unlocked the door, lunged inside, and grabbed one of the twenty-seven-pound Benét-Mercié machine guns and several thirty-round clips. Then Lucas, accompanied by several gunners with two more machine guns, ran to a crossing point near the railroad track and quickly set up the weapons. During the next hour and a half of fighting they leveled some twenty thousand rounds of machine-gun bullets into the main part of Columbus.

The Mexicans in the detachment approaching Columbus from the southwest poured into the main part of town. They battered down doors and opened fire on any house that showed a light. Several of the Villistas crashed their way into the Commercial Hotel on Main Street, looting and shooting as they burst through the rooms. Walton Walker was yanked out of his upstairs room, shoved down the stairs, and shot to death. His wife somehow escaped. Charles DeWitt Miller, an engineer, and Dr. H. M. Hart were thrown out of the hotel into the street, where they were killed and robbed. The Lemmon and Romney grocery store was set ablaze. The flames quickly spread to other adjacent buildings.

Lieutenant William A. McCain, his wife, and young daughter lived in civilian quarters south of the railroad tracks. As the firing started the three McCains and a young orderly who was staying with them fled into the brush away from the house. Minutes later the four were joined by Captain George Williams, armed with a revolver. The group was soon discovered and attacked by a Mexican bandit. In the brief struggle that followed, the three men easily overpowered the bandit and killed him.

The townspeople suffered unbelievable terror, brutality, and horror from the savagery of the Mexican bandits. The rifle fire of the Springfields was deadly accurate as the troopers, using the illumination of the burning buildings, caught the Villistas

Columbus—Main Street, *circa* 1916. During the early morning of March 9, 1916, Pancho Villa's bandits broke into and looted Sam Ravel's store.—*Courtesy Pancho Villa Museum.*

Pancho Villa (center) with "Dorados," his hand-picked body guard, *circa* 1913.—*Courtesy Pancho Villa Museum.*

in a crossfire. After about an hour and a half of battle the Villistas began to feel the sting of defeat and slowly began to withdraw toward Mexico. As the rear guard of the Mexicans was pulling away from Camp Furlong, Major Frank Tompkins ran from his home to a small promontory called Cootes Hill, south of the tracks. There he found Colonel Slocum commanding a few riflemen as they fired from the vantage point toward the retreating Mexicans. Dawn was just breaking. Twenty minutes later Major Tompkins and about thirty-two mounted cavalrymen chased the Villistas across the border and several miles into Mexico.

The final toll of casualties amounted to eight American soldiers, nine civilians, and about a hundred Villistas dead, along with numerous horses and mules. Several raiders were taken prisoner, along with some local Mexicans of questionable reputation. The prisoners were tried for murder and in June, 1916, seven of them were hanged in the jailyard at Deming, New Mexico.

During the next eleven months Columbus was the headquarters for the punitive expedition led by Brigadier General John J. Pershing. Troops numbering 4,800 men and 4,175 animals of the Seventh, Tenth, Eleventh, and Thirteenth Cavalry and the Sixth and Sixteenth Infantry regiments entered Mexico on March 15, 1916. The expedition fought a limited but successful campaign against Pancho Villa's army, destroying several bands of raiders and killing many of his officers and men.

On February 5, 1917, the last trooper of Pershing's Punitive Expedition marched across the international boundary south of Columbus into the United States. The dismantling of the camp at Columbus began at once, and by May of 1917 all vehicles, airplanes, and machinery had been shipped elsewhere. In 1919 Columbus still served as field headquarters for five thousand troops, but by 1923 the number had dwindled to sixty.

Today Columbus has a grocery store, tavern, motel, a couple of service stations, and the Pancho Villa Museum. A few ruins of the west portion of Camp Furlong and Cootes Hill have been attractively converted into the Pancho Villa State Park. The small population is slowly growing again, but the railroad station and some of the old adobe and wooden buildings of the picturesque border town remain as they did on March 9, 1916.

Above—Columbus after Villa's raid, 1916.—*Courtesy National Archives.*

Colonel Herbert J. Slocum, commanding officer of the Thirteenth Cavalry, stationed at Columbus during the raid.—*Courtesy National Archives.*

General John J. Pershing (1860–1948), commander of the punitive expedition into Mexico.—*Courtesy National Archives.*

Below—Columbus after the raid, 1916.—*Courtesy National Archives.*

Above—Army motorized equipment on the punitive expedition, 1916.—*Courtesy Pancho Villa Museum.*

Above—Columbus, Camp Furlong, now a state park. Lieutenant Lucas' quarters (center) and Cootes Hill with flag pole.

Columbus railroad station looking from the "big ditch" used by the Villistas as cover during their attack.

Cooks Peak

COUNTY: *Luna*
LOCATION: *about 29 mi. northeast of Deming*
MAP: *page 251*
P.O. est. 1889; discont. 1914.

A granite monolith that rises from the alluvial plain of Luna County was named for Captain Philip St. George Cooke of the Mormon Battalion, who passed through the area in the winter of 1846. Thirty years later, Ed Orr found ore while prospecting in the region, but his discovery failed to stimulate interest until two other prospectors, named Taylor and Wheeler, located the district's principal mines about 1880. In the summer of 1882, George L. Brooks supervised the grading of a road up the main canyon of the mountain and chose a campsite appropriately named for the prominent landmark. During the late 1870's the area of Cooks Peak had served as a veritable Apache stronghold. Because of the prevalent fear that the Indians might revisit their old haunts, soldiers from nearby Fort Cummings were engaged to stand guard during the construction of the road. After its completion, Brooks hauled the first load of silver- and lead-bearing ore from the camp. Many more tons were to follow as the town reached its greatest peak of prosperity in the early 1890's.

The camp of Cooks Peak was divided into an eastern and a western section and was comprised of the typical conglomeration of miner's shacks and chosen necessities. The saloon and dancehall allegedly stayed open day and night. The camp was no place for the religious or the morally conscious. A good priest made a few visits to the camp, but his works and presence passed unheeded.

Cooks Peak claimed to be a tough place, where killings were a common occurrence. Petty quarrels often terminated with the quick squeeze of a trigger. One day Thomas Dennis, a strapping Texan, was greasing his boots when Joseph Eswell, a slender, sickly fellow, advised him not to use lard because it would not shed water. Dennis' uncivil reply provoked Eswell into commenting that Dennis was getting so arrogant that nobody could speak to him. This set off a fusillade of angry words, during which Eswell frivolously threatened to beat Dennis to death with a shovel. A third party intervened at that point and induced Eswell to get to work. As Eswell turned to leave, Dennis drew a gun and without hesitating calmly shot and killed Eswell with one well-placed bullet. No doubt fearful for his own safety, Dennis went to Silver City, reported his crime to Sheriff Woods, and asked to be put in custody. Dennis claimed he acted in self-defense.

The silver depression in 1893 brought temporary suspension of work on most of the major properties at Cooks Peak, but by 1895 much of the mining had again resumed. In 1897 the camp reported the following: population, a hundred residents; daily stage and mail from Florida station, a distance of fourteen miles; twelve producing mines shipping twenty tons a day at an estimated value of $600; miners' wages $3.00 a day, and Mexican labor $1.50 a day.

A mill tailings pile and a couple of melted adobe ruins beside the tailings hint of those good years when mining fed prosperity to Cooks Peak.

General Philip St. George Cooke (1809–95), after whom Cooks Peak was named.—*Courtesy Museum of New Mexico.*

Miners at the Cooks Peak Mine, *circa* 1890.—*Courtesy Blachly Collection, University of Arizona, Special Collection.*

Mine buildings and tailings dump at Cooks Peak, *circa* 1890.— *Courtesy Schmit Collection, University of New Mexico Library.*

Cooks Peak: (1) saloon and post office, (2) store, (3) boarding house, *circa* 1890.—*Courtesy Blachly Collection, University of Arizona, Special Collections.*

Coolidge

COUNTY: *Mckinley*
LOCATION: *about 20 mi. southeast of Gallup*
MAP: *page 245*
P.O. est. 1888; discont. 1895. Re-est. 1926; discont. 1957.

The name Coolidge has been applied to two communities in western New Mexico. The site of the first settlement is located about three miles northwest of present-day Coolidge. The ruins that were left at the site of old Coolidge were removed by bulldozer about 1930. Today the old site is identified by the large log hogan that was constructed about 1935 by Harold L. Ickes, secretary of the interior under President F. D. Roosevelt.

A small settlement called Crane was named for Billy Crane, an early pioneer who at one time acted as a scout and teamster for Kit Carson. He owned a ranch called Bacon Springs, where he was contracted to cut and deliver hay to Fort Wingate for the cavalry horses.

In the early 1880's the Atlantic and Pacific Railroad constructed a main line across the territory, passing the settlement of Crane. The name of the embryo community was changed to Coolidge in honor of Thomas Jefferson Coolidge, a director of the A. & P.R.R. During the next few years, until 1888, Coolidge did not have a post office, but it made a fair showing as a tough little community with a trading post operated by John B. Hall and Charles Paxton, a general mercantile store run by C. L. Flynn, the Page brothers sawmill and lumber yard, and Dr. Burke, the resident physician. The settlement had no religious representation or school, and, as stories go, the law was administered by the citizens without recourse to constitutional proceedings.

The story is told of a stranger who got off the train one day in Coolidge and made his way to the combination general store, saloon, and post office. There he bought a three-cent stamp but was charged a nickel. When the stranger mentioned the error, the postmaster replied that he never sold anything for less than five cents. The stranger produced a postal inspector's badge and began to reprimand the postmaster for selling liquor in.a federal post office. The old storekeeper gathered up all of the post office supplies and mail, placed them in a box, and threw it out the door. He then explained to the postal inspector that a saloon paid better than a post office.

After a number of years the railroad transferred much of its business to Gallup, and Coolidge folded up. Mail service continued in the vicinity under the post office names of Dewey, Guam, and Perea. About 1926 the community of Coolidge was re-established at its present location on Interstate 40, with a trading post and service station.

Cooney

COUNTY: *Catron*
LOCATION: *about 15 mi. northeast of Glenwood*
MAP: *page 253*
P.O. est. 1884; discont. 1915.

While serving as a guide and scout at Fort Bayard in 1870, Sergeant James C. Cooney discovered high-grade silver and copper ore in the Mogollons. When his term of duty expired in 1875, Cooney organized a party that prospected the area and soon located the first claims. Frequent Indian raids, however, forced the men to temporarily abandon their mining properties. Two years later their claims were relocated and feverishly worked until April, 1880. At that time the Apaches, led by Chief Victorio, began their vicious assaults throughout the Frisco Valley. The miners on Mineral Creek were attacked and two men were killed. The body of one of the victims, Buhlman, was found at the entrance of his mining tunnel, but the remains of the other were not found until two years later. James Cooney and William Chick, who had gone to Alma to warn the settlers, were ambushed on their return to camp and both were killed. Their bodies were buried beside the road near the entrance of Cooney Canyon, where they had fallen. When news of his brother's death reached Captain

Cooney gold and silver mining camp, *circa 1910.—Courtesy Museum of New Mexico.*

James C. Cooney, killed by Apaches in 1880, was interred in this rock vault.

Michael Cooney in New Orleans, he resigned from his position as customs inspector and went to New Mexico to take over his brother's Silver Bar Mine. Several years later, in 1884, Captain Cooney had a vault hewn out of a large boulder a few hundred yards below the company's mill near the spot where his brother had been buried. Here the remains of James Cooney were interred. It seemed a fitting memorial to the man who gave his name to the booming camp on Mineral Creek. By 1889 the camp of Cooney claimed a population of six hundred, three operating stamp mills, a school, a church, and two hotels.

In September of 1911, Cooney was struck by a destructive flood. Eight houses were swept away by the rampant current that also caused considerable damage to other buildings, including the mill and plant of the Enterprise Mining Company.

Captain Michael Cooney met his demise in 1914 while combing the mountains for a lost mine.

Years earlier, in 1883, Cooney had grubstaked a man named Turner. The prospector supposedly found a mine on Sycamore Creek in the Mogollons, but he soon disappeared and was never heard from again. His skeleton was found six years later in Sycamore Canyon, showing that he had been the victim of an Indian attack. With the verification of Turner's death the alleged mine rightfully belonged to Cooney, and he became determined to find it. Several of his attempts to locate it ended in failure. Then, in October of 1914, Cooney looked for the mine again, but this time he never returned. As winter set in, parties were forced to give up their hopeless search for him. Four months later Cooney's body was discovered in Sycamore Canyon lying just a hundred yards from the spot where Turner's remains had been found.

The town of Cooney is gone. Only some rock foundations and rubble attest to its onetime existence.

Copper City

COUNTY: *Bernalillo*
LOCATION: *about 3 mi. east of Cuba*
MAP: *page 243*
P.O. est. 1883; discont. 1890.

The mineral deposits that gave rise to Copper City were first discovered by Indians and Mexicans early in the nineteenth century. In the 1880's, Copper City was founded when systematic effort was made to mine the deposits. During its short life it allegedly had, at one time, over five hundred residents, the usual number of saloons and stores, a restaurant, school, hotel, and butcher shop.

A tale is told of a buried treasure at Copper City. Two partners, Harris Dupont and F. D. Thompson, worked a mining claim near Copper City. Greed took hold of Dupont, and he began quietly caching away more than his share of the mine's profits. One day when Dupont had gone to town for supplies, Thompson discovered the hidden coins and realized he had been cheated. Thompson kept this discovery from Dupont while awaiting the perfect opportunity to deal out revenge. One afternoon, while Dupont was leaning over to inspect some mine equipment, Thompson hit him on the head with a hammer, killing him instantly. Covering the mine entrance and burying the gold coins, Thompson made a hasty departure for Texas. An innocent sheepherder who stumbled across Dupont's body and stole the miner's watch later was hanged for Thompson's revengeful crime. Years later Thompson returned to recover the money he had buried but was never able to find it.

Copper City is gone. Even the exact location is difficult to pinpoint. Partially hidden in overgrowth is the black slag pile from the thirty-ton smelter that once produced a daily carload of copper.

Shaft winch at Copperton.

Copperton

COUNTY: *Valencia*
LOCATION: *about 22 mi. southwest of Prewitt*
MAP: *page 245*
P.O. est. 1901; discont. 1911.

Copperton probably never boasted more than ten families. It had no school or church, just a small store. A business directory of 1905–1906 listed four mining companies at Copperton; a sawmill; J. Lukens, dairyman, rooms, and boarding; and Myra E. Jones, stationer and postmaster. The camp folded at about the time the post office closed. Although Copperton was a small camp with a life span of only one decade, there are several ruins left. Looking west from the road sign marked Copperton Canyon the observer can see a log winch and the remnants of a couple of log cabins half hidden in the aspen-tree meadow. A little farther down the gulch are half a dozen more log cabin ruins and several other ruins are on the knoll to the south.

Copperton, looking northeast, 1905.—*Courtesy F. C. Schrader, U.S. Geological Survey*.

Log cabin ruins at Copperton.

Council Rock

COUNTY: *Socorro*
LOCATION: *about 45 mi. northwest of Magdalena*
MAP: *page 247*
P.O. est. 1881; discont. 1883.

In January of 1881, Uncle Billy Hill discovered silver in the Iron Mountain District of Socorro County. This strike sent two prospectors named Davis and White into the region where they located the Old Boss Mine. By October of 1881, the town-site of Council Rock had been staked out and filled with almost a hundred cabins to accommodate the expanding growth. Anticipating a great demand, the eager real estate promoters sold lots for as high as $250 each.

The new village was called Council Rock, taken from the name of a large nearby rock which in earlier years had been used as a meeting place for Indians and white men.

Mining failed to support the town, which soon crumbled into obscurity.

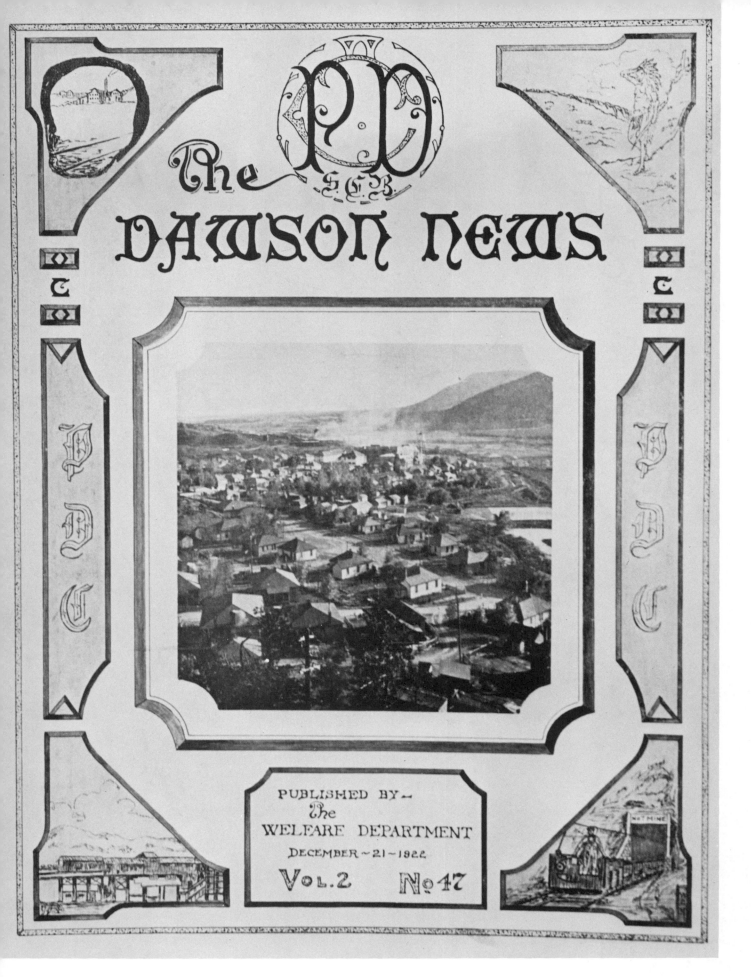

The D. D. N. S. C. B.

The Dawson News

PUBLISHED BY
The
WELFARE DEPARTMENT
DECEMBER ~ 21 ~ 1922
VOL. 2   No. 17

Front page of *Dawson News.*—*Courtesy Ruth Hart.*

View of coal tipple and homes at Dawson, *circa* 1945.—*Courtesy Ruth Hart.*

Dawson

COUNTY: *Colfax*
LOCATION: *14 mi. northeast of Cimarron*
MAP: *page 239*
P.O. est. 1900; discont. 1954.

In 1869, John Barkley Dawson bought from the Maxwell Land Grant twenty-three thousand acres of rich ranching land along New Mexico's Vermejo River. About 1895, coal was found on the land, and the first coal mine on Dawson's ranch opened in 1901. During that year the Dawson Fuel Company was organized, and a railroad was constructed from Tucumcari to Dawson. Phelps Dodge Corporation looked over the Dawson mines and found them favorable, hence in 1906 the company purchased the property and Dawson became a concern of the Stag Canon branch, a subsidiary of Phelps Dodge. The increasing market for coal and coke brought about rapid development. Dawson grew into a prosperous coal city, eventually supporting a population of nine thousand residents.

In keeping with its rise in importance, Dawson quickly improved the necessities and added the luxuries. A large number of modern homes were built. Shade trees, sidewalks, a hotel, a newspaper —*The Dawson News*—and a theater graced the town. For the sports minded there were a ball park, an athletic field, a swimming pool, golf course, bowling alley, and facilities for pool and billiards. In 1914 the new mercantile department store opened. Being strictly up-to-date, the store sold almost everything, including food, hardware, furniture, ready-made clothes, and shoes. It also contained a bakery and an ice plant that turned out five thousand pounds of ice every twenty-four hours. By 1919 the store had three branches and more than sixty employees.

The Dawson schools evolved from simple frame buildings into a modern grade school and a large stone and brick high school. The high school basketball and football teams were especially outstanding, and for years were in the top bracket. The big football game of the season with Raton was held on Thanksgiving Day and usually decided the district championship. The whole town of Dawson took an interest in the highschool sporting events. During a game all businesses were closed.

Dawson maintained a modern hospital staffed with five doctors. There was also a dispensary housing the doctor's offices, two dentist's offices, and a registered pharmacist. On the spiritual side, the town had a Catholic church with a resident priest and a Protestant Union Chapel.

The coal city had an interesting cosmopolitan makeup, representing a large range of nationalities. In addition to Americans from different places in the United States there were people from Italy, Greece, the British Isles, and Mexico; also some French and Germans, with a sprinkling of Japanese and Chinese. Many of these immigrants lived in the dozen or so miners' boardinghouses. During leisure hours and on Sunday the men entertained themselves by playing native games and cooking food of their country to treat friends and visitors.

Dawson's long life was scarred by two terrible mine tragedies. The unbroken rows of uniform silver crosses in Dawson's cemetery are a vivid reminder of those two nightmarish events that occurred years ago. On October 22, 1913, at 3:10 P.M. a sound was heard like the shot of a high-powered rifle, followed by a dull roar and a vibration of the earth. A solid mass of fire catapulted from the mouth of Mine No. 2, and moments later fifteen men stumbled from the tunnel, too dazed to know what had happened. Dawson stood shocked and silent as rescue crews began to retrieve the dead and some still alive. Two men from the Koehler Mine, on hearing the news, rushed to Dawson to offer assistance. Despite protests they entered the mine to help in the rescue work, but a sudden leak of escaping gas asphyxiated them. On that fatal day, 263 miners plus the two heroic rescue men lost their lives. Twenty-five others managed to escape.

On February 8, 1923, at two o'clock in the afternoon a powerful explosion crumbled the reinforced concrete mine entrance to Mine No. 1. The following hours seemed like a reinactment of the earlier

Residential street in Dawson, *circa* 1945.—*Courtesy Ruth Hart.*

disaster. There was no hope for the trapped miners. Miraculously though, two men did come out alive; 120 miners were not as lucky.

After a half century of life, Dawson's demise was brought about by circumstances and progress. Phelps Dodge Corporation was forced to cease mining operations at their Stag Canon branch. With the conversion from steam locomotives to diesel units the need for Dawson's coal decreased.

Dawson was sold to the National Iron & Metal Company of Phoenix, Arizona, who agreed to dismantle the town, and Dawsonites were given a thirty-day notice. It was not easy for many of them to leave the only home they had ever known and to see Dawson razed to the ground. Everything in Dawson, from pencil sharpeners to mine machinery, went on sale to buyers from all parts of the country. Two men from Albuquerque, Van Roush and Dugan Guest, purchased four hundred dwellings which they sold intact in groups or individually to be moved to another location or to be torn down for the material. The largest single item of

the town, the coal washer, was sold to a coal firm in Harlan County, Kentucky. Workmen from Kentucky took the huge plant down, loaded it in freight cars, and hauled it to Harlan County to be reassembled. The one exception to the sale was the Catholic church, which was given to the diocese by Phelps Dodge before the town was sold. The church was dismantled and the materials moved to other locations. The large main store building erected years earlier for $250,000 was razed at no profit. The high school, along with the opera house, hospital, and numerous other buildings gave way before the onslaught of wreckers, thus making final Dawson's cessation.

About all that is left today are the few homes of people employed by the Phelps Dodge ranch, two large brick smokestacks, shade trees, and some of the sidewalk. Half a mile south is the large cemetery. The rest of Dawson is scattered all over the country.

Dawson coal washer, *circa* 1925.—*Courtesy Museum of New Mexico.*

Dawson Catholic church, *circa* 1945.—*Courtesy Ruth Hart.*

Below—Advertisements from *Dawson News*, December 21, 1922.—*Courtesy Ruth Hart.*

Above—Boy Scout first aid class at Dawson, from *Dawson News*, December 21, 1922.— *Courtesy Ruth Hart*.

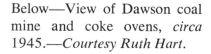

Phelps Dodge Company store at Dawson, *circa* 1945.—*Courtesy Ruth Hart*.

Below—View of Dawson coal mine and coke ovens, *circa* 1945.—*Courtesy Ruth Hart*.

Above—Phelps Dodge employees, from section hand to general manager, at their last celebration before the closing of the mine, spring, 1950.—*Courtesy Ruth Hart.*

Above—Notice from Phelps Dodge Corporation to residents of Dawson to vacate their homes. March 31, 1950.—*Courtesy Ruth Hart.*

Present view of coke oven smokestacks at Dawson.

Dawson cemetery. White iron crosses mark the graves of miners who died in the mine explosions of 1913 and 1923.

Diener

COUNTY: *Valencia*
LOCATION: *about 18 mi. southwest of Prewitt*
MAP: *page 245*
P.O. est. 1916; discont. 1931.

Copper mining was carried on at Diener but not very profitably. It was a small settlement of about ten cabins housing ten to twenty miners from California. Diener folded in the early 1930's.

On the south side of the road is a notched-log cabin, and on the north are the badly sagging, roofless ruins of two more cabins and several clusters of scattered wood. The rock and cement foundations of the mill, which burned down in the 1930's, are on the pine-covered sloping hillside.

Ruins of the copper mining camp of Diener in the Zuni Mountains.

Dolores, placer gold mining camp, *circa* 1895.—*Courtesy L. C. Graton, U.S. Geological Survey.*

Dolores

COUNTY: *Santa Fe*
LOCATION: *about 32 mi. southwest of Santa Fe*
MAP: *page 243*
P.O. est. 1887; discont. 1890. Re-est. 1894; discont. 1901.

Two decades before the magic word "gold" sent people rushing to California, New Mexico was experiencing a gold furor. The discovery produced the settlement of Real de Dolores, now more generally referred to as Dolores or Old Placers. There are two stories concerning the actual circumstances surrounding the initial find. One tells of a herd of livestock that strayed from some freighters. After searching for several days the men found the oxen in a canyon where there was a small spring. When one of the animals suddenly died, the men cut open its stomach and found a large gold nugget.

Believing the oxen had swallowed the gold while drinking from the spring, the freighters panned the spring, found gold, and triggered a gold rush. The more credible and less fanciful version claims that the Old Placers were discovered by a Mexican herder from Sonora who followed his strayed sheep into the Ortiz Mountains and found a rock similar to gold-bearing ore he had seen in Sonora. When the rock proved to contain gold, news of it spread, and the inevitable rush began. It is interesting to note that in those days it took three months for the news of the gold discovery to reach Missouri, eight hundred miles away.

Prospectors hurried north from Mexico and other parts of the country to wash out the gold-laden sands and gravels. Their labors were carried on under great disadvantages due to the scarcity of water, which forced the miners either to carry the dirt to the water, two miles away, or pack water in barrels to the workings. Regardless of the crude methods employed, an estimated $300,000 to $500,000 of gold was extracted. The eager gold seekers established a busy town. References disagree as to the population of Dolores, but figures fall somewhere between two thousand and four thousand persons. Hundreds of adobe homes and businesses cropped up along the numerous long streets, shaping Dolores into a city of considerable magnitude.

In 1833 gold quartz veins, the source of the placer deposits found five years previously, were discovered by a Spaniard named Don Cano on the Santa Rosalia Grant about half a mile from Dolores. Jose Francisco Ortiz owned the property, but being unskilled as a miner he took into partnership Don Demasio Lopez. Under Lopez's competent management the Sierra Del Oro or Ortiz Mine began to produce quantities of gold. Struck with gold greed and wishing to cash in on a larger share of his mine profits, Ortiz listened to the advice of some unscrupulous men, who talked him into breaking his partnership with Lopez and forming a new one with them. The new management, however, proved to be utterly inefficient, and the mine failed to produce. About 1840, rumors of richer fields shifted the scene of activity away from Dolores in the Ortiz Mountains to the New Placers

in the San Pedro Mountains. The New Mexico Mining Company acquired the Ortiz Mine in 1864 and the following year built a twenty-stamp mill. It was the first stamp mill erected in New Mexico.

A population figure for 1870 listed 150 people at Real de Dolores. In 1883 it was reported that the ruins of the adobe dwellings, vestiges of the roads, and partially-filled pits from the booming placer days of 1828 gave Dolores the appearance of almost total desolation. Four years later a report of Dolores stated that a healthy growth existed, but no boom was anticipated for the town.

Thomas A. Edison erected a large plant at Dolores in 1900 in hopes of extracting gold with static electricity. The operation closed down after a few unsuccessful experimental attempts, and Edison turned his attention to other undertakings. One of his projects involved finding a metal to use in making a heat-resistant filament for his electric light bulb. Edison never found the substance, yet, ironically, it lay within his reach at Dolores. In 1950 scheelite, an ore of tungsten, was found in an old cut made half a century earlier by Edison.

An old general store and saloon now serves as a private ranch headquarters, and the rest of the site of Dolores is marked by numerous rock tailings piles.

71
D

Right—Advertisement from *Los Cerrillos Rustler*, December 14, 1888.—*Courtesy Highlands University Library*.

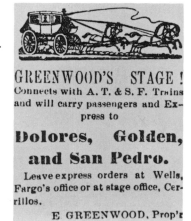

GREENWOOD'S STAGE !
Connects with A. T. & S. F. Trains and will carry passengers and Express to

Dolores, Golden, and San Pedro.

Leave express orders at Wells, Fargo's office or at stage office, Cerrillos.

E. GREENWOOD, Prop'r

Ortiz Mine, chief gold producer of the Old Placer District around Dolores, *circa* 1895.—*Courtesy L. C. Graton, U.S. Geological Survey*.

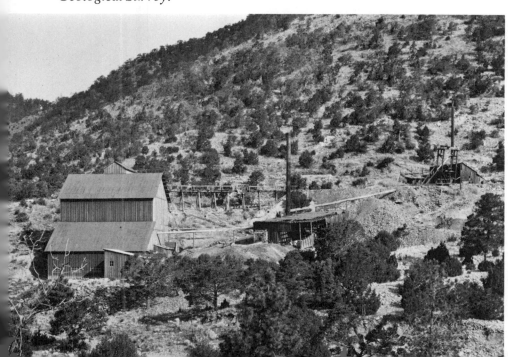

Elizabethtown, looking south, 1901.—*Courtesy Museum of New Mexico.*

Elizabethtown, present view, looking south from the cemetery.

Elizabethtown

COUNTY: *Colfax*
LOCATION: *5 mi. north of Eagle Nest*
MAP: *page 239*
P.O. est. 1868; discont. 1931.

Launched by a feverish gold rush in the mid-1860's, Elizabethtown, or E-town as it was more often called, exploded into a raw, lusty, vigorous camp of seven thousand residents. Today, however, only shabby suggestions of E-town's long and indelible life have survived. Half a dozen old buildings and a cemetery stand guard over a silent town.

Elizabethtown's beginning followed the frantic discovery of gold on Willow Creek in 1866. Thousands of hopeful Argonauts sucked up by the cry of "gold" converged at the new Eldorado. During the next year, gold was found in every creek and gulch around Baldy Mountain, and the Moreno Valley was turned into a frenzy of mining activity.

About 1868, John Moore and others established a townsite and named the new settlement in honor of Moore's daughter, Elizabeth. Elizabethtown claimed two singular distinctions. It was the first incorporated town in New Mexico, and in 1869 it became the first county seat of the newly formed Colfax County.

After surveying and naming the camp, the next problem to be tackled was an ample water supply to profitably work the gold fields. Captain N. S. Davis, a United States Army engineer was employed by parties from Fort Union and Las Vegas to investigate diverting water from Red River. The outcome was the organization of the Moreno Water and Mining Company and the commencement of the big ditch project. Certainly a most remarkable engineering feat of its day, the ditch was built between May 12 and November 13, 1868, with as many as 420 men working at a time. Covering a distance over forty miles and costing $300,000, the aqueduct bridged arroyos, was suspended from steep walls, and was even lifted seventy-nine feet over a valley floor by twenty-three hundred feet of trestle. Because of evaporation and seepage, however, the completed ditch was never as successful as had been anticipated.

March, 1868, reported Elizabethtown with about a hundred buildings. John Moore is credited with erecting the first house and first store in the town. Other businesses quickly sprang up, so that by 1869 the increasing population patronized five stores, seven saloons, two hotels, three dance halls and a drugstore. That year E-town published its first newspaper, *The Lantern.*

A certain amount of notoriety is linked with E-town because of some unsavory characters and desperate crimes committed there. Joseph Antonio Herberger, a member of the vigilantes, committed his atrocities under the guise of that organization. In the spring of 1868, Herberger and other vigilantes captured, hanged, and riddled with bullets murderer "Pony" O'Neil. This act seems to have set off Herberger's latent violence and unbalanced nature. A few months later, in a saloon, Herberger beat Captain Keefer to death with a piece of stovewood because of a disagreement over a whisky bill. His next victim was saloonkeeper Greeley, whom he shot twice and killed because of a petty jealousy. Arrested and convicted of murder, Herberger spent two and a half years in the Santa Fe penitentiary.

Acting in self-defense turned "Wall" Henderson into a pathetic victim and a notorious character of E-town's history. In 1869 a number of men jumped Henderson's mining claims. When Henderson told the men to leave, one of them sprang at Henderson and attempted to beat him with a shovel. Henderson stopped his assailant with a well-placed bullet, instantly killing him. Tried for murder in Mora County, Henderson was acquitted and soon returned to E-town, where he was plagued by continued abuse from the friends of the man he had killed. One day in a saloon, Ned O'Hara threatened to smash Henderson's head with a rock, and, again acting in self-defense, Henderson shot his attacker. Although O'Hara did not die, Henderson was guilt-ridden and remorseful for his deeds and began drinking heavily, becoming violent and argumentative. He soon joined up with a gang of desperados and further increased his notoriety by killing saloonkeeper Joseph Stinson. Although Henderson killed only two men, and both circumstances were probably justified under the loose code of those days, he nevertheless gained rank among the more desperate characters of E-town.

No doubt the most macabre of E-town's stories revolved around the gruesome activities of Charles Kennedy, owner of a traveler's rest on the road between Elizabethtown and Taos. Several people who stopped there mysteriously disappeared and were never heard from again. Finally one day, Kennedy's wife fled in terror to E-town and reported that her husband had killed their baby. Officers were sent to arrest Kennedy while others, acting upon information supplied by his wife, began searching the house. A variety of partially charred human bones were found burning in the fire, and further investigation unearthed two skeletons beneath the house. When the rumors began circulating that Kennedy's lawyer was going to buy his freedom, an irate mob snatched Kennedy from custody, threw a rope around his neck, and dragged him through the streets, strangling him to death.

In 1871, E-town's prosperity began to slacken. People moved on and houses were torn down. Soon the town was reduced to about a hundred residents, and for a number of years it slumbered in semi-desertion.

About the turn of the century, Elizabethtown once again felt a pulse of activity with the installation of a big dredge christened "Eleanor." The Oro Dredging Company, headed by H. J. Reiling, built a dam three miles from Elizabethtown, constructed a large boat, and hauled the heavy dredge machinery from the railroad at Springer. It took two weeks for the 21,000-pound boilers to be hauled the fifty-five miles to E-town. In August, 1901, the assembled dredge, costing $100,000, was put into production. With the dredge handling four thousand cubic yards of dirt a day and operating around the clock, Elizabethtown again entered a phase of prosperity.

The town was thriving well when a fire broke out in September of 1903. Starting in the second floor of Remsberg's store, the flames spread rapidly throughout the town. Losses were heavy, with only Herman Froelick's general store escaping destruction. The fire proved a hard blow for E-town; one from which it never fully recovered. Gradually E-town began to dwindle, and although mining continued until World War II, E-town's prosperous era had long since passed. Vandals eventually destroyed the Mutz Hotel and the Catholic church. In 1956 the old schoolhouse was sold for salvage.

Present ruins of Remsberg's Store.

Hydraulic mining along Moreno Valley, *circa* 1900.— *Courtesy Museum of New Mexico.*

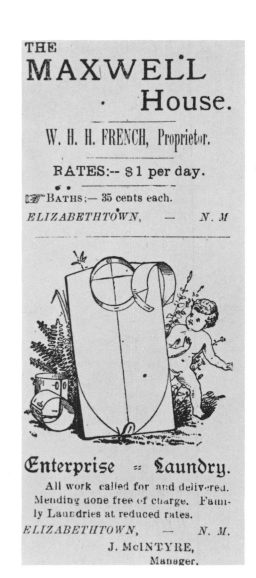

Advertisements from *Mining Bulletin*, January 25, 1900.—*Courtesy Colfax County Courthouse.*

Below—Elizabethtown, *circa* 1890: (1) Remsberg's Store, (2) John Pierson Store, (3) Froelick Store.— *Courtesy Museum of New Mexico.*

Independence Day in E'town.

Grand Celebration by the Mountain Metropolis.

There will be a celebration held in E'town on the Forth of July. The committees are hard at work. They are as follows;

ARRANGEMENTS COMMITTEE.

C. J. Dold, W. C. Whitescarver, Wm. Edling.

ROCK DRILLING COMMITTEE.

J. Zwergle, T. B. Stevens, J. C. Kelso.

RACING COMMITTEE.

A. J. Poak, Dr. L. L. Cahill, W. Simmons.

FIRE WORKS COMMITTEE.

Peter Perry, Norman Perry.

PROGRAM.

Sunrise Salute.

10 A. M.   Music by Band.
            Prayer by L. O. Haberstich.
            Declaration of Independence
                Florence C. Morse.
            Music by Band.
            Address by E. C. Abbott.
            Song Miss Elizabeth Argue.
            Music by Band.

11 A. M.   Rock Drilling Contest,
                Single and Double.

AFTERNOON.

1 P. M.   Races.

Potatoe Race.   Old Man's Race.
Shoe   "   Boy's   "
Sack Race Men.   Foot   "
Sack   " Boys.   Burro Race fast.
Wheelbarrow Race.   Burro   " slow.
Three Legged "   Greased Pig.
            Music by Band.

4 P. M.   Horse Race best 2 in 3 ¼ mi.
           Pony   " best 2 in 3 300 yd.
           Ladies "   ¼ mi.

EVENING.

8 P. M.   Fire Works on Tailings
                East of Town.
           Music by Band.

9 P. M   Grand Ball at both Halls.

Though the skies were dark and lowering a good crowd gathered in Elizabethtown for the Fourth of July celebration and at 10 A. M. Chairman Dold called the assembly to order. The band played the opening piece, the Declaration of Independence was listened to and Hon. E. C. Abbott began his address. All this time the mists had been gathering and the women with little ones and the girls with new hats cast anxious glances around. Taos Co. seemed to be the storm centre and soon the Taos mountains were obscured from view. Then the rain began. Mr. Abbott with the crowd running after went into Pritchards hall and the program was finished as well as could be, while the rain beat furiously on the big iron roof. The speaker was obliged to raise his voice and even then could scarcely be heard by those nearest, such was the din of the storm. However the band could be heard easily and E'town never felt more pleased that we had such a good one. The chairman announced that on account of the mud and water the races would be on the 5th. and all went home as soon as the rain would let them, and staid there till evening. At 8 o'clock there was a fine display of fire works and a band concert followed by a dance in both halls which was well patronized. About 80 couple danced 'till the "we sma hours", Geo. Downey kept them supplied with ice cold lemonade and other temperanc drinks, but they all lived through the evening and at 12 o'clock repaired to the "Miners Inn" where a good supper was served. The races came off on the 5th. and the following gives the names of the winners:

Fast Burro Race,   Jay Hammond,
Slow   "   "   Joseph Raught,
Boys Foot Race,   Roy Pearson,
Boys Sack Race,   Allen Perry,
Shoe Race,   Norman Perry,
Boys Shoe Race,   Louis Morse,
Potatoe Race,   Norman Perry,
Girls race,   Nellie Pritchard,
3 legged Race,   Louis Dold and
                       Allen Perry.

Horse Race, Time 28 sec. John Zwergle first money, F. Bain second money.

Pony Race, Time 19 ¼ sec. 300 yards Manus Gallagher first money, W. H. H. French second money.

The committees who had the celebration in charge deserve much praise they wo k d hard, harder than any one would think, and

---

Left—Elizabethtown's Fourth of July program, from *New Mexican Miner*, June 22, 1900. Right—Follow-up news article of Fourth of July celebration from *New Mexican Miner*, July 6, 1900.—*Courtesy Colfax County Courthouse.*

Below—Advertisements from *New Mexican Miner*, May 18, 1900.—*Courtesy Colfax County Courthouse.*

Above—Elizabethtown school closing exercises. *New Mexican Miner*, May 18, 1900.—*Courtesy Colfax County Courthouse.*

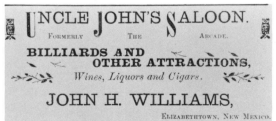

Elizabethtown, New Year's Day celebration, 1896. Left, Henry Pritchard's Store; Right, Mutz Hotel.—*Courtesy Museum of New Mexico.*

Below—Elizabethtown, drugstore and post office, 1899.—*Courtesy Museum of New Mexico.*

BED ROCK PRICES!

FOR CASH ONLY.

Dry Goods, Notions, Boots, Shoes and Hardware at 25 per cent discount.
Men's Suits from $5 upward.
Fine Negligee Overshirts from 65 cents to $1.10.

GROCERIES

14 pounds granulated sugar	$1 00	1 gallon can golden syrup	$ 60
20 pounds oatmeal	1 00	1 plug Horseshoe tobacco	45
7 packages Arbuckles' coffee	1 00	1 plug Climax tobacco	45
1 case corn	2 40	1 quart bottle good whisky	75
1 case tomatoes	2 65	1 quart bottle imported port wine	1 00
4 cans sardines	25	1 quart bottle A1 blackberry brandy	65
2 cans salmon	25	1 quart bottle beer	30
15 pounds dried grapes	1 00	20 bars White Eagle soap	1 00

Everything in proportion for cash only.   Doors and window sash in stock.

Henry Pritchard,

ELIZABETHTOWN - - - - - - NEW MEXICO.

Above—Advertisement from *New Mexican Miner,* May 7, 1898.— *Courtesy Colfax County Courthouse.*

Advertisement from *Mining Bulletin,* January 4, 1900.—*Courtesy Colfax County Courthouse.*

First and Last Chance
SALOON.
If You want a Good Time, Go and see Louie & Ed.
ALL KINDS OF LIQUORS AND CIGARS.
ELIZABETHTOWN, — N. M

Elizabethtown church, 1943.—*Courtesy Library of Congress.*

Above—Advertisement from
The Black Range, October 6,
1882.—*Courtesy Highlands
University Library.*

Left—Engle, view of the Santa Fe station.

Engle

COUNTY: *Sierra*
LOCATION: *17 mi. east of Truth or Consequences*
MAP: *page 251*
P.O. est. 1881; discont. 1955.

Once a thriving cattle town and the shipping point for mining supplies to western New Mexico, Engle is only a vestige of its colorful past. Several adobe buildings, the sun-baked façade of a church and yellow station buildings of the Atchison, Topeka and Santa Fe Railroad are gradually deteriorating. A few people still live there, keeping Engle from becoming totally deserted.

In 1879 Engle was built as a station on the A.T. & S.F. Railroad. Several conflicting stories are told about the origin of its name. One tale states that the station is the namesake of R. L. Engle, one of the engineers who supervised the railroad construction, but by mistake the name was registered with the post office department as Angle. It stayed that way for six months before being cor-

rected. Another story claims that the station name was originally spelled Engel. When a paint crew for the railroad was lettering the name they changed it to Engle; so the spelling of the name was changed in the railroad timetable in order to match the one on the station.

In the early 1880's Engle was locally referred to as Rogers' Ranch after Alex Rogers opened a general store. Rogers' Store supplied ranchers and miners in the northern portion of the Black Range Mountains and served as headquarters for the Southwestern Stage Company that ran a tri-weekly, four-horse coach to the mines at Fairview (Winston), some fifty miles west, for a $7.50 fare.

Although Engle reported a small population of forty persons in 1884, it claimed several business establishments; Armstrong Brothers' General Store, the Humboldt Hotel and Humboldt Mining Co., with David Branson its president, a saloon, express agent, blacksmith, boardinghouse, and a cotton gin mill. Water was piped about four miles by steam pump from Del Muerto Spring, providing Engle with an abundant supply.

Colonel David Branson, the financial mainstay of the community, was said to have fought in the last battle of the Civil War and to have given the final command to cease firing. The engagement took place on May 12 and 13, 1865. Branson was sent out from the general camp on Brazo's Island at the mouth of the Río Grande with his command of about three hundred mixed troops of the Second Texas Cavalry, First Missouri, and Thirty-Fourth Indiana regiments to capture a herd of Confederate cattle. During the battle with the Texas Cavalry, the Union ship *Quaker City* arrived with the news of the South's surrender.

The early 1900's brought an influx of cattle drives to Engle Station from as far east as Tularosa. Many herds such as the seventeen thousand head of the Bar Cross outfit brought in during the spring of 1917 gave Engle an economic boost. Trail drivers stopped for a while to blow their pay at the Hickcock Saloon, Thompson Saloon, and the Blue Goose brothel. More than likely they raised a little hell, as was the case with Jesse Ake. Jesse and some of his companions were watching a slow-moving work train traveling north out of Engle. Deciding to have a little fun with the workers whose heads were sticking out of the open gondola, Jesse whipped out his lariat and in a flash dropped the lasso around the neck of Ramon Aragon. Before anyone realized what was happening, Ramon was jerked head-first out of the open car and came

crashing down into the cinders with a broken neck. Ake fled south toward the Organ Mountains, pursued by law officers from Hillsboro and Las Cruces; he was never captured.

The construction of Elephant Butte Dam in 1915 bolstered Engle's economy at least for a couple of years. A railroad spur was built west from Engle for twelve miles, to the east bank of the Río Grande, and nearly all building materials and workers were supplied out of Engle. At that time Engle had a thriving five hundred people. Jitney Jack Smith, Earl Lovelady, Festus Heffernan, and several others began bus service to Hot Springs, present-day Truth or Consequences. Each competitor worked independently, trying to undercharge and outdrive the others. Probably because he was the only mechanic, Heffernan finally won out, operating the only bus service in Engle.

After completion of the Elephant Butte Dam in 1916 the town was reduced in size, in 1919 reporting two hundred persons and in 1926, seventy-five. In 1930 a road leading east to Tularosa was graded. Engle residents hoped it would also be paved, improving their economic condition. The paving was never done. In the early 1940's the area east of Engle was restricted by the United States government as the location for the first A-bomb test site, and closed to all direct travel in that direction. This final action shattered Engle's last hope for survival.

Engle, adobe building.

Adobe ruins, Engle.

Below—Engle, Santa Fe railroad station, 1890.
—*Courtesy Museum of New Mexico.*

Right—Advertisement from *The Black Range*, October 6, 1882.—*Courtesy Highlands University Library.*

Estey City

COUNTY: *Lincoln*
LOCATION: *about 37 mi. southwest of Carrizozo*
MAP: *page 241*
P.O. est. 1901; discont. 1903. Re-est. 1904; discont. 1910.

Estey City has long since disappeared. Only old mine dumps serve as a reminder of its past existence.

Copper minerals had been known to exist in this region for many years, but it was not until the turn of the twentieth century that an effort was made to extract them. The new townsite on the southeastern edge of the Oscura Mountains was the namesake of David M. Estey, of Owasso, Michigan, the promoting force behind the Estey Mining and Milling Company, which at one time controlled about three hundred claims in the district. By July 31, 1901, the little but promising copper camp boasted of its 250 citizens, fifty dwellings, a large general merchandise store, one saloon, a post office, and a mill. Expansion was rapid. Churches, a school, a large hotel capable of accommodating sixty guests, electric lights, installation of water pipes, erection of a smelter, building of new businesses, and a doubling population followed the promising mining activities.

Times were favorable. The various mining companies and their eastern backers had little doubts as to Estey City's propitious future.

These auspicious days were to be short-lived. Trouble was brewing in the form of the European panic of 1901–1902, which forced the price of copper downward. In May of 1902, Estey City donned the gloom of a ghost town. Mining ceased, the El Paso and Northeastern shut down the Oscura Station, which had served as Estey City's transportation link, mail service stopped, and only four families from the former population of five hundred remained. However, by midsummer of that year the situation had taken a favorable upswing. Copper was once again in demand. The Dividend Mining and Smelting Company bought up the Estey Mining and Milling properties and revived both mining and Estey City. Other mining companies rushed in to purchase claims, the post office reopened, and vacant houses were quickly reoccupied. Once again Estey City was alive and busy.

The conditions, the times, and other unforeseen factors contributed to the town's eventual death about 1910. Today the site of Estey City is inaccessible to the curious tourist, since it lies within the boundaries of the restricted White Sands Missile Range.

Abandoned Estey City, looking west, 1917.—*Courtesy N. H. Darton, U.S. Geological Survey.*

Faywood Hot Springs, today.

Faywood Hot Springs

COUNTY: *Grant*
LOCATION: *29 mi. northwest of Deming*
MAP: *page 255*
*P.O. est. as Hudson Hot Springs 1879;
discont. 1881.*

The people and buildings that made Faywood Hot Springs a fancy resort are now gone, and its story has been added to New Mexico's history. All that remain are several adobe foundations near the still-bubbling mineral hot springs on a lush green knoll.

In the early 1880's, Richard Hudson acquired the hot springs property. Believing the waters to have healing and medicinal powers, Hudson built a resort hotel there called Hudson Hot Springs. The hotel probably functioned for almost a decade before it burned down about 1890.

A. R. Graham cemented the sides of the spring in 1893, and while pumping out some of the water to prevent leakage he discovered many interesting relics attesting to the fact that the spring had been in use long before Hudson Hot Springs Hotel graced the place. Among the objects found were earthen vessels, copper spoons, stone hammers, and flint tools. A human skull and bones were also removed from the depths of the spring. They probably were the remains of the unfortunate Indian who had been tossed into the hot water. The story is told that in the days when the Apaches

freely roamed the area a squad of cavalry was sent to warn a family living just west of the hot springs of an impending Indian raid. The soldiers camped the night at the hot springs and the next day intercepted an Indian attack as they swooped down on the innocent settlers. Taken by surprise, the Apaches fled in confusion, one of their band falling wounded near the spring. With cruel hatred for the red man, a soldier deliberately picked up the injured brave and dumped him into the hot cauldron. Later the soldier was court-martialed for his atrocity, but was acquitted.

Sometime in the 1890's the hotel was rebuilt, and in 1897, Hudson Hot Springs reported a population of thirty-five, daily mail service and stage service to Hudson station on the Atchison, Topeka and Santa Fe Railroad five miles away, Methodist and Presbyterian church services held once a month, and a public school open for three months of the year, with livestock, fruit, agriculture, and the hot springs as its resources. The Hudson Hot Springs Sanitarium Company owned the hotel and applauded the benefits of the waters for kidney, blood, and rheumatic diseases.

Probably before the turn of the century the hotel came into the possession of Mr. T. C. McDermott, and the place took the name of Faywood Hot Springs, a combination of the names of J. C. Fay and William Lockwood, McDermott's partners. Faywood Hot Springs Hotel could accommodate nearly a hundred guests. It was a large, spacious one-story rectangular building, with a long veranda that seemed to stretch indefinitely along the length of the hotel. An enthusiastic reporter, attempting to convey the vastness of the place, stated that the building seemed to roam all over the desert and that it had miles of veranda. The hotel was decked with a huge cheerful fireplace, and every room opened to the outside with large windows for comfortable ventilation. A big closet, a marble washstand with hot and cold water, and radiator heat embellished each of the many rooms. The comfortable accommodations coupled with the healing waters of the hot springs served as a lure to patrons from all parts of the country. A. J. Spaulding, the millionaire sporting goods manufacturer, was one of the hotel's enthusiastic devotees.

T. C. McDermott was a man of ingenuity and was always thinking of ways to utilize the spring's hot water. One of his inventions involved using the water to heat a new-style incubator he had designed. The incubator was nothing more than a long box filled with various pipes, but it proved successful. Out of seventy-five eggs set inside the box, sixty hatched.

The Faywood Hot Springs Hotel existed for many years. The hotel and McDermott and Company, bottlers of mineral water, were listed in a 1940 business directory. Eventually the clientele decreased, causing the hotel to close. The property was sold, and Faywood Hot Springs Hotel was torn down.

Springhouse at Faywood Hot Springs, *circa* 1940. The springs flow a volume of 140,000 gallons a day at 142° F.—*Courtesy New Mexico Record Center and Archives.*

Faywood Hot Springs resort, *circa* 1900. *Courtesy Museum of New Mexico.*

Fleming, *circa 1884.—Courtesy Museum of New Mexico.*

Advertisement—*Courtesy Museum of New Mexico.*

Fleming

COUNTY: *Grant*
LOCATION: *about 11 mi. west of Silver City*
MAP: *page 255*
P.O. est. 1883; discont. 1887.

Following the discovery of the Old Man Mine in 1882, Fleming launched its career as a promising silver camp. The budding settlement was named in honor of Jack Fleming, a prominent, enterprising citizen and one of the owners of the Old Man Mine. A force of eight men were soon engaged in grading a road from the embryo camp to Silver City and were paid three dollars a day plus board for their labor. Building commenced at a rapid rate as two saloons, one general merchandise store, and a boardinghouse opened up within one week during May of 1883. Town lots sold for fifty to seventy dollars each, and in a short time over two

blocks had been snatched up. Caught up by the throbbing pulse of prosperity, a man offered to pay two thousand dollars for a one-fifth interest in the Fleming townsite.

In view of the expanding possibilities, three men from Silver City, M. B. Mikesell, Thomas Kendall, and a Mr. Ross, laid off a second townsite about half a mile below Fleming and began sinking wells and selling lots. The name Penrose was proposed for the lower townsite, which by mid-May, 1883, claimed a butcher shop, bakery, one store, a corral, two saloons, and a blacksmith shop. Twenty lots had been sold at prices varying from fifty to a hundred dollars.

Fleming camp enforced definite ethnic restrictions. Chinese were not allowed in the camp, and Mexicans could not work in the mines, although they were not prohibited from working for themselves.

The first murder at Fleming occurred in October, 1884, and caused a considerable stir in the camp. Several miners on their way to work one

Old Man Mine at Fleming, *circa 1885.—Courtesy Museum of New Mexico.*

Advertisement from *The Black Range*, April 27, 1888.—*Courtesy Highlands University Library.*

morning looked into the tent bakery run by a Negro named John Woods. Inside lay Woods, dead from a gunshot in his skull. Justice Givens and Deputy Sheriff Cantwell arrived from Silver City to hold an immediate inquest. The condition of Woods's tent plainly indicated that the motive had been robbery, but there were no clues to lead to the arrest of the assassin. As a result of the crime the townspeople pleaded for a deputy to be appointed at Fleming. There was obviously a sprinkling of tough characters among the 250 to 300 population, yet the town had no officer of the law.

Less than two months later another shooting occurred, helping to boost the unsavory reputation that Fleming was quickly gaining. James Hunter, while under the influence of whisky, got into a dispute with a man named Vail in front of the Parlor Saloon. Vail's friend James O'Connell intervened, drew his revolver, and struck Hunter on the head. In his second attempt to deal a blow, the gun discharged, shooting Hunter over the left eye. Hunter staggered into the Parlor Saloon and fell unconscious, and O'Connell was quickly arrested.

Hunter's wound proved not fatal, and he lived to tell the tale.

Fleming enjoyed other social diversions besides liquor. The town had a baseball club that challenged the teams of Deming, Silver City, and El Paso. Skating matches were held at Fleming's rink until it was converted into a billiard hall, and there was also talk of erecting a bowling alley.

Indian scares continued to be a threat throughout most of Fleming's life. A group of about forty men elected officers and organized a company for the protection of the town against Apaches. Not to be outdone by the men, the ladies organized a second company, calling themselves the Calico guards. It was jokingly rumored among the men that some members of the Calico guards could shoot as well with both eyes closed as they could through a globe sight.

The Old Man Mine was worked steadily until 1888, and intermittent work continued until 1893. Meanwhile, Fleming faded into a ghost town. A padlocked gate bars the road that leads to the site of Fleming.

Idle headframe and coal loading chutes at Gamerco.

Gamerco, power plant smokestack, today.

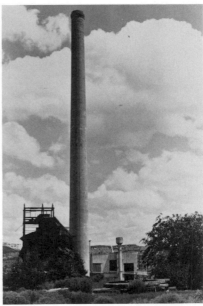

Gamerco

COUNTY: *McKinley*
LOCATION: *3 mi. north of Gallup*
MAP: *page 245*
P.O. est. 1923; discont. 1964.

The Gallup American Coal Company began sinking shafts into coal deposits north of Gallup in 1920, and two years later the newly formed camp of Gamerco witnessed hoisting of the first coal. Even before mining was underway the town was platted, and the Gallup American Coal Co. moved abandoned homes from Heaton, a nearby coal camp, to Gamerco, in addition to new ones that were being constructed. The town was supplied with a company store, meat market, hotel, clubhouse, shower house for the miners, and an executive office building. Recreation facilities of a golf course, swimming pool, tennis courts, and ball park were soon added. The town had a resident physician and a nurse.

Mine practices were fully professional at Gamerco's eight-hundred-foot shaft, and the company stressed safety. Ninety per cent of the underground employees had United States Bureau of Mines certificates for rescue and first aid. The men were supplied with electric lamps, only permissible low heat explosives were used, and electric haulage replaced mules along thirty miles of underground track.

The miners' and other employees' homes of frame construction had two to four rooms and were furnished electricity and free water. This meant plenty of vegetable gardens, lawns, and an attractive town.

Miners working on the surface received $5.60 for a seven-hour day; those underground were paid more. No one was allowed to work more than five days a week. The five hundred men on the payroll were not unionized and preferred to keep it that way. Strikes had occurred at various mines around Gallup; one in 1917 when the striking United Mine Workers were broken up by the National Guard, another in 1922, resulting in increased wages, and a third in 1933, when the militia was again called out to break up strikers of the National Miners Union.

Today Gamerco is still an occupied residential area but all of the mines have closed. Many old buildings, a giant steel headframe, and a towering smokestack from the power plant remain.

Gardiner

COUNTY: *Colfax*
LOCATION: *3 mi. west of Raton*
MAP: *page 239*
P.O. est. 1897; discont. 1940.

Coal was discovered in Dillon Canyon about 1881 by James T. Gardiner, geologist for the Santa Fe Railroad, and in 1882 the Old Gardiner Mine, or Blossburg No. 4, as it was called, began production. In 1896 the Raton Coal and Coke Company took over operation of the mine, and during the next few years was accompanied by the St. Louis, Rocky Mountain & Pacific Railroad in building a battery of coke ovens, and the town of Gardiner started to grow.

In 1905 the Blossburg Mercantile Co., Gardiner Saloon, a Catholic church, a Methodist Episcopal church, the Raton Coal & Coke Co. Hospital, and a population of about four hundred people made their homes in Gardiner. The hospital, staffed by Dr. J. T. Bils, Dr. Hubbard, and several nurses, was well equipped with operating room, modern laboratory, and the latest X-ray transformer.

As the community expanded more homes were constructed of concrete blocks, and a few were even built of adobe. The Gardiner Saloon, operated by Joe Di Lisio, had a partition built through the center room so that the black and white patrons could drink separately. For a short time the arrangement worked fine—until fights broke out and the partition was smashed.

As Gardiner matured and became more sophisticated, auxiliary activities developed, such as the Gardiner Ladies Club, a local band, the Gardiner Reading Circle, soccer, basketball, and baseball teams, and a sportsmen's club. The people enjoyed surprise parties for respected citizens, revival meetings, and ice cream socials. During the early 1920's Gardiner was at its zenith. Mr. Van Houten, president of the Rocky Mountain and Pacific Co. always attended the Gardiner eighth-grade graduation ceremony held at the Raton Country Club. The gracious occasion was climaxed by a delicious dinner, and Mr. Van Houten handed out presents to the graduating students.

During the Great Depression men lost their jobs when the mines closed, and Gardiner began the downhill slide. After the close of the Gardiner Mine in 1939, a few families remained during World War II to ship residual coke breeze to smelters throughout the southwest. The machine shop was finally disconnected in 1954, the three hundred coke ovens went into ruin, and Gardiner was a ghost town.

Today only scattered foundations, a few isolated company buildings, a locomotive house, and the long lines of deteriorating brick coke ovens line the mouth of Dillon Canyon. The remains of an abandoned power plant at the Gardiner Mine farther up the canyon add to the haunting beauty of this picturesque valley.

Gardiner, looking northwest, *circa 1902.—Courtesy Evelyn Shuler.*

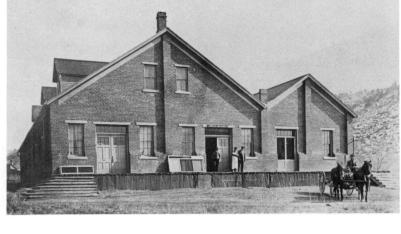

Gardiner Store, *circa* 1915.—*Courtesy John Southwell.*

Right—Miners outside the engine room, *circa* 1915.—*Courtesy John Southwell.*

Left—Mine haulage motor and miners, *circa* 1915.—*Courtesy John Southwell.*

Right—View of coal washing plant and storage bins at Gardiner, *circa* 1925.—*Courtesy Evelyn Shuler.*

Above—Gardiner looking north-east, 1939.—*Courtesy New Mexico Record Center and Archives.*

Engine house at Gardiner, *circa 1915.—Courtesy John Southwell.*

Present engine house at Gardiner.

Above—Gardiner ovens where coal from surrounding mines was converted to coke, *circa* 1915.—*Courtesy John Southwell.*

Left—Present condition of coke ovens.

Below—Ruins of Gardiner coal washing plant and storage bins.

Georgetown, general view looking east, 1940.—*Courtesy Library of Congress.*

Georgetown

COUNTY: *Grant*
LOCATION: *18 mi. northeast of Silver City*
MAP: *page 255*
P.O. est. 1875; discont. 1903.

Silver gave birth to Georgetown. As early as 1866, prospectors probing the hills just west of the Mimbres River discovered the valued metal which gave rise to subsequent mining operations and the camp. By the early 1870's a small settlement was taking root around the Mimbres Mining and Reduction Company's activities. The camp was named for George Magruder, of Georgetown, D.C., who was vice-president of the mining company.

Georgetown turned into a success story. The rich ore of the mines prompted population growth and buildings sprang into being. Georgetown, a well-planned community, was divided into three sections. The business center captured the middle position and was flanked on the north by the better

residential area, Catholic church, and grade schools, and on the south by the town jail, miners' quarters, and questionable establishments. Across the gulch from the town tucked in the hills were the mines. There were many of them; the Naiad Queen, McNulty, Satisfaction, McGregor, Uncle Sam, Extension, and others. After the ore was extracted it was hauled to the company's two mills on the Mimbres River by ox teams, horses, and mules.

A. C. Lowery started the town newspaper, the *Silver Brick*, later changed to the *Georgetown Courier*, in August, 1881. The eighties proved to be the most prosperous decade for Georgetown. One of the peak years, 1888, listed a large variety of businessmen from butchers to wagonmakers and a population of twelve hundred. In addition, the town was heir to an assortment of stores and saloons, schools, churches, boardinghouses, the National Hotel, a theater, skating rink, and brewery.

Georgetown had its Apache scares, cattle rustlers, sicknesses, and tragedies, as well as its dances, holiday gatherings, political rallies, and fun. It combined the ups and downs of a typical mining community. Glamorous but reckless and bold, Georgetown contained the restless, the righteous, and the self-vindicating. In January, 1890, a desperado began terrorizing Georgetown. Apparently unprovoked, he started taking pot shots at citizens. Officers attempting to arrest the gunslinger became fearful of his aim and were compelled to fall back. Later, however, a second attempt at arrest proved more successful. While taking the offender to jail the officers were met by a mob of masked men who forcibly took the prisoner from custody, dragged him to a tree, hanged him, and riddled his body with bullets. The victim's identity was never known, nor did it matter. He had broken the law and had paid for his crimes.

Early one morning a bad fire broke out in the two-story company store. Little could be done to smother the blaze, since there was inadequate water and no fire-fighting equipment. The town residents looked on from the skating rink as the fire gutted the store's interior, broke through the floor-ing to the basement, and began exploding the stored kegs and barrels of oil, kerosene, and paint. As the roof crashed in, the raging fire spread next door to the Chinese restaurant and then on to the butcher shop before it was finally brought under control. A few days later a crew from the mines demolished the scorched walls of the store and retrieved the safe. This fire proved an ominous turning point for Georgetown. The company never rebuilt the store, and after 1893, when the price of silver slumped, Georgetown was doomed. The year 1897 listed a population of two hundred, and by 1903 this figure was cut in half. Soon weeds took over the once busy streets, and neglected adobe buildings began to crack and gradually melt into heaps of mud.

Not much is left of Georgetown today. There are some scattered rocks indicating onetime building foundations and a lone adobe wall. The most interesting feature is the Georgetown cemetery with many legible epitaphs.

92
G

Ruins of store building in Georgetown, 1940.—*Courtesy Library of Congress.*

Abandoned home in Georgetown, 1940.—*Courtesy Library of Congress.*

Georgetown–Silver City stagecoach. Photographed in Silver City, *circa* 1880's.—*Courtesy Museum of New Mexico.*

Georgetown cemetery.

Gibson

COUNTY: *McKinley*
LOCATION: *3 mi. northeast of Gallup*
MAP: *page 245*
P.O. est. 1890; discont. 1947.

The coal camp of Gibson has disappeared. About all that is left is its history.

Prospecting in 1882 led to the discovery of the Gallup Mine that nurtured the community of Gibson. The Crescent Coal Company was organized with John Gibson as mine superintendent. John was a popular figure, whose name was chosen for the town.

Gibson developed into a sizable community with a hotel, company store, hospital, meat market, Catholic church, and a school open ten months of the year. The Gallup Mine proved to be a profitable coal property until about 1902, when fires broke out in the mine. The Crescent Coal Company invested thousands of dollars in an attempt to control the smoldering blazes, but their efforts were not effective, and they were forced to abandon the Gallup Mine.

About that time the American Fuel Company acquired the property and placed it under the management of the Colorado Fuel and Iron Company. A population of six hundred was reported for Gibson in 1905. In 1917 the plants and all coal and surface rights became the property of the Gallup American Coal Company, and in 1919 Gibson listed twelve hundred occupants.

Sinking of new shafts at nearby Gamerco in 1920 and the first hoisting of coal two years later necessitated the closing of the older mine properties at Gibson. When work discontinued at Gibson, the population decreased. However, many Gallup American employees continued to have their homes in Gibson and the Gibson store remained open.

Gibson's obituary appeared in the late 1940's, when the dwindling demand for coal erased the community from the map.

Gibson, *circa* 1910.—*Courtesy Gallup Public Library*.

Above—Class of children at the Gibson school, date unknown.—*Courtesy Gallup Public Library.*

Baseball team of the American Fuel Company at Gibson, 1909.—*Courtesy Gallup Public Library.*

Abandoned coal dumping chute at the Gibson Mine.

Glen-Woody bridge across the Río Grande and the buildings at Glen-Woody, looking south, *circa* 1900.—*Courtesy Holder Collection, Kit Carson Museum.*

Glen-Woody

COUNTY: *Taos*
LOCATION: *14 mi. southwest of Taos*
MAP: *page 241*
P.O. none

Glen-Woody was a short-lived gold camp that proved to be a financial failure. In the late 1890's W. M. Woody, who had been operating placer mines on the Río Grande, discovered a large body of low-grade gold in quartz on the east bank of the river about a mile below the village of Pilar. About that time, however, the Klondike gold rush lured him away for a few years. Returning to Taos around the turn of the century, Woody proceeded to interest Eastern capitalists in developing the ore body. Glen-Woody camp, established in 1902 by the Glen-Woody Mining and Milling Company, sprang up on the west side of the river. A fifty-ton mill and cyanide tanks were installed on the east bank, and a large flume was built about a mile north. Over the river hung a suspension bridge built on some of the piers of an old government bridge which had been burned during an Apache raid in the 1870's. Some work was done at Glen-Woody, but the venture proved unsuccessful and forced abandonment. For years the hotel and buildings of Glen-Woody slowly rotted away. The property eventually became the possession of Ashley Pond, a former chief of the Santa Fe Fire Department, who used the place to entertain fishing parties.

Today cars whiz by on U.S. 64 between Santa Fe and Taos, never aware that the town of Glen-Woody once existed.

Glorieta

COUNTY: *Santa Fe*
LOCATION: *18 mi. southeast of Santa Fe*
MAP: *page 243*
P.O. est. 1880 to present.

Early Spanish settlers named the southern terminus of the Rocky Mountains "Glorieta," or bower, as suggested by its rolling mountain slopes covered with a dense growth of cottonwood and pine trees.

In the 1830's and 1840's wagons passed along the Santa Fe Trail from Independence, Missouri, across La Glorieta Pass. During the period prior to the Civil War, when travel along the trail was at its peak, the Pigeon's Ranch served as a hostelry and stage station between Las Vegas and Santa Fe. The ranch was named Pigeon as a nickname given to its Franco-American proprietor, Alexander Vallé, because of his broken English or, as another story relates, because of his peculiar manner of dancing at parties, Vallé was an obliging host and eventually his accommodations were expanded to include a store and saloon.

The Civil War brought Glorieta its only note of fame, although it was a few years later that the village had its beginning. The famous battle of La Glorieta Pass took place between Confederate General Henry H. Sibley's Texas Cavalry and the Federal troops commanded by Colonel Edward R. S. Canby and led by Colonel John P. Slough and Major John M. Chivington of the First Regiment of Colorado Volunteers. The fighting commenced with the battle of Apache Canyon on the west side of the pass on March 26, 1862. The decisive engagement was fought two days later, east of the pass at Pigeon's Ranch. The battle involved artillery, infantry, and cavalry, and lasted without interruption for several hours. The Texans slowly advanced against the troops under Colonel Slough, but in the meantime Major Chivington wiped out the Confederate supply encampment at Johnson's Ranch west of the pass. More than a fourth of the Federal and Confederate troops engaged in combat were either killed or wounded. The Union casualties were estimated at about 150 and the Confederates totaled some 250. When the action ended, the dead were interred in an open field east of Pigeon's Ranch. The destruction of their supply train was the turning point in the Confederates' attempt to occupy New Mexico Territory.

In 1879, when the Atchison, Topeka and Santa Fe Railroad came over La Glorieta Pass, a small village began to grow a few miles west of Pigeon's Ranch and soon took over as a mining and lumbering supply center for the district. In the year 1884 the majority of the working force of some 250 population reportedly was employed by four saw-

Pigeon's Ranch, occupied by Union troops during Battle of Glorieta Pass, *circa* 1870's.—*Courtesy Museum of New Mexico.*

mills and the Silver Lode Mining Co. The businesses consisted of the Glorieta House, two general stores, and two saloons. In the next five years Glorieta became known as the headquarters from which sportsmen reached the hunting and fishing grounds of the upper Pecos River.

Shortly after World War II the Southern Baptist Assembly chose Glorieta as headquarters for their western leadership center. Construction of the Southern Baptist facilities began in 1950, and throughout the next ten years approximately five million dollars were poured into the project. Today several thousand young Southern Baptist students attend conferences during the summer at the Glorieta headquarters. The town itself maintains a small mercantile store, a gift shop, La Silla Grande Restaurant, the Rio Grande Press, which occupies the former school building, and a sprinkling of dwellings.

General Edward R.S. Canby (1817–73), commander of the Union army, the Department of New Mexico, at the time of the Glorieta battle.—*Courtesy National Archives.*

View of Glorieta, *circa* 1897.—*Courtesy Museum of New Mexico.*

Gold Dust

COUNTY: *Sierra*
LOCATION: *4 mi. northeast of Hillsboro*
MAP: *page 251*
P.O. none

Little is known and nothing seems to be left of Gold Dust. It was a tent town in 1881, when scores of eager Argonauts diligently dug for gold in Gavilan Canyon, Flap Jack Gulch, and other arroyos and ravines. That year Chief Victorio and a band of Apaches descended on Gold Dust in a surprise raid. About thirty men were working in Flap Jack Gulch when the Indians attacked the tent community half a mile away. Cries brought the men running from the diggings, but by the time they arrived, the Apaches had galloped off, after firing several shots into the tents.

John Butecke lived on a mining claim near the Gold Dust placers. While hunting in the Black Range, Butecke came upon a large bear that he tried to shoot but only wounded. The enraged bear rushed at Butecke and seized his outthrust rifle in its mouth. After a terrific fight, Butecke managed to point the rifle barrel at the bear and kill it. Though terribly scarred for life, Butecke claimed the rare distinction of wrestling with a bear and surviving, and he had a rifle stock well marked by the bear's teeth.

Exactly when Gold Dust folded and died is debatable. In later years, when the gold furor faded, the area became ranching country. Today four or five weathered old ranch buildings, believed to have been built in the 1920's, remain near the site that once was Gold Dust. Just north of the buildings are hundreds of cone-shaped mounds, the results of past gold dredging.

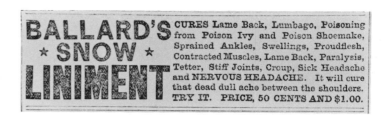

Advertisements—*Courtesy Highlands University Library.*

Buildings at the site of Gold Dust.

Golden

COUNTY: *Santa Fe*
LOCATION: *33 mi. northeast of Albuquerque*
MAP: *page 243*
P.O. est. 1880; discont. 1928.

New gold placer deposits were discovered at the base of the San Pedro Mountains about 1840. Rich gold deposits referred to as the Old Placers had been found in the Ortiz Mountains some twelve year earlier, and now the prospectors and miners with their dry washers and bateas were coming to the new strike in search of wealth. Soon the community of El Real de San Francisco developed, along with the neighboring settlement of Tuerto to the north. The two villages and surrounding vicinity probably never contained more than a few hundred people and consisted almost entirely of Mexicans and Indians who lived in adobe dwellings and brought the crudely scraped ore on burros to the valley, where they used water to concentrate the gold.

Placering continued intermittently during the next forty years, interrupted by the Mexican War and the Civil War. About 1880, eastern capital and southwestern politicians formed several companies: the Canyon del Agua and San Pedro Mining Company, Mammoth Mining Company, and the Gold Bullion Company to develop the New Placer mines. Gradually the townsite known as El Real de San Francisco had its name changed to Golden and had begun to expand its services to the incoming population. By 1882 Golden consisted of three general merchandise stores, a hotel, and the Madden & Maxwell Saloon. Two years later the town had expanded to claim about four hundred persons, *The Retort* newspaper operated by Colonel R. W. Webb, a tri-weekly stage to the railroad station at Wallace for a fare of $2.50, a constable, shoemaker, blacksmith, justice of the peace, lawyer, and a couple of stamp mills.

Colonel Webb was a colorful character and, by virtue of his position as Golden's only newspaper man, spoke out against the evils of the day. He accused the Canon del Agua and San Pedro syndicate, which for a short time had General Ulysses S. Grant as its president, of shutting out the small mine operators in order to monopolize the placer mines. The most dramatic episode of the conflict between the syndicate and the small mine owners took place in May of 1883. One day as the mine supervisors left for dinner, eleven men from Golden, armed with revolvers and rifles, took over the mine. For several days the company officials tried to rid the mine of the trespassers by threats to starve, smoke, and shoot them out. Finally, having had no success by threat of force, the syndicate agreed to certain compromises that would benefit the small mine owners, and a truce was called.

Golden also had its menace of bandits and rustlers that Colonel Webb was always ready to challenge. He ran editorials in *The Retort* identifying the toughs by name. Occasionally Webb served as the town marshal. Finally he gave up the losing battle with the syndicate, folded up *The Retort*, and moved to Las Vegas, New Mexico.

After 1884, Golden's population dropped, the buildings deteriorated, and the mines east of the town lay idle. In 1910 a Franciscan priest, Fray Angelico Chaves, assigned to mission duty south of Santa Fe, repaired the church of San Francisco at Golden. The original church is said to have been erected in 1830; however, most of the structure above the foundation has been replaced.

Today the church of San Francisco, surrounded by its *camposanto*, overlooks a few of Golden's dilapidated rock, adobe, and mud-chinked buildings scattered throughout the valley.

Above—Catholic church and cemetery at Golden.

Left—Stock certificate owned by L. Bradford Prince, Territorial governor of New Mexico (1889–93), and investor in mining properties around Golden.—*Courtesy New Mexico Record Center and Archives.*

Below—Golden, present view of abandoned dwellings.

Gold Hill cemetery.

with the intention of a surprise attack. Seeing the American flags blowing from the poles, they concluded that General George Crook had assembled a large troop of cavalry and infantry there. The Apaches quickly canceled their intended raid and headed southeast.

Gold Hill's active life continued for more than twenty years. In 1897 the camp reported a population of 125 and school six months of the year. By 1905 the population had dropped to thirty.

Today the Gold Hill Ranch occupies the site of the onetime mining camp. The only remaining trace of Gold Hill is the cemetery that rests on a hill just beyond the ranch.

Gold Hill

COUNTY: *Hidalgo*
LOCATION: *about 15 mi. northeast of Lordsburg*
MAP: *page 255*
P.O. est. 1886; discont. 1906.

David Egelston, a forty-niner prospector, and two partners, Robert Black and Tom Parke, located the Gold Chief Mine in September of 1884. During the following months they developed the property as other prospectors began arriving in the area, forming a loosely knit community. By May, 1885, parties returning to Silver City from Gold Hill gave glowing descriptions of the fabulous wealth of the camp, but disclosed that the lack of water and good society made the place undesirable for immediate occupancy. A month later, however, Gold Hill began to acquire a hopeful appearance, with a gradually increasing population busily engaged in building and developing their camp. Tom Parke opened the Pioneer boardinghouse, and Robert Black was the leading camp merchant. Still in its infancy, Gold Hill cheerfully claimed that no Indians, births, deaths, or marriages had been reported to disturb the peace of the camp.

To celebrate the Fourth of July, 1885, Bob Howland unfurled two American flags over Gold Hill. Little did he realize that his patriotism saved the camp. Geronimo and a band of ninety warriors had positioned themselves in view of the camp,

Grafton

COUNTY: *Sierra*
LOCATION: *about 37 mi. northeast of Truth or Consequences*
MAP: *page 251*
P.O. est. 1881; discont. 1904.

Grafton got its start as a mining camp in the early 1880's, and by 1883, with seventy-five houses, ranked second in importance to the four Black Range towns of Chloride, Grafton, Fairview (later Winston), and Hermosa. The opening of the Grafton Hotel, operated by A. P. Dyer (owner of A. P. Dyer & Co. general store) and Billy Kellem, was reported in December of that year. The hotel claimed to be unsurpassed for convenience, because the post office and express office were under the same roof as the hostelry. A. P. Dyer served as landlord, postmaster, express agent, agent for the Southwestern Stage Company, waiter in the dining room, and chamber man. Billy Kellem was the cook. Grafton also had R. T. Howe's saloon, N. Uptegrove's saloon, and F. H. Winston & Company general store. The Grafton school began in January, 1884, with seven pupils and Miss Nellie Russell of Robinson as the teacher. Voluntary contributions from the townspeople paid Miss Russell's monthly salary of sixty dollars.

Being in the vicinity of the Ivanhoe, Alaska, Occidental, and other valuable mines, Grafton became a town of considerable activity. In the early years of its life it boasted a population of over three hundred, but by 1892 the camp had only fifteen houses and twenty persons. Even after Grafton was practically deserted, work was still being done on the Ivanhoe property. At one time the mine was partially owned by Colonel Robert G. Ingersoll, American politician and professional agnostic. The story goes that one day he and his engineer appeared at the Ivanhoe Mine, which at that time was no more than a prospect. Ingersoll liked the name of the property and the engineer liked the looks of it, so before the day was over they had purchased it for sixty thousand dollars. For several years Ingersoll spent time each summer at Grafton.

A couple of old buildings, said to have been used at one time as headquarters of the operators at the Ivanhoe and Emporia mines, are all that remain today.

Advertisement from *The Black Range*, October 6, 1882.—*Courtesy Highlands University Library*.

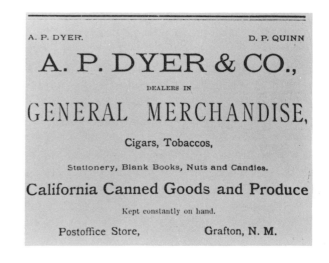

A. P. DYER.   D. P. QUINN

A. P. DYER & CO.,

DEALERS IN

GENERAL MERCHANDISE,

Cigars, Tobaccos,

Stationery, Blank Books, Nuts and Candies.

California Canned Goods and Produce

Kept constantly on hand.

Postoffice Store,   Grafton, N. M.

Grafton, hewn log cabin.

Graham

COUNTY: *Catron*
LOCATION: *7 mi. northeast of Glenwood*
MAP: *page 253*
P.O. est. 1895; discont. 1904.

The community of Graham, also called White-water, situated at the mouth of Whitewater Canyon, at one time housed about two hundred people and functioned as a mill town. Gold and silver deposits discovered about 1889 in the mountains above the canyon produced the development of several mines, including the Confidence, Blackbird, Bluebird, and Redbird. The narrowness of Whitewater Canyon made it impossible for a mill to be built at the mines, and so the canyon mouth was selected as the mill site. John T. Graham constructed the mill in 1893 and gave his name to the young town that was beginning to take shape.

Although water ran plentifully in the high mountain reaches of Whitewater Creek, it was often dry at the mill site. Therefore, the problem of supplying enough water to meet the demands of the mill's steam generator and the needs of the townspeople was solved with the construction of a four-inch water pipe that commenced in the mountains and terminated three miles down the canyon at Graham. Built at the same time as the mill, the small pipe was packed in sawdust and encased in wood to prevent freezing. By 1897, with the installation of a larger generator, an eighteen-inch pipe was built parallel to the smaller pipeline in order to answer the increasing needs for water. The two water lines were considered quite an engineering feat. Holes had to be drilled into the hard rock walls to brace the supports for the pipes, and in some locations the lines were placed twenty feet above the rough canyon floor. The men who walked the eighteen-inch pipeline to keep it in repair called it the "catwalk."

The mill never proved to be as successful as was hoped. When it closed for good in 1913, the town of Graham died. Graham and Whitewater Canyon had a few dubious claims to fame. The town blacksmith was William Antrim, whose wife's son was the infamous Billy the Kid. The seclusion of Whitewater Canyon served at various times as a sanctuary for Geronimo's and Nana's Apaches, and later for Butch Cassidy and the Wild Bunch.

Nothing is left of Graham today except foundation ruins of the mill. Whitewater campground now stands at the mouth of the canyon, and the water lines, long since torn down, have been replaced today by a metal catwalk. Thousands of annual visitors enjoy walking on the catwalk as it weaves up the canyon, following the same course of the old pipes.

Graham, mill ruins at the mouth of Whitewater Canyon.

Miners at the Confidence Mine near Graham. Man at center with full beard is William Henry Harrison Antrim, Billy the Kid's stepfather, *circa* 1890.—*Courtesy Blachly Collection, University of Arizona, Special Collections.*

Hachita and Old Hachita

COUNTY: *Grant*
LOCATION: *Old Hachita—9 mi. west of Hachita*
              New Hachita—37 mi. southeast of
Lordsburg
MAP: *page 257*
P.O. est. 1882; discont. 1898. Re-est. 1902
to present.

In the Little Hatchet Mountains a mining camp named Hachita took shape about 1875. There were silver, lead, and copper mines, among the best being the Hornet, King, and American. Turquoise mines were also worked at Hachita and were claimed to be the most valuable in the Territory. Hachita reported a population of three hundred in 1884, as well as steam smelting works, three saloons, two general stores, and several mining companies. By September, 1890, only twenty-five men were working the mines of Hachita, but the camp was reported to be lively and industrious. The American Mine worked fourteen men and claimed that they could work more if they had mule teams to move the ore dumps out of the way. The Hornet Mine reported bustling activity, rich ore, and prosperous returns.

The daily monotony of camp activity was interrupted when it was learned that a man named George Forget, who was working at the American, had a price on his head—a reward of two hundred dollars for his arrest. Forget denied he was the wanted man, but the next day when a sheriff from Tombstone, Arizona, arrived at Hachita, Forget had conveniently disappeared. The sheriff told the men at the camp that eighteen months before, Forget had been a prisoner in the Tombstone jail on charges of stealing forty pounds of ore. The sheriff felt Forget's offense was minor, so allowed him a great deal of freedom. Forget awaited his chance, and when the sheriff stepped into one of the cells, leaving his keys in the lock and his gun in the office, Forget locked the sheriff in the cell, took his gun, and walked out of the jail. A few days after his disappearance from Hachita, Forget was picked up at Separ Station, and he confessed to being the wanted man.

Hachita began to dwindle in importance during the 1890's. A couple of years after the turn of the century, railroad tracks were laid about nine miles east of Hachita. A railroad town sprang up and took the name of the fading mining camp. Henceforth, Hachita was the railroad town, and the original bearer of the name became known as Old Hachita. The post office moved to "new" Hachita, and the center of activity shifted to the community at the junction of the El Paso & Southwestern and the Arizona & New Mexico Railroad. Hachita included about two hundred inhabitants, Hachita Merchantile Co., Hotel Hachita, two saloons, meat market, boardinghouses, and a restaurant.

Located in the hot, dry desert of southern Grant County, the Hachita saloons no doubt seemed an oasis to the miners and cowboys in the area. An unfortunate incident occurred in November of 1908. Two drunk cowboys staggered up to Conductor Herbert Faulkner, who was standing near the caboose at the Hachita railroad station. Without any warning and for no apparent reason, they gunned him down. The wounded conductor was quickly placed on the train and rushed to a hospital in El Paso, where his fate remained questionable.

Today the railroad is gone, but Hachita remains. Only about fifty people still live there. Main Street boasts a mercantile store and gas pump, a bar, cafe, and a couple of deserted buildings. On the back streets there is a post office, school, deserted adobe church, and some interesting old occupied houses along with unoccupied ones. Old Hachita, nestling in the Little Hachet Mountains, claims a private home, half a dozen or so old buildings, head frames, and mine dumps.

Old Hachita, one of the present buildings.

New Hachita, looking south.

New Hachita, Main Street.

Hagan and Coyote

COUNTY: *Sandoval*
LOCATION: *Hagan—20 mi. east of Bernalillo*
           Coyote—3 mi. west of Hagan
MAP: *page 243*
P.O. est. as Hagan 1902; interm. to 1931.

Completely deserted now, the couple of dozen adobe ruins of Hagan and the similar few melting adobes of Coyote stand silent and eerie. Reached only by dirt roads, and miles from a paved road, the ruins seem to loom up like a mirage from the floor of the rolling desert country. The two towns are located on the Una De Gato arroyo, about three miles apart. Hagan and Coyote were the products of coal mines and led parallel lives, though Hagan proved to be the heartier of the two.

Founded two years before Coyote, Hagan outlived it by about twelve years.

Hagan began in 1902 with the discovery of coal fields and the organization of the New Mexico Fuel and Iron Company. As the Hagan Mine began successfully to produce, the Sloan Mine was opened three miles to the northwest, establishing Coyote about 1904.

Both towns seemed to be the victims of projected railroad promises that failed to materialize. About the time of Coyote's beginning, talk centered on the building of the Albuquerque Eastern Railroad through Hagan and Coyote, linking Tijeras with Algodones. Despite the fact that the idea was pigeonholed in 1905, the towns managed to survive the economic disappointment. For the next four years, Hagan supported a population of about sixty and a general merchandise store. Then, in 1909, the shelved railroad project was actually started, giving great hope and impetus to both Hagan and Coyote. When the roadbed was within a few miles of Hagan, work abruptly stopped and was never continued. The Albuquerque Eastern Railroad proved as transitory as a dream.

Though lacking railroad connections, Hagan and Coyote managed to survive. A decade later, new rumors of the construction of a railroad began to circulate. Still a pipe dream however, the projected idea faded, this time dealing a death blow to Coyote. The small camp had never been given a chance to grow up to economic maturity. Hagan muddled through this third crisis, to be rewarded in 1924 by the long-anticipated railroad and an economic boost. The Rio Grande Eastern Railroad, a 12.6-mile branch of the A. T. & S. F. line, boosted Hagan into its prime. A power plant, shop, warehouse, and new company buildings magically sprang up. The town listed a population of five hundred, the Hagan Power and Electric Company, the Tonque Clay Products manufacturers of tiles and bricks, the Orange Hotel, and the Hagan Mercantile Company. Coal mining, metal mining, and stock raising were the principal industries.

Hagan's glory was brief. Six years later, as the coal incline was driven downward, a thin bed of shale between the coal beds increased in thickness until there was more shale than coal. Economically, it did not pay to continue operations, and Hagan was forced to die. The property was leased in 1939 and worked briefly. When the mines closed for good, people drifted away. By 1950, no one was left at Hagan.

Hagan, adobe ruins looking southeast.

Ruins of a company building at Hagan.

Left—Coyote, adobe walls.

Hematite

COUNTY: *Colfax*
LOCATION: *about 6 mi. southeast of Red River*
MAP: *page 239*
P.O. est. 1897; discont. 1899.

Located on west Moreno Creek near Red River Pass about three miles up the gulch from Elizabethtown, Hematite was a short-lived placer camp. Rich ore veins discovered in the fall of 1895 were responsible for the birth of the place. May, 1896, found Hematite doing well, with a modest population of two hundred, a boardinghouse, a store, and the Athens Mining and Milling Company preparing to erect a stamp mill. Many claims were staked, and placer gold was found, but apparently not enough to keep Hematite alive for very long. In a few years it had become a ghost. Not a trace remains of Hematite today.

Hermanas

COUNTY: *Luna*
LOCATION: *about 32 mi. southwest of Deming*
MAP: *page 257*
P.O. est. 1903; discont. 1925.

Hermanas functioned for a number of years as a small railroad town on the El Paso & Southwestern Railway. Farming and stock raising as well as some mining companies were listed as the principal in-

Hermanas, deserted section house.

dustries. The community was named for the Tres Hermanas Mountains a few miles to the east, where ore deposits, principally of silver and lead, had been worked for many years but never had attained production of great importance. Hermanas' population in 1907 was claimed to be 150, and probably it never exceeded that number. Various businesses listed during the years were Mrs. E. W. Faulkner's restaurant and hotel, two groceries, Wells Fargo & Company Express, and, of course, a post office.

Today a deserted, shabby section house still stands. On the opposite side of the road is a roofless rock building.

Hermosa

COUNTY: *Sierra*
LOCATION: *about 28 mi. west of Truth or Consequences*
MAP: *page 251*
P.O. est. 1884; discont. 1929.

About 1880, the lure of gold and silver sent countless prospectors to explore the Black Range in Sierra County. In spite of the great risk of death at the hands of hostile Indians, prospecting resulted in the discovery of such mines as the American Flag, Palomas Chief, Ocean Wave, Antelope, Pelican, and others. Shortly following the initial strike at the American Flag Mine in 1883, J. C. Plemmons brought a herd of cattle to graze near the future site of Hermosa. Convinced of the prosperity of the area, he foresightedly built a store and house and began the first merchandising business in Hermosa. Others settled down in the newly formed camp as additional businesses and residences took root. Mrs. D. C. Rogers, the only white woman in the area for two years, ran the camp's first boardinghouse.

Apaches constantly plagued the early settlers of Hermosa. They stole stock from the camp and made threats on men's lives. Once, during a valiant attempt to drive the white men from the area, the Indians surrounded the mine diggings and kept the men at bay for eleven days. Mrs. Rogers sought refuge in a mine tunnel. The persistent and hardy miners stood their ground and finally forced the Apaches to leave.

By the late 1880's, Hermosa was prospering, with a hotel, saloon, blacksmith shop, meat market, livery stables, post office, merchandise stores, and a twice-weekly stage. Gradually refinements crept into the camp with the Hermosa Literary Society, schoolhouse, and church. Dances and various social and holiday events added variety to the daily life.

In June of 1889, the town was hit by a destructive flash flood. A number of business concerns and residences were carried away by the raging waters.

Before the decade of the 1890's had passed, Hermosa was on the decline. The population gradually fell from a reported 150 in 1897 to 60 in 1905.

What is left of Hermosa today has been absorbed into a ranch. The old hotel and a one-room hewn-log post office stand side by side as the last relics of the onetime mining camp. On the east side of the road to the north of Hermosa rests the cemetery. True to its name, Hermosa still can boast of its beautiful mountainous setting.

Opposite page—J. C. Plemmons Store at Hermosa, *circa 1888.—Courtesy Blachly Collection, University of Arizona, Special Collections.*

Advertisements from *The Black Range*, August 17, 1888.—*Courtesy Highlands University Library.*

Fourth of July program at Hermosa, from *The Black Range*, June 8, 1888.—*Courtesy Highlands University Library.*

1892
1939

Sierra County courthouse at Hillsboro, *circa* 1900.—*Courtesy Black Range Museum.*

Hillsboro

COUNTY: *Sierra*
LOCATION: *33 mi. southwest of Truth or Consequences*
MAP: *page 251*
P.O. est. 1879 to present.

Hillsboro is not a ghost town, and its residents resent its being called one. It was a mining town, they say, but never a ghost town. Hillsboro boomed and faded with mining, but it has never died, and it seems unlikely that it will. It is too charming and pretty a place, composed of a quiet tree-lined street of quaint old buildings. There are two churches, a Catholic and a Community Mission; a school up to six grades; a store; a garage, and the interesting Black Range Museum. The town is unincorporated, but about a hundred persons have made their homes within the community.

Hillsboro's hell-raising boom days began in April, 1877, when two prospectors, Dan Dugan and Dave Stitzel, found some float on the east side of the Mimbres Range. Although Dugan proclaimed the pieces worthless, Stitzel pocketed a few and had them assayed at a mill on the Mimbres River. When the samples assayed at $160 in gold per ton, the two hurried back to the site of their find and staked out the Opportunity and Ready Pay mines. In June of that year, Frank Pitcher and Dugan located the famous Rattlesnake Mine. As news of gold seeped out, people made a beeline for the district. By August, 1877, the first house in Hillsboro had been built. In November, placer gold was discovered in Snake and Wicks gulches, causing other gulches to be combed and scraped for the elusive metal. That winter George Wells, a mine operator, cashed in ninety thousand dollars in gold dust and nuggets he had mined from Wicks Gulch.

As yet the aspiring mining camp was still unnamed. In December, 1877, each prospector wrote on a piece of paper his choice for the town's name. The papers were put into an old hat, shuffled around, and one slip impartially drawn from the lot. The name selected was Hillsborough (later shortened to Hillsboro).

Menacing Indians proved to be a constant threat during Hillsboro's infancy. In 1880, four companies of soldiers stationed at Hillsboro and three hundred miners protected the town. Yet even frequent Apache raids did not stop the feverish pace of the eager prospectors and miners. Hillsboro was to produce six million dollars in gold and silver.

Hillsboro, brick walls of the Sierra County courthouse.

The town soon had seven hundred people and all the necessities of a prosperous community. There was a public school, church, four hotels, three stamp mills, the *Sierra County Advocate* newspaper, stores, and saloons. Hillsboro grew into the largest settlement and county seat of Sierra County. The handsome brick- and stone-trimmed courthouse erected in 1892 was the scene of the 1898 trial for the Fountain murder, one of New Mexico's most celebrated unsolved crimes.

Judge Albert J. Fountain was returning home to Las Cruces from Lincoln in January, 1896, having secured indictments against two cattlemen, Oliver Lee and William McNue. Traveling with Fountain in the buckboard was his eight-year-old son, Henry. They stopped for the night at La Luz and the next morning continued their journey. Fountain was aware of three horsemen trailing them, but, though urged by a passing mailman to return to La Luz for safety, the Judge impatiently drove on, eager to reach Las Cruces. Neither he nor his son ever reached their home. The next evening the mailman stopped at the Fountain house and learned that the Judge and his son had not arrived. Officials were immediately informed, and a posse was organized to search the route the Judge had taken. All that was ever found was the abandoned

buckboard. Fountain had had enemies, but also many friends who were positive that Oliver Lee lurked behind the Judge's disappearance. Two years later three men, Oliver Lee, William McNue, and James Gilliland were tried in the Hillsboro courthouse for the murder of Fountain and his son. The trial lasted for three grueling weeks while people jammed into Hillsboro to learn the details and outcome of the famous case. Evidence failed to support a conviction, and the jury returned a verdict of not guilty. The prisoners were freed, and the mystery shrouding the Fountain murder case remained unsolved.

Hillsboro continued a healthy growth, claiming twelve hundred residents by 1907. A flood on June 10, 1914, caused considerable damage to the town. A sudden rain swelled the creek, which overflowed and poured down Main Street. The destructive waters uprooted trees, crumbled buildings, and snuffed out the life of pioneer resident Thomas Murphy, first sheriff of the county.

As the years passed Hillsboro began feeling stiff competition from Hot Springs (now Truth or Consequences). Hillsboro relinquished its claim as the county seat to Hot Springs in 1938. Its palmy days were over, and Hillsboro slipped quietly into its present leisurely pace of life.

Above—Hillsboro, *circa* 1900. —*Courtesy Museum of New Mexico.*

Above—Mail cart on Hillsboro's Main Street, *circa* 1900.—*Courtesy Black Range Museum.*

Above—Hillsboro Main Street, today.

Right—Hillsboro, Black Range Museum and Library.

Looking through jail door and walls of the Sierra County courthouse at Hillsboro.

Jicarilla

COUNTY: *Lincoln*
LOCATION: *27 mi. northeast of Carrizozo*
MAP: *page 249*
P.O. est. 1892; discont. 1942.

Known placer mining in the Jicarillas dates back as far as 1850. Those were the days when native Mexicans worked the stream beds, separating the gold from the dirt in a wooden bowl called a "batea." In the 1880's, with the advent of the American miners, prospecting for the lode deposits was undertaken. From the influx of prospectors the settlement of Jicarilla formed. Some two hundred people dotted the area with crude shacks and homes. In 1905, E. H. Talbert ran the general store, Joe Long operated the local saloon, and A. H. Norton served as justice of the peace. Two years later the Jicarilla schoolhouse was built. The logs for the rectangular-shaped building were cut and hewn in the canyon on the east side of Ancho Peak, then dragged down the mountain to the chosen school site about a mile south of Jicarilla proper. The school functioned for many years and the building also doubled as a Saturday night dance hall.

Jicarilla seemed to have reached its peak during the depression years of the 1930's, when it served as a haven to as many as three hundred destitute families who could sometimes make as much as $7 a week mining. Wild turkeys in the Jicarillas provided food for many empty stomachs during those years. At the height of the Depression more than sixty children attended the Jicarilla one-room log school. When jobs became available again, people moved on, and Jicarilla began to die.

A log saloon constructed in 1908 functioned as a post office and store from about 1914 to 1927. Later it became the home of old-timer Adolf Lobner. In 1962 the cabin was totally destroyed by a fire in which Lobner lost his life.

Today a false-front building, formerly the Jicarilla store and post office and dating from the 1930's, still stands. Only one family lives at Jicarilla the year round. The log school also remains, the windows now covered with rusty corrugated iron sheeting.

Jicarilla, log schoolhouse.

Johnson gold dredge at Jicarilla, *circa* 1900.—*Courtesy Museum of New Mexico.*

Johnson Mesa

COUNTY: *Colfax*
LOCATION: *16 mi. east of Raton*
MAP: *page 239*
P.O. est. as Bell 1891; discont. 1933.

Johnson Mesa is unique. Rising two thousand feet above the valley floor of Raton, this sky island is a land unto itself. The mesa top, stretching seven by fourteen miles, is grassland and gently sloping hills, crisscrossed with barbwire fences and dotted with cattle and deserted farm buildings.

The mesa was named for Lige Johnson, who settled just south of the mesa at a place called John- son Park. He let his cattle graze the mesa top, so soon it also bore the name of Johnson. In the early 1880's, Marion Bell, a railroad construction worker on the Santa Fe Railroad (not a miner as some reports claim), led a group of fellow "tie hackers" up to the mesa top to try their skill at farming. It proved to be a successful venture. Soon

miners from the Blossburg Mine, wishing to sup- plement their income by farming also, settled on Johnson Mesa. Mining at Blossburg was somewhat sporadic, and at times labor difficulties temporarily closed the mine. Carrier pigeons were used to fly the message that the Blossburg Mine was working to a headquarters building on the mesa.

The people of Johnson Mesa raised potatoes, oats, grain, and other crops, and then eventually branched out into cattle ranching. Following the flood of hopeful farmers, a post office was estab- lished as Bell and functioned in connection with a small general store. At one time there was a family living on every 160 acres. There were five schools for the mesa children, one with an enrollment of seventy-five. The mesa also offered three years of high school.

St. John Methodist Episcopal Church was com- pleted in 1899. It was dedicated on August 14, and for many years that day was commemorated by a day of celebration. There would be a morning service, picnic, ball game, and other entertainment. Every represented denomination used the church. During the late 1920's and 1930's, a priest offered mass at the church once a month. The Fourth of July, another day of celebration on Johnson Mesa, included horse races, foot races, and a rodeo. During the summer months dances were held every week at a dance pavilion that was built on top of a large hay barn.

Times were often hard for the mesa people. Winters were very severe, and many times the families would be snowbound. A flu epidemic in 1918 took several lives. The mesa had no hospital, but Dr. Morgan took care of the people's medical needs.

Marion Bell left Johnson Mesa in 1914 and died in Raton in 1930. The Pat Berry family settled on the mesa in 1884. Mr. Berry worked at the Bloss-

burg Mine off and on until 1904, and then chose to remain on Johnson Mesa. His descendant, Frank Berry, bought the old Marion Bell house in McBride Canyon in 1928. Through the years the house has been expanded and modernized. Mr. and Mrs. Frank Berry live there today, one of the few remaining families on Johnson Mesa.

After World War I people started leaving the mesa. The conditions were too challenging and severe. People wanted an easier way to make a living. Today five families make their homes on Johnson Mesa during the summer, but no one lives there in the winter. St. John Methodist Episcopal Church stands empty and silent, facing a weed-grown cemetery. The church pulpit reposes in the Raton Museum, along with furnishings of the Bell post office.

Summer social at St. John Episcopal Church on Johnson Mesa, *circa* 1905.—
Courtesy Joe Young.

Marion Bell homestead in McBride Canyon on Johnson Mesa, *circa* 1928.— *Courtesy Frank Berry.*

Left—Looking across Johnson Mesa, old hay baler in foreground.

Below—Johnson Mesa, present view of St. John Episcopal Church and cemetery.

Kelly, looking west, *circa* 1920.—*Courtesy C. H. Gorden, U.S. Geological Survey.*

Kelly

COUNTY: *Socorro*
LOCATION: *29 mi. west of Socorro*
MAP: *page 247*
P.O. est. 1883; discont. 1945.

J. S. Hutchason, known as "Old Hutch," is credited with being the father of the Magdelena mining district. His discoveries spawned the mining camp of Kelly. Hutchason was poking around the Magdelena Mountains in the spring of 1866 when he found rich lead outcroppings. He staked the Juanita Mine and, three weeks later, the Graphic Mine. In those early days the ore was smelted locally in adobe furnaces called "vassos," and then the metal was hauled by ox team to Kansas City.

Probing farther around the hills, "Old Hutch" found another promising prospect, which he obligingly turned over to a friend, Andy Kelly, who operated a local sawmill. Kelly gave his name to the mine and worked it for a time, but when he failed to do the required assessment work, Hutchason jumped the claim.

Meanwhile, prospectors attracted to the area about 1879 laid out a townsite on the west slope of the Magdelena Mountains and named it for Kelly.

In the late 1870's Hutchason sold his Graphic Mine for thirty thousand dollars. He also sold the Kelly Mine, which in turn was resold to Gustav Billing for forty-five thousand dollars. In 1881 Billing erected a smelting plant near Socorro at Park City which treated ore from the Kelly and other mines until 1893. In 1896, with the construction of the Graphic Smelter, Magdelena became the smelting town for Kelly. It treated the ore there until 1902.

With the advent of the 1880's, the small camp of Kelly began to experience a promising growth and much activity. A branch line of the Atchison, Topeka and Santa Fe reached Magdelena, four miles from Kelly, in 1885. Daily stages ran to Magdelena, a school, two hotels, a resident doctor, and the usual assortment of stores and saloons served Kelly. The camp also boasted a fine water system with pipes conducting mountain spring water throughout the town. With the increasing influx of miners, sleeping accommodations were scarce. Supposedly, the two hotels rented beds in eight-hour shifts.

About the turn of the century, as lead and silver were being wrenched from the earth, a discarded greenish rock was being tossed high on the waste dump piles. Cory T. Brown of Socorro shipped away some of the rock to have it tested. It turned out to be a valuable zinc carbonate called smithsonite. Brown, in partnership with J. B. Fitch, immediately leased the Graphic property and began stripping the dumps of the smithsonite. Kelly's second era of prosperity dawned as others leased

properties and began doing the same thing. In 1904 Brown and Fitch pocketed a tidy sum by selling the now-celebrated Graphic Mine to Sherwin-Williams Paint Company. Billing sold the Kelly Mine to Tri-Bullion, who then built a smelter at Kelly.

Kelly began to boom with prosperity as it reaped the profits of smithsonite. The camp became the state's leading producer of zinc. Kelly expanded to include two schools; three churches, a Catholic, Methodist Episcopal, and Presbyterian; and a moving picture parlor. By 1931 the smithsonite deposits were exhausted. Gradually, mining throughout the district began to decrease, allowing Kelly to die. Today some mining is still being done near Kelly, but the prosperous camp that once had a population of three thousand no longer claims any residents. The only intact building is the white-stucco-front Catholic church, where mass is still offered once a year. Adobe and rock ruins dot both sides of the dirt road beyond the church. Extensive mine workings, tailings dumps, old mine buildings, and headframes stand rusted and neglected farther up Kelly Canyon. Facing the church on the hillside is Kelly's cemetery.

Upper Kelly, 1915.—*Courtesy G. F. Laughlin, U.S. Geological Survey.*

Advertisement from the *Socorro Chieftain*, June 19, 1884.—*Courtesy Highlands University Library.*

Ruins of the Tri-Bullion Mill and Taylor headframe at Kelly.

122
K

Below—Empire Zinc Co. plant. Tri-Bullion Mill and Taylor head-frame, looking north, 1915.—*Courtesy G. F. Laughlin, U.S. Geological Survey.*

Catholic church at Kelly.

Right—Kelly cemetery looking south toward the Catholic church.

Below—Advertisements from *Socorro Chieftain*, October 24, 1885.—*Courtesy Highlands University Library*.

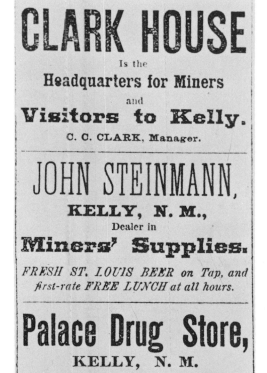

Kingston, *circa* 1887.—*Courtesy Cloudman Collection, University of New Mexico Library.*

Kingston

COUNTY: *Sierra*
LOCATION: *9 mi. west of Hillsboro*
MAP: *page 251*
P.O. est. 1882; discont. 1957.

At its height, Kingston boomed with seven thousand people, twenty-two saloons, three hotels, and three newspapers: *The Clipper, The Shaft,* and *The Sierra County Advocate.* As the nucleus of a rich silver district, the town was born following the discovery of the Solitaire Mine by Jack Sheddon in early August, 1882. Other mines were located, claims staked, and the inevitable stampede followed. A. Barnaby opened a tent store which quickly became the hub of the growing tent town. On August 26, the Kingston townsite was surveyed, and by late fall the new and promising camp

had lured eighteen hundred people. Main Street lots sold for as high as five hundred dollars apiece.

At first Kingston was a tent city, and before many people had constructed permanent cabins, winter set in. It was a cold winter, bringing with it a smallpox epidemic. The only doctor in town was Dr. Guthrie, who ordered the largest tent in town to be turned into a hospital. The Kingston people bravely rose to the occasion by supplying cots and bedding for the hospital. Reliable nurses seemed somewhat more difficult to obtain. The first two men to offer their services as nurses were drunk most of the time, having hired themselves out in payment for a daily jug of whisky from the doctor. The next nurses were three women from the red-light district. With honest concern and devotion they unselfishly plunged into the task of saving lives. Although seven men had died under the dubious care of the first two nurses, none died after that. The dead were buried at the site of the tent, and the smallpox epidemic was soon past.

Kingston's history is chock-full of tales and lore. It was a fun-loving, fast-drinking, and hard-working mining town. Its stories run the gamut from Kingston's first Christmas and the opening of a new dance hall, the Casino, where everyone was invited and everything was free, to the entanglement of man and bear during a foot race on the Fourth of July; from the tent lodginghouse where lower berths were preferred to the upper ones because stray bullets from the nearby saloons sometimes ripped through the canvas walls, to the numerous Apache raids and Indian scares. James McKenna's *Black Range Tales* tells it all. Kingston lays claim to citizens Albert Fall and Edward Doheny, who were later involved with the notorious Teapot Dome Scandal during the administration of President Harding in the early 1920's; a performance at Kingston's theater by Lillian Russell; the local wit of Sheba Hurst, now an immortalized character in Mark Twain's *Roughing It*; and the domain of Apache chiefs Geronimo and Victorio.

Kingston had about everything but a church. A suggestion for one brought a generous response as hats were passed in saloons and miners tossed in coins and nuggets. The total collection of fifteen hundred dollars was enough to build the church.

During the 1880's and 1890's, Kingston yielded a large production of silver. By 1904, $6,250,000 worth of silver had been extracted from the district. Then the deposits became depleted, the price of silver declined, and Kingston became essentially inactive.

Several bad fires and the ravages of time have greatly reduced Kingston's buildings, but its quiet serenity and partial desertion now serves as a retreat for artists. Upon leaving N.M. 180 and entering Kingston's dirt Main Street, the first stone building to be seen on the south side of the road is the old Victorio Hotel, originally three stories high. There is the Black Range Lodge and the old Percha Bank. Across the road from these are a double-roofed brick building originally an assay office and a bell hanging from posts which was used to announce the arrival of mail. Tucked on either side of the main dirt road are other buildings and homes.

Printing the first daily newspaper at Kingston, 1896.— *Courtesy Museum of New Mexico.*

Above—Kingston, *circa* 1885. View of Main Street.—*Courtesy Blachly Collection, University of Arizona, Special Collections.*

Left—Inside store at either Kingston or Hillsboro, *circa* 1880's.—*Courtesy Black Range Museum.*

Below—Kingston Main Street, *circa* 1880's: (center) Occidental Hotel, (far right) Opera House.—*Courtesy Black Range Museum.*

Right—Pin-up of the kind sold to miners and cowboys, date unknown.—*Courtesy Museum of New Mexico.*

Below—Homes at Kingston, *circa* 1880's. —*Courtesy Black Range Museum.*

Below—Picnic under the pines near Kingston, *circa* 1890.—*Courtesy Black Range Museum.*

Assay office, Kingston.

Brass bell at Kingston, once used to signal the arrival of mail.

Kingston cemetery.

Koehler

COUNTY: *Colfax*
LOCATION: *16 mi. southwest of Raton*
MAP: *page 239*
P.O. est. 1907; discont. 1957.

Most of Koehler is gone. The Kaiser Steel Corporation purchased the property in 1955 and razed all of the buildings except for a small office, one shop, and the processing plant. The town was named after Henry Koehler, president of the American Brewing Company of St. Louis, Missouri, and also chairman of the Maxwell Land Grant Board of Directors. The townsite of Koehler and the coal mines were on what was once part of the Maxwell Land Grant.

Koehler's days as a vital coal mining camp began about 1906 with the opening of the first coal mine. The St. Louis, Rocky Mountain & Pacific Company, with its railroad and coal interests, owned the property. By 1907 Koehler camp claimed a thousand people, a post office, a company general store, and the newly completed two-story school. Koehler gradually expanded, embracing 210 beehive coking ovens, the coal washing plant, an electrical generating plant, three boardinghouses, bath houses, amusement hall, meat market, 158 homes, and, eventually, eighteen hundred people.

As in many company-owned camps, the employees rented their adobe homes from the company. Each look-alike dwelling was lighted with electricity provided by the company power plant. People bought provisions from the company store (always called the Blossburg Merchantile Company in the St. Louis, Rocky Mountain Company-owned camps) and quenched their thirst in the company-owned saloon.

Life in many of the coal camps was similar. Relaxation from the weekly monotony of hard work often took the form of baseball games. Each town organized a team which competed with neighboring ball clubs on Sundays and holidays. Koehler's arch rival was the Van Houten team. Dances, picnics, and a variety of other activities also added to Koehler's social life.

The Koehler school caught fire and was totally destroyed in December, 1923. Fortunately the flames were noticed in time for all teachers and students to evacuate before the structure burst into an uncontrollable blaze. Since there was no efficient way of bringing water to the fire, the volunteer firemen stood around helplessly, watching the building burn to the ground. Koehler's days were already numbered. The camp closed in 1924, and people scattered to other mining camps. For the next twelve years Koehler was a ghost town. In 1936 the Koehler mines reopened, and the town was given a second life. Demands for coal were decreasing, though, and Koehler felt little encouragement. Eventually Kaiser Steel Corporation purchased the property, and Koehler, as a coal town, died.

129
K

Below—Koehler, *circa* 1915, mine employees' homes.—*Courtesy Evelyn Shuler.*

Above—Miners' clubhouse at Koehler, *circa* 1915.—*Courtesy Evelyn Shuler.*

La Bajada

COUNTY: *Santa Fe*
LOCATION: *26 mi. southwest of Santa Fe*
MAP: *page 243*
P.O. est. 1870; discont. 1872.

Sandwiched between the famous La Bajada Hill and the Santa Fe River is the sleepy community of La Bajada. Only about six families live there amid the adobe ruins of a past era. La Bajada residents still farm along the Santa Fe River, as verified by small patches of corn and a few grazing animals. Most of the people moved away in the early 1940's, when the call of big cities promised greater opportunities than farming.

La Bajada dates back to pre-Rebellion times (Pueblo Revolt, 1680). Supposedly, Governor don Diego de Vargas visited La Bajada during the reconquest in 1692. Later, and for many years, La Bajada served as a vital stopping place for stages, freight wagons, and then automobiles after their harrowing hairpin descent from La Bajada Hill. The hill was far better known than the little farming village at its base. The road that crept over it, zigzagging for more than a mile down the steep, black basalt cliff, was on the old Santa Fe Trail linking Santa Fe and Albuquerque. In 1932 the La Bajada route was sacrificed for a new highway five miles southeast of the old grade.

There was a little mining done near La Bajada on the old road. La Bajada Mining Company organized in 1923 and made a small shipment of ore in 1928.

One of the most interesting ruins at La Bajada is the melting adobe shell of the Catholic church. Beside it stand the wooden fences and crosses of long-neglected graves. The church reputedly dates back to sometime near 1831. The gabled roof that once graced the structure was built about 1918.

130
L

Right—La Bajada, present view looking west.

Left—Adobe mission and cemetery at La Bajada.

La Belle

COUNTY: *Taos*
LOCATION: *about 8 mi. northeast of Red River*
MAP: *page 239*
P.O. est. 1895; discont. 1901.

Named for Mrs. Belle Dixon, wife of one of the early day prospectors and investors in the property, the now-vanished town of La Belle boomed for a number of years as a gold mining camp.

La Belle received its name on August 28, 1894, and by December of that year there were already eighty buildings, including three saloons, one hotel, one restaurant, one mercantile store, a butcher shop, blacksmith shop, and one feed store. Soon a cry rang out for a much-needed school-marm, since the population swelled to six hundred by March, 1895. By July, the sixteen-by-thirty-two-foot frame school building was almost completed, along with numerous other additions to the town. La Belle now featured *La Belle Cresset* newspaper, five general stores, four livery barns, six saloons, two barber shops, two laundries, a new jail which was reported never to have accommodated anyone, and three hotels. The Southern Hotel was a large structure moved laboriously from Catskill and claimed four stories and eighty rooms. It was probably the same hotel that was reported to be a twenty-thousand-dollar building that was sold to the highest bidder for fifty dollars when La Belle died.

More popular was the Exchange Hotel, owned by Mr. and Mrs. Nadock, which later became known as the Nadock Hotel. Its modest fourteen rooms were rarely empty, since the hotel served as the official stop for the twice-weekly stage that inevitably arrived in camp loaded with newcomers. The Nadock's fourteen-year-old daughter, Annie, helped at the hotel by waiting on tables and cleaning rooms. The notorious outlaw and train robber Black Jack Tom Ketchum and his brother Sam were occasional visitors at the Nadock Hotel, since they had a ranch a short distance from La Belle. When dances were held at the hotel the two handsome brothers were sought after as partners by the La Belle girls, and Annie always danced with one or the other of them. Black Jack's life as an outlaw was exposed after the train robbery near Folsom, New Mexico, on July 11, 1899, in which Elza Lay

(see Alma) and G. W. Franks also took part. Black Jack was captured and convicted of killing Sheriff Edward Farr during the ensuing flight and showdown with the posse after the robbery. On April 26, 1901, Black Jack was hanged at Clayton, New Mexico, and as the trap door sprang the amateurishly adjusted noose tore his head from his body. Sam Ketchum died less dramatically, from a bullet-shattered arm and blood poisoning. The story of Black Jack concludes with the tale that he buried several thousand dollars somewhere near La Belle. If he really did, no one has been fortunate enough to prove it.

At the time of Black Jack's death, La Belle was also gasping for breath. The high hopes that had appeared so promising proved to be unfounded. The ore was low-grade, and by 1910 only ten hangers-on remained, still hoping to "strike it rich" someday. Eventually even these hardy souls were forced to move on, finally admitting that La Belle would never live again.

Tom "Black Jack" Ketchum, train robber. He was hanged at Clayton, N.M., April 26, 1901.—*Courtesy Field Collection, University of New Mexico Library.*

Lake Valley

COUNTY: *Sierra*
LOCATION: *18 mi. south of Hillsboro*
MAP: *page 251*
P.O. est. as Daly 1881; discont. 1882. Re-est. as Lake Valley 1882; discont. 1955.

Lake Valley's inception followed the discovery of silver ore in 1878 by cowboy prospector, George W. Lufkins, who found a piece of float which he had assayed. In spite of the fact that the piece assayed high, Lufkin never realized much from his find. It is claimed that he received a mere $10.50 from the property, a fact that may well be disputed. Ironically enough, very near to where Lufkin found his float was the celebrated Bridal Chamber, where over three million dollars in horn silver was extracted. In the early 1880's two miners struck an ore vein which they promptly sold for a hundred thousand dollars. Two days after the sale, it was discovered that the ore vein ran into a subterranean room. Named the Bridal Chamber, it proved to be one of the richest single ore bodies of silver ever discovered. On the day of the discovery in 1881, George Daly, the owner of the property, was killed by Apaches.

The town of Lake Valley was started in September of 1882, but another townsite called Daly, after George Daly, had preceded it by a year. The short-lived Daly was soon relocated and renamed after a small lake in the area which now is dry. Before long, Lake Valley had stamp mills, smelting works, three churches, a school, two weekly newspapers, numerous saloons, hotels, stores, shops, and a reported thousand people in 1884. At first water had to be carted into Lake Valley from a well about a mile from the town. Later, an extensive pumping machine and pipeline were constructed from the lake about three miles away.

Lake Valley, 1890. Arrival of the Santa Fe eight-wheeler on the branch line from Nutt. Monument Peak in the background.—*Courtesy Schmit Collection, University of New Mexico Library.*

Life was unpredictable in Lake Valley. During the first week of July, 1884, it seemed to be a target of misadventure. H. M. Sinclair's store was robbed of firearms valued at $100, two houses caught fire, and during the excitement $153 were stolen. A third house burned that week, asphyxiating its occupant, William Davy, an employee of one of the mines. As five hundred people helplessly watched, unable to save Davy, a Chinese was held up on Main Street and robbed of thirty dollars.

Stages ran between Lake Valley and Nutt, a station on the Atchison, Topeka and Santa Fe Railroad. The trip cost $2, and the distance was fourteen miles. Soon a branch of the railroad was extended to Lake Valley. Then coaches ran daily from Kingston through Hillsboro to Lake Valley, to join the railroad. In 1888 J. W. Orchard purchased the Kingston–Lake Valley Stageline. His wife Sadie was supposed to have been an adept horsewoman who broke many of the stagecoach horses and sometimes drove the Concord coaches.

One day the stage was carrying a large sum of money from Kingston to Lake Valley, thence to be sent on to Las Vegas. Feeling slightly nervous about the possibility of a holdup, Bill Holt, an Orchard driver, stopped the stage a few miles out of Hillsboro on the pretext that he wanted to check one of the horses. While a passenger held the reins, Holt skillfully removed the hay from the horse collar, stuffed the money into the empty cavity, and buckled the pad back over the collar. A few miles farther on, several armed, masked men held up the stage and demanded the money. Holt calmly told them that the money had been sent on a previous run. Although the bandits searched the coach, they failed to find the money. It arrived safely at its destination, and Holt received a hundred-dollar reward from the grateful Orchards.

Intense mining operations at Lake Valley continued under the management of the Sierra Grande Company until August, 1893, when the mines were closed. Later they reopened under new management. With the passing of years mining decreased, Lake Valley's population began to shrink, and the town began to crumble with disuse and neglect. Today it is only a ghostly shadow of its former prosperous self. Weathered adobe and wood buildings, vacantly staring glassless windows or tightly boarded openings, sagging roofs, and debris are all that remain. A substantial old garage, a small adobe church, a school, and two occupied houses are the most noteworthy remaining features. On the southwest side of the road overlooking Lake Valley is the cemetery.

133
L

Lake Valley, mill and concentrator, *circa* 1890.— *Courtesy Schmit Collection, University of New Mexico Library.*

Left—The Orchard Stage Line had headquarters at Lake Valley. Photograph probably taken in Hillsboro, *circa* 1890.—*Courtesy Black Range Museum.*

Below—Advertisement for the Orchard Stage Line.—*Courtesy Museum of New Mexico.*

LAKE VALLEY STABLES

LAKE VALLEY CITY, N. M.

Livery, Feed and Sale Stable.

Rigs and Saddle Horses

Furnished to all parts of the Range. Accommodations furnished for Miners and Campers.

Blacksmiths and Wagonmakers.

HAY AND GRAIN FOR SALE.

DOHNEY & CO., Proprs.

he Scenery along this Line is Grand, the Towns are Prosperous and Hotel Accommodations Good

Horses are Changed every Ten Miles, making the run from Lake Valley to Kingston in Five Hours.

J. W. ORCHARD,

United States Mail, Express and Stage Line.

NEW FOUR HORSE CONCORD COACHES.

Leave Lake Valley daily, on the arrival of trains, for Hillsboro and Kingston, always connecting with trains on the A., T. & S. F. Railway going East.

LAKE VALLEY, - - NEW MEXICO

Above—Advertisement from *The Black Range*, October 6, 1882.—*Courtesy Highlands University Library.*

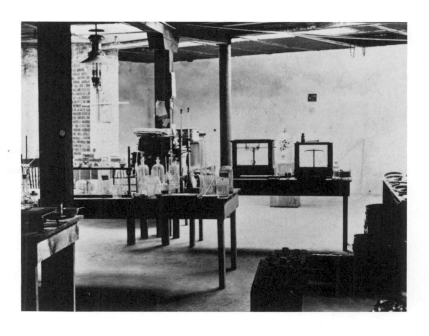

Right—Inside an assay office at Lake Valley, *circa* 1890.—*Courtesy Schmit Collection, University of New Mexico Library.*

Above—Abandoned stone garage, Lake Valley.

Weathered headboard in Lake Valley cemetery.

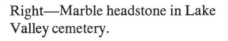

Right—Marble headstone in Lake Valley cemetery.

Below—Cemetery, looking north toward Lake Valley.

La Ventana, Main Street, with El Nido Hotel Bar in background.

La Ventana

COUNTY: *Sandoval*
LOCATION: *14 mi. south of Cuba*
MAP: *page 243*
P.O. est. 1925; discont. 1932.

La Ventana thrived as a coal camp from the mid-1920's to the early 1930's. Long before this time, however, the village existed. Land was fertile along the Río Puerco, attracting Spanish-speaking people who settled near its banks, but times were difficult for these early settlers of La Ventana. This was Navaho country and the Indians were reluctant to share it. Greater in number than their Spanish neighbors, the Navahos easily swept down on the unsuspecting village, stealing whatever they could. Because of this constant threat, La Ventana was deserted sometime during the 1870's.

The first family to resettle in La Ventana after its desertion was the Padilla family, who arrived in 1914. Young Florentino Padilla often scampered over the lintel of the window rock located east of La Ventana that gave the town its name. In 1919 the lintel collapsed, so now there is only a large gap remaining. Florentino herded sheep as a young boy and later went to work in the coal mines during La Ventana's active years.

The Santa Fe, San Juan and Northern Railroad pushed through La Ventana and beyond in 1927. In 1930 five coal and coke companies were reported working at La Ventana. The town listed El Nido Hotel, which was built about 1925 and boasted sixteen rooms, general merchandise stores, restaurants, a stage line, post office, school, and a population of 150. The depression years brought La Ventana's life to an end.

In the mid-thirties the abandoned San Juan Mine caught fire. For several years it burned unchecked, until the entrance was sealed off in 1939. Somehow the fire is still being nurtured by oxygen and today continues smoldering beneath the earth.

La Ventana is a jumble of deserted buildings and the El Nido Bar Lounge run by Florentino Padilla. He and his family are the only residents of La Ventana.

Stone wall ruins at La Ventana.

Leopold

COUNTY: *Grant*
LOCATION: *11 mi. southwest of Silver City*
MAP: *page 255*
P.O. est. 1904; discont. 1914.

Copper discoveries made in the Burro Mountains in 1871 initiated several periods of mining followed by inactivity. Eventually, mining interest was revived in 1902, giving birth to Tyrone and its sister town, Leopold. Growing up around the workings of the Burro Mountain Copper Company, Leopold was named after Asa F. Leopold, an important figure in the town. By February, 1905, the Burro Mountain Copper Company boasted being the largest individual quartz mining company in New Mexico, supplying employment to almost two hundred men who worked in the mine and mill at Leopold. Two years later Leopold claimed over twelve hundred people in its neigh-borhood and forty two-room cottages in the process of construction. T. M. Bates opened his new grocery, dry goods, and hardware store midway between Leopold and Tyrone; a Miss Ross had a confectionary stand; and a bakery and a barber shop were also added to Leopold's businesses. There was Brown & Co. general mercantile and blacksmiths, Burro Mountain Copper Company Hotel, Burro Mountain General Merchandise store, a stage line, justice of the peace, deputy sheriff, and a school. A mine tunnel fitted with an iron grillwork door served as the town jail.

In 1909 Phelps Dodge Corporation purchased the Burro Mountain Copper Company holdings and in 1912, after further acquisitions of surrounding properties, moved their local headquarters from Leopold to Tyrone. With activity no longer centered in Leopold, the town relinquished its post office and eventually died. Nothing remains of Leopold today.

Lincoln

COUNTY: *Lincoln*
LOCATION: *32 mi. southeast of Carrizozo*
MAP: *page 249*
P.O. est. 1873 to present.

Lincoln, New Mexico, the focal point of the Lincoln County War, is today a monument of historical value.

In 1849 Spanish pioneers settled in the lush green valley of the Río Bonito and soon sustained a little community that they called La Placita del Río Bonito, the Little Town by the Pretty River, and later shortened to La Placita. The village consisted of a few adobe buildings around a plaza and was fortified by a thick-walled, circular stone tower. During the 1850's and 1860's, frequent raids of Mescalero Apaches drove the residents into the "Torreon" for protection. In the late 1860's the town included some forty adobe houses and about four hundred people.

In 1869, Captain Saturnino Baca, encouraged by Lawrence G. Murphy, who was the post trader at Fort Stanton, Major William Brady, and Dr. J. H. Blazer, sponsored a bill in the New Mexico Territorial Legislature to create a new county. The bill passed, and, upon the request of Captain Baca, the county was called Lincoln, commemorating the famous President. La Placita, one of the largest villages in the new county, had its name changed to Lincoln. Major William Brady was appointed sheriff, and thus began Lincoln, New Mexico.

Four years later L. G. Murphy & Co., with representatives James J. Dolan and Emil Fritz, were ordered to leave Fort Stanton on the charge of unwholesome business practices with the military and Indians. The Murphy company moved to Lincoln, where they had a small business interest. There they built a large stone two-story structure known as the Murphy Store. The Murphy-Dolan enterprise aligned itself with leading territorial politicians known as the Santa Fe Ring under the leadership of Samuel B. Axtell, governor, and Thomas B. Catron, United States district attorney. Through the generosity of these influential friends, L. G. Murphy & Co. was given contracts to supply beef and flour to the army at Fort Stanton and the Mescalero Apache reservation west of Lincoln. In an attempt to enhance profits, the company of Murphy and Dolan employed Jesse Evans and his rustler associates to supply them with cattle to fill the contracts.

A well-educated lawyer, Alexander A. McSween, and his wife, Susan, moved from Kansas to Lincoln in the spring of 1875. McSween, a man of firm religious principles and high professional ideals, at once began to increase his opposition to the unscrupulous Murphy-Dolan faction. Early in November of 1876 a young Englishman, John H. Tunstall, arrived in Lincoln. Having a sizable trust provided by his father's successful mercantile firm in London, John had set out to make his fortune by developing long-range business investments. He acquired land and developed ranches on the Río Peñasco and Río Feliz. In April, 1877, he ventured into joint partnership with Alex McSween and formed the John H. Tunstall & Co. mercantile business. The new store was under construction when Tunstall also started the Lincoln County Bank. John S. Chisum, a shrewd businessman and highly respected rancher in the Pecos River valley served as the bank president with McSween as vice president and Tunstall as cashier. The new business establishments intensified the antagonistic attitude of the Murphy-Dolan party.

From the early years of Lincoln, troublemakers, outlaws, and riff-raff seemed to gravitate there. Juan Mes and his three brothers, Paz, Jesús, and Juanito, killed Oliver Thomas in Lincoln in December, 1875. As a result, a detachment of the Ninth Cavalry from Fort Stanton killed six of the gang at their hideout on the Río Hondo. Juan Gonzales, Nica Meras, and Jesús Largo were horse thieves in Lincoln County and usually sold their stolen stock in Chihuahua, Mexico. William Bonney, alias "Billy the Kid," came to Lincoln County in 1877 from western New Mexico and in a short time developed a friendly regard for Tunstall and McSween.

When Colonel Emil Fritz died in the summer of 1874, L. G. Murphy placed the settlement of the Fritz estate in the hands of the newly arrived Alex McSween. When the case was settled, after three years of court proceedings, J. J. Dolan, successor to L. G. Murphy & Co., claimed that the Fritz estate of some $7,100 was equal to Fritz's indebtedness to the Murphy Store. The stubborn refusal of Alex McSween to believe this claim or to be intimidated and forfeit the estate as payment greatly increased hostilities, and complications began to develop.

McSween was unjustly arrested for embezzlement of the Fritz estate and then released on bail. Sheriff Brady, under the pretext of law, attached joint property of the Tunstall and McSween store worth about thirty thousand dollars to be held in judgment against McSween's embezzlement charge. In addition to this property value, Brady threatened to secure the cattle of Tunstall's Río Feliz Ranch as extra legal measures against McSween. On February 17, 1878, Tunstall rode to the ranch to advise his employees that it was best for them to allow the cattle to be impounded, since that would be the least violent and best solution at the time. The next morning, Tunstall, accompanied by Dick Brewer, John Middleton, William Bonney, and Robert Widenmann, rode toward Lincoln driving a small herd of horses. At a point on the trail when Tunstall was momentarily out of sight of the others, Sheriff Brady's men, the ones sent to collect the Tunstall cattle, swooped down out of the hills and gunned Tunstall to death. A formal coroner's inquest concluded that James J. Dolan, Jess Evans, George Hindman, and several others composed the band that had killed Tunstall. McSween made considerable effort to have the responsible parties arrested, but Sheriff Brady refused to permit a constable to serve the warrants, claiming that as a legal posse the killers were immune from arrest.

Public resentment against the Murphy-Dolan clan heightened to the point where James Dolan requested, from his military friends at Fort Stanton, a guard to be posted at his store. At this time Dolan had acquired L. C. Murphy & Co. and changed the name to J. J. Dolan & Co.

McSween knew that with Tunstall out of the way, he would logically be killed next. The charge of embezzlement was still over his head, and this alone was enough to give Dolan's men a reason for justifiable murder. Because of these feelings, McSween left Lincoln to hide in the hills. At about the same time several friends and former employees of John Tunstall formed a band of vigilantes calling themselves the Regulators. Dick Brewer, the leader, acquired warrants for the murderers of Tunstall and set out with his men to find them. On March 4, the Regulators jumped five of the murderers southeast of Lincoln on the Río Peñasco. In a running battle that lasted some five miles, the Regulators captured Frank Baker and George Morton. During the return trip to Lincoln along the Agua Negro River, Morton, Baker, and a Regulator by the name of McCloskey were ambushed and killed by unknown assailants.

The heated feud between the Regulators and the Murphy-Dolan party blew up again on April 1. As Sheriff Brady, George Hindman, and three other men left the Dolan store and headed for the courthouse up the street, they were fired upon from the shadows of the Tunstall store. Brady died seconds after he was mortally wounded and Hindman, fatally hit by a single bullet, was blown backwards. When the firing stopped five of the Regulators, with the exception of Billy the Kid, rode from behind the Tunstall Store and left town. Billy had received a thigh wound, so remained in Lincoln for a day and then uncomfortably left town.

The battle of Blazer's Mill occurred three days later. The Regulators, led by Dick Brewer, included Frank and George Coe, Billy the Kid, and several other riders. At eleven o'clock on a Thursday morning they rode up to the grist mill buildings of Dr. Joseph Blazer, several miles southwest of Lincoln on the Río Tularosa. Later in the day, while the Regulators were inside eating dinner, Andrew "Buckshot" Roberts, one of the men for whom Brewer had a warrant, rode up. Through a window the Regulators saw Roberts approach and, in an attempt to take him without a fight, sent Frank Coe outside to encourage him to give up. After much talking and no success, George Coe, John Middleton, and Charlie Bowdre went outside to make the arrest. Roberts was still talking to Frank Coe when he saw the three men come around the corner. Bowdre ordered Roberts to give up, but before Roberts could draw and shoot he got a slug in the stomach. Suffering terrible pain, Roberts dragged himself into a doorway and, after stuffing a mattress across the door for a barricade, began firing at the Regulators. In a flash his shots cut off Bowdre's belt buckle, removed George Coe's trigger finger, hit Middleton in the chest, and grazed Billy the Kid's arm. Everyone dived for protection, and Dick Brewer ran for cover to some logs near the sawmill, in sight of the action. As he eased his head above the logs for a look, Robert's bullet hit him between the eyes at a distance of some 140 paces. The remaining Regulators fled, leaving Brewer dead and Roberts to die the next day.

During the next two months, the spring term in court at Lincoln issued warrants for the murderers of Brady and Hindman and sent troops from Fort Stanton to try to find Alex McSween. On May 14, Regulators raided Dolan's cow camp southeast of Lincoln on the Río Pecos, killing one herder and wounding two others.

In the early part of June, 1878, George W. Peppin succeeded William Brady as sheriff and renewed every effort to arrest McSween and his followers. During this same time a federal investigation was being conducted by Judge Frank Warner Angel of the Department of Justice, with the assistance of McSween. Alex McSween and several loyal followers were continually on the move. For a time they would hole up at San Patricio, a little Mexican village about fifteen miles south of Lincoln, and other times they hid out at the Chisum ranch. The evening of Sunday, July 14, Alex McSween and about fifty of his followers rode into Lincoln and barricaded themselves in strategically located buildings. McSween and eleven men, including Billy the Kid, Tom O'Folliard, and Jim French, holed up in the McSween building due west of the Tunstall Store. Sheriff Peppin's men, who had been away from Lincoln, returned and positioned themselves in the old Torreon and the Wortley Hotel. Upon the arrival of more Peppin reinforcements the next day, intermittent shooting broke out between the two factions and lasted for four days.

On the morning of Friday, July 19, at the request of Sheriff Peppin, Colonel Dudley arrived at Lincoln with a detachment of officers and thirty-five enlisted men. The soldiers mixed with Peppins men, making it risky for McSween's men to fire. About noon a couple of Peppin's deputies poured coal oil at one corner of the McSween house and set it ablaze. During the entire afternoon the shooting became more violent as McSween's men were forced to move from room to room, the flames slowly advancing through the ceiling of the adobe building. At one point Mrs. McSween, who was amidst the action, appealed to Colonel Dudley to intervene and call a truce, but Dudley refused.

The smoke became almost unbearable as darkness approached. It was now the time for an escape, and Billy the Kid, Jim French, and Harvey Morris made their break from the flaming oven and headed through the east gate under heavy gunfire. Morris was killed at the gate and the other two dashed to safety along the brushy bank of the Río Bonito. McSween and the nine others, however, waited too long. As they fled the blazing building, four of them, including McSween, were forced to take cover behind a nearby woodpile. The others made it to the chicken coop a few yards farther. After about ten minutes, McSween and three others tried for the east gate but found it blocked by Peppin's gunmen and dashed back to the woodpile. Someone yelled that they wanted to surrender, and Peppin's deputy, Bob Beckwith, replied that he would accept. As Peppin's men entered the east gate to take over, shots were fired,

El Torreon, Lincoln, *circa* 1940.
—*Courtesy Fulton Collection, University of Arizona, Special Collections.*

and Beckwith was killed, along with McSween and two of his men, Francisco Zamora and Vicente Romero.

Although it took a few more killings and a few months longer for law and order to be restored, the climax of the Lincoln County War was over.

Judge Frank Angel's investigation paid off, and General Lew Wallace replaced Governor Axtell, Thomas Catron resigned as United States attorney, George Peppin resigned as sheriff, and Colonel Dudley was relieved of his command. Billy the Kid went on to make his daring escape from the Lincoln County Courthouse, originally the Murphy-Dolan Store. James Dolan, although he lost his company to the foreclosure of Thomas Catron in 1878, gained control of the Tunstall Store and ranch and by 1882 was back in the mercantile business.

Lincoln continued to serve as a supply center for ranches and mines in the vicinity and in 1888 reported a population of about eight hundred residents. Gradually the population decreased, and in 1913 the county seat was moved to Carrizozo. The Lincoln County Courthouse then became a community center and later a school. In 1937 the state of New Mexico took over the old courthouse and began restoration and preservation.

Today the Main Street of Lincoln is a beautifully preserved monument to the Lincoln County War, thanks to the remaining citizens. Many old buildings and appropriately placed plaques recall to the visitor that today Lincoln is much the same as it was a hundred years ago.

View of Lincoln, looking northeast, date unknown. (1) Murphy-Dolan Store, (2) Wortley Hotel, (3) Site McSween home, (4) Tunstall Store, (5) Dolan home.—*Courtesy Fulton Collection, University of Arizona, Special Collections.*

Left—left to right, seated, Colonel Emil Fritz, Major L. G. Murphy. Standing, J. J. Dolan and unidentified clerk. This was L. G. Murphy and Co. who moved to Lincoln in 1873 and became part of the Lincoln County war.—*Courtesy Fulton Collection, University of Arizona, Special Collections.*

Right—Major William Brady. Sheriff Brady's posse killed John Tunstall. In turn, Brady was murdered on Lincoln's Main Street, April 1, 1878.—*Courtesy Fulton Collection, University of Arizona, Special Collections.*

Below—Present view of J. J. Dolan home and plaque telling its history.

OLD DOLAN HOME

Built in 1888 by J. J. Dolan, who took part in the L.C. War on the Murphy side, and afterwards was conspicuous in county affairs. In later times the building served as a hotel, the most familiar name being Bonito Inn.

OLD LINCOLN COUNTY MEMORIAL COMMISSION 195?

Right—Lincoln County courthouse, *circa* 1888. Sheriff Jim Brent and deputies in foreground.—*Courtesy Fulton Collection, University of Arizona, Special Collections.*

Present-day plaque with history of Murphy-Dolan Store.

MURPHY - DOLAN STORE

Built 1874, as place of business and residence of L. G. Murphy & Co., a dominant factor in area in 1870's, and headquarters of the Murphy faction during Lincoln County War. Firm failed, and store became county gov't and judicial center for 33 years.

OLD LINCOLN COUNTY MEMORIAL COMMISSION 1960

Below—Former Murphy-Dolan Store, Lincoln, *circa* 1920. Stairs have been added.—*Courtesy Fulton Collection, University of Arizona, Special Collections.*

Present view of Lincoln County courthouse, originally the Murphy-Dolan Store, now a museum.

TUNSTALL-McSWEEN
STORE

J. H. Tunstall and A.
A. McSween erected
1877. A focal point in
Lincoln County War
in which both part-
ners were slain. De-
spite looting by Seven
Rivers group, build-
ing continued as a
store under pioneer
merchants, notably
John M. Penfield.
OLD LINCOLN COUNTY MEMORIAL COMMISSION 1950

Above—Tunstall-McSween Store, Lincoln, when it was the Penfield Store,
circa 1920.—*Courtesy Fulton Collection, University of Arizona, Special
Collections.*

Above—Present plaque
with history of Tunstall-
McSween Store.

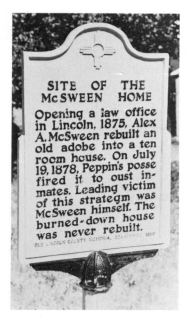

SITE OF THE
McSWEEN HOME

Opening a law office
in Lincoln, 1875, Alex
A. McSween rebuilt an
old adobe into a ten
room house. On July
19, 1878, Peppin's posse
fired it to oust in-
mates. Leading victim
of this strategm was
McSween himself. The
burned-down house
was never rebuilt.
OLD LINCOLN COUNTY MEMORIAL COMMISSION 1950

Left—Present plaque with history of
McSween home.

Below—Inside the Tunstall Store when it was a store
and post office operated by J. M. Penfield, *circa*
1920.—*Courtesy Fulton Collection, University of
Arizona, Special Collections.*

Above—Alexander A. McSween, lawyer, exposed the Murphy-Dolan faction. Killed by Murphy-Dolan gang July 19, 1878.—*Courtesy Fulton Collection, University of Arizona, Special Collections.*

Below—John H. Tunstall, Englishman, merchant. Killed by Murphy-Dolan gang February 18, 1878.—*Courtesy Fulton Collection, University of Arizona, Special Collections.*

Above—Susan McSween, wife of A. A. McSween. Died at White Oaks, N.M., 1931—*Courtesy Fulton Collection, University of Arizona, Special Collections.*

Below—John S. Chisum, cattle rancher, friend of Tunstall and McSween. Died 1884. —*Courtesy Fulton Collection, University of Arizona, Special Collections.*

Old photo of Wortley Hotel, date unknown.—*Courtesy Fulton Collection, University of Arizona, Special Collections.*

Present view of Wortley Hotel and plaque giving its history.

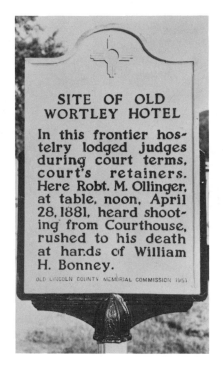

SITE OF OLD
WORTLEY HOTEL

In this frontier hostelry lodged judges during court terms, court's retainers. Here Robt. M. Ollinger, at table, noon, April 28, 1881, heard shooting from Courthouse, rushed to his death at hands of William H. Bonney.

OLD LINCOLN COUNTY MEMORIAL COMMISSION 1951

Below—Present-day view of the Torreon and plaque.

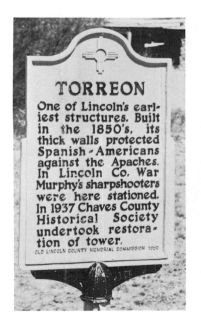

TORREON

One of Lincoln's earliest structures. Built in the 1850's, its thick walls protected Spanish-Americans against the Apaches. In Lincoln Co. War Murphy's sharpshooters were here stationed. In 1937 Chaves County Historical Society undertook restoration of tower.

OLD LINCOLN COUNTY MEMORIAL COMMISSION 1950

Madrid

COUNTY: *Santa Fe*
LOCATION: *24 mi. southwest of Santa Fe*
MAP: *page 243*
P.O. est. 1896; discont. 1966.

Rows and rows of vacant company houses stand weathered and forlorn in varying degrees of disrepair. A crumbling church, a deserted hotel, the abandoned school buildings, and the rusty ruins of the Madrid coal-processing plant are some reminders left from Madrid's prosperous years as a coal mining town. The place is not totally deserted. About sixty-five people live there, and a few businesses, a restaurant, tavern, gas station, and an antique shop are in operation. The Old Coal Mine Museum and a summer melodrama company attract tourists to the ghost town.

Madrid produced both anthracite and bituminous coal, a unique and unusual condition. It was recorded that coal was being taken from the Madrid fields as early as 1835. The town dates from about 1869, when coal mining was being conducted there on a limited basis. In the 1880's, the Santa Fe Railroad became interested in the Madrid coal to supply their steam engines. The railroad extended a spur line from Waldo five miles to Madrid and began intense mining operations.

Madrid reached its peak coal production in 1928, with its best years ranging from 1920 to the end of the 1940's. It was a company-owned town controlled by the Albuquerque and Cerrillos Coal Company and geared toward supplying all the needs of the employees. There was a six-room hospital, a doctor available at all times, a garage and service station, hotel, company store, schools, and churches. Madrid had a fine baseball park with an electric scoreboard and a field lighted for night games, a tennis court, golf course, and a shooting range. Madrid's social and civic activities were generally sponsored by the Madrid Employees

Madrid, looking northeast, *circa* 1925.—*Courtesy Museum of New Mexico.*

Club, which was largely responsible for making Madrid an outstanding town. Everyone working at Madrid was an automatic member of the club, unless excluded by personal choice. Dues were seventy-five cents a month. The Employees Club sponsored the baseball team, the Madrid Miners; the annual Fourth of July celebration; the annual childrens' Easter egg hunt; the thirty-piece Madrid Band, and the most noted of all Madrid's activities, the famous Christmas celebrations. During the Christmas season, Madrid played host to thousands of visitors who came to view the town's fabulous Christmas display. Over forty thousand electric bulbs were used to light up Madrid. Main Street was decorated with garlands and pillars, each house had a lighted Christmas tree, on the mountain were life-size figures depicting biblical scenes, and the ball park held a fanciful toyland display. From the first week of December until after New Year's, Madrid was transformed into a spectacularly illuminated yuletide fairyland. Then World War II broke out, and the annual displays were discontinued, never to be revived.

The population dwindled as miners left their jobs to take part in the war. By the end of the war many of Madrid's former buyers had switched to other sources of fuel. Madrid coal was no longer in demand.

In 1954 the whole town was put up for sale. The reported sale price of $250,000 would buy as advertised:

ENTIRE TOWN
200 HOUSES, GRADE AND HIGH SCHOOL,
POWER HOUSE, GENERAL STORE, TAVERN,
MACHINE SHOP, MINERAL RIGHTS
9,000 ACRES, EXCELLENT CLIMATE,
FINE INDUSTRIAL LOCATION

There were no takers. Today, Madrid waits like an empty shell, either to be totally destroyed or, perhaps, once again to feel the pulse of life.

Madrid, abandoned homes.

Fourth of July parade in Madrid, *circa* 1930.—*Courtesy Museum of New Mexico.*

Right—Miners' homes decorated for the yuletide season, 1940—*Courtesy New Mexico Record Center and Archives.*

Madrid, 1940. View of Christmas displays on hillside.—*Courtesy New Mexico Record Center and Archives.*

Coal tipple and railroad yard at Madrid, 1940.—*Courtesy New Mexico Record Center and Archives.*

Below—Old hotel on Madrid's Main Street.

Below—Madrid, present view.

Malone

COUNTY: *Hidalgo*
LOCATION: *about 15 mi. northeast of Lordsburg*
MAP: *page 255*
P.O. est. 1884; discont. 1888.

The mining camp of Malone was named for the discoverer of the district, John B. Malone. Prior to 1884, placer mining was plentiful in the area, and then lode deposits were discovered. Malone took root about the summer of 1884. It was never a very large camp. In 1885 it reported a population of fifty plus a company of soldiers under charge of Lieutenant Sands. The businesses consisted of two saloons and a small supply store which also contained the post office.

Malone had more than one period of activity. In 1904 the International Mining and Milling Company was engaged in setting up machinery in the concentrator and working the mines. Since forty men were involved in the work, a petition was circulated in hopes of re-establishing a post office.

The camp is gone, but the wood and corrugated iron buildings of a later homestead are at the site.

Malone, mine winch.

Mentmore

COUNTY: *McKinley*
LOCATION: *5 mi. west of Gallup*
MAP: *page 245*
P.O. est. 1917 to present.

An operating combination store and post office plus about ten houses in good repair remain at the once-active coal town of Mentmore. The townsite is privately owned.

The first coal mine, named Dilco, was opened about 1913 by the Direct Coal Company. Originally the camp was also named Dilco, but when a post office was established the name became Mentmore. In 1918, George Kaseman of Albuquerque purchased the Dilco Mine property and the Morris Mine located a mile to the north. He combined the properties under the name of the Defiance Coal Company.

The town of Mentmore, built around the mines, comprised a company store, school, homes, and the power plant. The employees lived in the company-owned frame houses of two to four rooms that were equipped with electricity and running water. Eight grades were taught at the Mentmore school, and free bus transportation to Gallup was supplied for the high school students. The population was about five hundred persons.

The mines closed at Mentmore in 1952, and since then the town has been dormant.

Mentmore, company homes.

Midnight and Anchor

COUNTY: *Colfax*
LOCATION: *Midnight—about 4 mi. northwest of Red River*

Anchor—about half a mi. east of Midnight

MAP: *page 239*
P.O. est. as Midnight 1895; discont. 1898.

High in the Cimarron Mountain Range rests a handful of deserted log cabin ruins at the edge of a pine clearing. The small, crudely constructed hovels mark the site of Midnight, a short-lived gold mining camp. The far removed mountain burg was settled by a group of miners and their families about 1895, when a post office was established. Several groups of claims known as the Midnight, Memphis, Caribel, Edison, and Anchor were worked in the vicinity of the village. Small investments in mining equipment and much hard labor yielded enough gold to sustain life in the camp for about three years. In 1897 the population of about two hundred used the services of the Ellis & Co. general merchandise store, Hays & Co. blacksmith, and a justice of the peace. Mail and passengers came tri-weekly from Catskill some fifty-eight miles to the east, and school was held three months of the year. The native gold and silver ore from four producing mines was sent to Denver for treatment.

The lack of free-milling ores and land litigation problems are the reasons given for Midnight's abandonment. It is said that the decision to close the Midnight Mine was made so suddenly that thirty-two log buildings in the process of construction were left unfinished.

About half a mile east of Midnight was the mining camp of Anchor. The settlement's life was brief, and it is doubtful that it supported any businesses or much of a population.

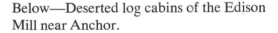

Left—Midnight, log cabin ruins.

Below—Deserted log cabins of the Edison Mill near Anchor.

Mineral City

COUNTY: *San Miguel*
LOCATION: *about 25 mi. west of Las Vegas*
MAP: *page 243*
P.O. est. 1881; discont. 1883.

For a number of years, starting in the early 1880's, the mining camp of Mineral City existed. In late summer of 1881, Mineral City was acclaiming its accessibility with a tri-weekly stage running between the camp and Las Vegas. Twenty-eight cabins and twenty-five or thirty tents and brush houses dotted the district. The camp contained the twenty-room Fairview Hotel with its barber and billiard hall, the Hilty Brothers general merchandise store, and the *News* weekly newspaper. Probably by the late 1890's, the ore had played out and the miners had drifted away. The elegant Fairview Hotel eventually burned down, and Mineral City, at the junction of the Tecolote River and Blue Canyon, disappeared.

154
M

Modoc, 1904. View of Modoc lead mine and camp.—*Courtesy Museum of New Mexico.*

Advertisement from the *Las Vegas Optic*, April 6, 1882.—*Courtesy Highlands University Library.*

Modoc

COUNTY: *Doña Ana*
LOCATION: *about 7 mi. south of Organ*
MAP: *page 253*
P.O. est. 1901; discont. 1903.

In the late 1870's the Modoc Mine was located at the foot of the granite bluffs of the Organ Mountains, and it was worked at intervals from 1879 to 1905. It produced mostly lead, with some silver and copper. A small camp of frame buildings and a mill were built about seven hundred feet below the mine. A rope tramway conveyed the ore to the mill, and then the concentrate was shipped to the Deming smelter. During the mine's period of activity it produced an estimated $200,000, mostly in lead. Modoc camp died when the mine stopped producing.

Mogollon

COUNTY: *Catron*
LOCATION: *13 mi. northeast of Glenwood*
MAP: *page 253*
P.O. est. 1890; discont. 1973.

Tucked away in a narrow defile of Silver Creek Canyon, which winds its way through the precipitous Mogollon Mountains, rests the quiet town of Mogollon. Its two dozen or so stone and wooden buildings and several nearly collapsed shacks line a once-bustling thoroughfare. An art gallery is in the former J. P. Holland General Store, and the Silver Queen Museum has a home in the old stone Coates & Moore merchandise establishment. At the east end of town, St. Francis Catholic Church occupies a location at the intersection of Jack Canyon and Silver Creek. A narrow dirt road winds north up Jack Canyon past the site of the Spanish red-light district. There it bends west around a mountain slope and past rusty machinery and abandoned mine buildings, a few of which are private residences, to the Little Fanny Mine buildings that are perched on top of an extensive fan-shaped tailings dump.

Early in the eighteenth century, Don Juan Ignacio Flores Mogollon served as the Spanish governor of lands from present New Mexico to the Pacific coast. Later the extensive mountain range of western New Mexico was given his name, and amid the mountains of this locality grew the gold and silver mining camp of Mogollon.

Prospecting in Silver Creek Canyon went hand in hand with the development of the mines at Cooney camp a few miles to the northwest. James Cooney, sergeant of the army stationed at Fort Bayard in 1870, discovered silver veins in the Mogollon Mountains. Some eight years later, after Cooney's hitch in the military, he returned to the mountains to work the rich gold and silver deposits. After James Cooney's death at the hands of Victorio and his hostile Apaches, Captain Michael Cooney moved west from New Orleans to continue development of his brother's mining properties and search for new prospects.

By 1889 mines were developed in Silver Creek Canyon and became the bonanzas known as the Maud S. and Deep Down mines. John Eberle, discoverer of the Last Chance vein, built the first log cabin in Mogollon. Harry Herman started a sawmill and lumber trade and donated timbers for the construction of the first jail. On occasion, when "Uncle Harry" went on a drinking bout and was thrown into his own jail, he swore that when released he would burn the place down. The town buildings were constructed of lumber, a post office opened in 1890, and the first school was added about 1892.

From early in its life, Mogollon was plagued by a series of fires and floods. The first big fire of 1894 wiped out most of the town buildings, but ambitious citizens immediately rebuilt, using stone and adobe. Other fires followed in 1904, 1910, 1915, and 1942, each one claiming lives and destroying property. With the melting snows and heavy spring rains, yearly floods occurred. The years of 1894, 1896, 1899, and 1914 witnessed disastrous torrents of water that swept down the mountain slopes and through the canyon, washing away tailings dumps, bridges, houses, and people.

Although the devastation by nature threatened to destroy the town several times, new mines—including the Little Fanny, Champion, McKinley, Pacific, and Deadwood—and the older producers extracted approximately one and a half million dollars of gold and silver in 1913, or about 40 per cent of New Mexico's precious metals for that year.

The Silver City and Mogollon Stage Line provided daily service, hauling passengers, freight, gold, and silver bullion some eighty miles between the towns in fourteen and a half hours. Holdups were not frequent, but occasionally, when they occurred, they created great excitement. Shortly before Christmas in 1912 a plot to rob the stage line of a five-thousand-dollar mine payroll was exposed. Five determined law officers from Mogollon laid a counterplot to prevent the crime. Two days before the shipment, Captain Fred Fornoff, Sheriffs McCart and Blair, and their two deputies posted themselves along the road where the robbery was supposed to occur. The stage passed the law officers without incident, but was robbed a few miles farther on. Upon receiving word of the holdup and a description of the thieves, the officers split into two groups. One group rode to Alma, where, based on the description of the bandits, they arrested three local merchants. The other group rode to the site of the holdup where they met a posse from Mogollon. From previous information and implicating evidence, the deputy leading the Mogollon posse was arrested as an accomplice in the robbery.

Late one afternoon C. A. Freeman, manager of the Mogollon Mercantile Company, his clerk, William Clark, and bookkeeper, R. E. Burns, were in the store following the delivery of a three-thousand-dollar payroll from Silver City. Two Mexican bandits armed with 30-30 Winchesters entered the store unnoticed and walked quickly to the cashier's office. When the startled Freeman turned to ask what they wanted, the Mexicans fired simultaneously. Both Freeman and Clark fell to the floor dead. Burns was then ordered to the safe, forced to open it, and to hand over the three thousand dollars. The killers hurriedly left, mounted, and struck out for the mountains to the east. Burns recognized one of the bandits, and a short time later a posse apprehended the two, killing one in a fight and capturing the other.

The community expanded to a population of fifteen hundred by 1915, with electricity, water, and telephone facilities. The school offered education to about three hundred children, and Catholic and Presbyterian churches administered to the spiritual needs of the people. In addition to the four merchandise stores, five saloons, and two restaurants, the town had extras including a hospital with three physicians; John Anderson, photographer; Pridemore & Howe, Auto Line; the Midway Theatre; Fert King, ice maker; a bakery; and two red-light districts, "Little Italy," the home of eighteen white girls at the west end of town and the Spanish section on the east.

During World War I, the demand for gold and silver dropped, and many of Mogollon's mines shut down. The population in 1930 had dropped to a reported two hundred. In 1934 the price of gold was raised from $20.67 per ounce to $35.00. This impetus created a temporary rejuvenation of life at Mogollon, with the population reportedly zooming to a thousand residents in 1938. World War II again caused a slash in the demand for precious metals, and this turn of events, accompanied by the devastating fire of 1942, almost finished the town. In 1950 the Little Fanny was the only mine in operation; today it is shrouded in silence.

Mogollon, miners' shacks at the Little Fanny Mine.

Mogollon, present view of Main Street.

J. P. Holland General Store on Main Street in Mogollon.

Above—Mogollon community band, 1909.—*Courtesy James Giles.*

MAURICE COATES   IRWIN MOORE

Coates & Moore

Mogollon, New Mexico

Wholesale and Retail Dealers ...in
Groceries
Provisions
Dry Goods
Clothing
Hats and Shoes

MINING SUPPLIES

Goods delivered to any part of the mountains

Advertisements from *The Mogollon Mines*, 1915.—*Courtesy James Giles.*

C. A. Marriott's
U. S. Mail,
Parcels Post,
Wells, Fargo
& Co. and
Marriott's
Express

Silver City
to
Mogollon

Mogollon—Main Street
after the flood of 1914.—
Courtesy James Giles.

Right—Advertisement from *The
Mogollon Mines*, 1914.—*Courtesy
James Giles*.

Below—Mogollon during the fire of
1915.—*Courtesy James Giles*.

Above—Little Fanny Mine, producer of gold and silver, looking north, date unknown.—*Courtesy James Giles*.

Right—Present view of the Little Fanny Mine, looking south.

Below—Stamp mill at the Last Chance Mine at Mogollon.—*Courtesy James Giles*.

Below—Gold and silver bullion, 1938.—*Courtesy James Giles*.

Mogollon Main Street, date unknown.—*Courtesy James Giles.*

Navajo coal mine, 1914. Standing, Japanese miners. Kneeling, left to right, J. J. McDermott, mine superintendent; Dr. Noonan, mine doctor.—*Courtesy Gallup Public Library*.

Navajo

COUNTY: *McKinley*
LOCATION: *about 3 mi. northeast of Gallup*
MAP: *page 245*
P.O. *none*

The opening of the Navajo coal mine by the American Fuel Company produced the camp of Navajo. Frame houses of two to four rooms supplied with water and electricity were built for the miners. A store and a hotel operated at the camp for a few years. About 1922, the Gallup American Coal Company sank the shaft at Gamerco, less than a mile west of Navajo, and the center of coal mining activity shifted there. The Navajo Mine closed, but many of the miners still lived at Navajo while working at Gamerco. In the mid-1930's Navajo reported a population of six hundred. Today there is no one. The houses were moved, and all that is left at the site of the camp are a few mine dumps and foundations.

Nutt

COUNTY: *Luna*
LOCATION: *19 mi. southwest of Hatch*
MAP: *page 251*
P.O. *est. 1881 interim. to 1939.*

Nutt, originally the terminal of the Atchison, Topeka and Santa Fe Railroad, served a vital role during the silver mining years at Lake Valley, Kingston, and Hillsboro as a point of arrival and departure for passengers and freight. In the early 1880's, hundreds of hopeful miners and merchants arriving daily at Nutt Station to pursue their dreams of wealth and adventure at one of the booming mining camps were met by the following notice posted at the station:

HO! FOR THE GOLD AND SILVER MINES
OF NEW MEXICO
Fortune hunters, capitalists, poor men,
sickly folks, all whose hearts are bowed down
and ye who would live long, be rich, healthy,
and happy: come to our sunny clime and see
for yourselves!

The railroad was extended to Lake Valley in 1884, so Nutt lost most of its population and its status as terminal but for many years still maintained an important role as station and trading post.

On September 25, 1886, Nutt Station was visited by two men who accosted Agent Farmer at gunpoint, robbed the place of $8.65, and then forced Farmer to walk a considerable distance with them from the station. When they finally left him, the unharmed Farmer quickly returned to Nutt, gave an alarm, and a posse took up pursuit of the robbers. One of the posse members, Henry Harvey, was shot by the fleeing fugitives and died the next day from his wound. Public indignation ran high. A second posse was organized and succeeded in capturing the two villains the following dawn. The men, Jim Gould, alias "Kid Allen," and Charles Clark, were immediately taken to Silver City to protect them from a possible lynching.

Nutt is now reduced to a few remnants—a windmill, a water tank, and a couple of deserted buildings.

Nutt.

Oak Grove

COUNTY: *Grant*
LOCATION: *about 10 mi. southwest of Silver City*
MAP: *page 255*
P.O. *none*

A little-known town that existed in the 1880's was Oak Grove. Situated in the Burro Mountains about ten miles southwest of Silver City and nestled appropriately in a grove of oak trees, the town had a population in December of 1882 of three hundred people, mostly miners and wood choppers. Oak Grove functioned as a direct result of the Queen City Copper Company, whose smelter and works were erected there, thus giving cause for a town. The company had a large building containing the furnaces, a blacksmith shop adjoining it, plus houses for the employees. In addition to the company buildings and smelter, Oak Grove had two general stores, a hotel, two restaurants, a saloon, a laundry, and a daily and tri-weekly line of stages between Silver City and Lordsburg.

How long Oak Grove lived and when it died is not known, but there is nothing left of the place today.

Organ

COUNTY: *Doña Ana*
LOCATION: *14 mi. northeast of Las Cruces*
MAP: *page 253*
P.O. *est. 1881 interim. to present.*

The town of Organ has had two lives. New Organ is a modern-day community on U.S. 70, with many of its residents presently employed at the White Sands Missile Base. Old Organ was a mining town, and its few remaining landmarks on a dirt road just north of the highway have been engulfed by the present town of Organ.

Mining in the Organ district began in the late 1840's with the discovery of the Stevenson-Bennett Mine. The mining camp of Organ was patented as a township on February 26, 1885, and during that year had a population of about two hundred. The town's peak population was claimed at eighteen hundred. The Torpedo Mine, discovered in 1899, was another highly productive operation that boosted the growth and economy of the community. Organ had seven saloons, a Catholic church, a two-teacher schoolhouse, two smelters, two stores—one owned by L. B. Bentley and the other, across the street, operated by M. C. Logan —and a tunnel jail which was originally a powder magazine.

One of Organ's old-timers, noted for his heavy drinking, often passed out to sleep off the effects of a drunken spree. One day L. B. Bentley found the old man sleeping in the street. After loading him into a wheelbarrow, he carted him off to the tunnel jail, dumped the inebriated form on a mattress, left the jail door open, and returned to his store. The next morning, curious to see if the old fellow had sobered up, Bentley returned to the jail and was surprised to find the man dead. On leaving the jail, Bentley found an empty Yellowstone-label whisky bottle tossed in an arroyo. Picking it up, he returned to the jail, and as a fitting token to the old man who had drunk himself to death, Bentley placed the bottle snuggly into the man's hand. Meeting several men on his way back to his store, Bentley told of the old man's death and mentioned that if they went to the jail they could see what killed him. For several weeks after that, Billy Viscarra, who ran a saloon across from Bentley's Store, noticed a marked decline in his sale of Yellowstone whisky. Bentley, on the other hand, was selling Green River and Old Taylor whisky and seemed to be doing a good business. Viscarra was a good sport when he found out the reason for his lack of sales, telling Bentley he would have played the same joke on him had the opportunity occurred.

L. B. Bentley and family came to Organ in 1903, established a store and assay office, and stayed on long after the mines closed. Bentley died in Organ about 1955. His store and assay office building remains standing and is now a privately owned residence.

Organ, present view of Bentley Store, now a private residence.

Right—Organ, *circa* 1915. Men on horseback (left) Mr. Dunwoody, mining promotor (right) L. C. Bentley, merchant.—*Courtesy Herman Wisner.*

Organ, *circa* 1915, L. B. Bentley's store and assay office.— *Courtesy Herman Wisner.*

Bentley Store, *circa* 1930.— *Courtesy Herman Wisner.*

Right—M. C. Logan, Organ merchant, had his coffin built in advance and kept in his store.—*Courtesy Herman Wisner.*

Below—Organ school, *circa* 1900.—*Courtesy Herman Wisner.*

Orogrande

COUNTY: *Otero*
LOCATION: *36 mi. south of Alamogordo*
MAP: *page 253*
P.O. est. as Jarilla Junction 1905; discont.
1906. Re-est. as Orogrande 1906 to present.

Prospecting started as early as 1879 in the Jarilla Mountains and by 1905 had triggered a gold rush. The discovery of a gold nugget described to be the size of a man's finger caused Jarilla Junction, a station on the El Paso and Northeastern Railroad built in 1897, to be renamed Orogrande. With promises of great prosperity the newly-acclaimed town quickly constructed a hundred houses, laid a fifty-five-mile water pipe from the Sacramento River to the townsite, and began publishing a weekly newspaper, *The Oro Grande Times*. For several years Orogrande was the hub of intense mining activity. Mining companies were organized, real estate offices opened, and the town claimed two thousand residents. So overcrowded were living conditions that many residents lived in hastily erected shacks and tents. One boarding-house rented the same beds to both the day and night shift mine workers for six months without either group knowing about the other one. One morning a man working graveyard shift happened to get off work early, only to find his bed occupied. He was so irate about the situation that he pulled a gun and killed the sleeping occupant.

The mines were quickly being depleted of gold, and after the initial excitement had subsided there appeared to be less gold than had been anticipated. Promoters got scared and began planting placer gold. One even put gold dust in a shotgun and peppered a cliff with the gold flakes. Although gold was the most sought-after treasure, it was not the only valuable mineral discovered in the Jarilla Mountains. There were also copper, iron, silver, and turquoise deposits. In 1906 the Southwest Smelter and Refining Co. built a smelter at Orogrande to treat the ores, but there was not enough custom smelting, so the $180,000 structure was abandoned.

Today Orogrande is reduced to a post office, a few businesses, and about fifteen families. Just north of Orogrande, half hidden in the desert vegetation, are the concrete foundations and slag pile of the smelter.

Otero

COUNTY: *Colfax*
LOCATION: *5 mi. south of Raton*
MAP: *page 239*
P.O. est. 1879; discont. 1880.

Nothing is left of Otero, the town that for a short time was the end of the track for the Atchison, Topeka and Santa Fe Railroad in New Mexico. When the tracks reached Otero in 1879 a festive celebration was held honoring Governor Miguel A. Otero of the Territory of New Mexico, for whom the town was named.

For a few months, Otero was a busy railroad town, and then the division point of the railroad was moved north to Raton, and the people and town moved with it. Although short-lived, the town claimed a newspaper, the *Otero Optic*, first printed on May 22, 1879, and a few noteworthy characters. There was Dolores Martinez, a gargantuan madame who established a popular dancehall at Otero. Her three-hundred-and-fifty-pound figure earned her the appropriate nickname of "Steamboat." Dr. T. O. Washington practiced medicine at Otero for awhile, until his quick temper ruled his actions during a quarrel and he stabbed a neighbor to death. He moved to Raton, where his unprofessional advances to a woman patient got him into trouble. When the young woman's fiance and a group of angered companions threatened Washington, officials put the doctor into protective custody in the Otero jail. The mob captured Washington anyway and escorted him to the Otero railroad yards, where they flung a rope over the framework of the water tank and lynched him.

Above—Miguel A. Otero (1859–1944), New Mexico Territorial governor, 1897–1906, for whom Otero was named.—*Courtesy Museum of New Mexico.*

Park City

COUNTY: *Socorro*
LOCATION: *about 1 mi. southwest of Socorro*
MAP: *page 247*
P.O. est. 1892; discont. 1894.

Gustav Billing, a German immigrant, built a smelter just southwest of Socorro in 1881. Around the smelter grew Park City, a dirt road lined with adobes. Businesses included the two-story Baca Hotel, Park City Store, Palace Saloon, Park City Saloon, and the Smelter Saloon. There was a school and a population of about three hundred. A spur railroad line ran from Magdelena to the Billing Smelter, carrying ore from the mines at Kelly.

Several years after the smelter was built, Gustav Billing and his family went to Germany for a visit, and while he was there, Billing died. In 1893 the Billing Smelter was sold to the American Smelting and Refining Company and finally was closed. Sometime in the early 1900's the smelter was dismantled, and gradually the town was torn down.

During Park City's active years a frequent visitor to the town recalled passing a house and through a window noticing a man inside carrying a large, wrapped bundle that looked suspiciously like a body. Stopping to investigate, the visitor discovered that it was the man's wife, who had died during the night. The man explained that since he had no more use for his wife he was going to bury her. Before the casual interment took place, however, the man's two adult sons were notified and were able to convince their father that Mother deserved a more proper and ceremonious burial.

Today only two houses of the original Park City remain. One is deserted and the other has been converted to a present-day residence.

GUSTAV BILLING

SMELTING WORKS

SOCORRO, N. M.

Will buy Smelting Ores, and Gold, Silver and Lead Ores, from date.

Sampling promptly done.

Assays carefully made, and cash paid as soon as assayed.

Above—Advertisement from *The Socorro Bullion,* October 24, 1885.—*Courtesy Highlands University Library.*

Woodcut of Billings Smelter at Park City, from Wm. G. Ritch, *Aztland, The History, Resources and Attractions of New Mexico.* D. Lothrop & Co., Boston, 1885.

Parsons

COUNTY: *Lincoln*
LOCATION: *about 8 mi. south of Nogal*
MAP: *page 249*
P.O. est. 1888; discont. 1926.

In the mid-1880's a gold strike by R. C. Parsons gave birth to the mining camp of Parsons. The camp claimed a population of several hundred persons and the usual assortment of businesses, trades, and professions. There was a general merchandise store, boardinghouses, livery stable, school, blacksmith, and justice of the peace.

About the turn of the century a large, two-story eighteen-room mansion was built at Parsons to house visiting stockholders and various guests. It played host to such noted people as a Mr. Studebaker, of Studebaker wagon fame, and Mary Roberts Rinehart (1876–1958), American writer of detective fiction. John M. Rice was Parsons' postmaster for many years, during which time the post office was housed in a corner of the inn's dining room.

Today the Parsons Hotel is still standing and still operating. The rest of the mining town is reduced to scant ruins of a mill and piles of wood from collapsed buildings.

Below—Advertisement from *New Mexico Interpretor*, May 23, 1890.—*Courtesy Highlands University Library.*

WHITE MOUNTAIN
HOTEL.
PARSONS CITY, N. M.

Board by the day or week, Table supplied with the best the market affords. Good rooms, and the best of beds. Prices reasnable.
GEORGE DILLARD, PROP.

Below—Parson Hotel.

Opposite page—Rusted classifier used to separate size gradation of ore.

Paschal

COUNTY: *Grant*
LOCATION: *about 15 mi. southwest of Silver City*
MAP: *page 255*
P.O. est. 1882; discont. 1883.

The Burro Mountain copper camp of Paschal is gone. In its day it claimed both the honor of being the first camp in the Burro Mountains and also one of the leading copper camps of the country. In 1879 the St. Louis Mine was discovered by Colonel J. W. Fleming, John Swisshelm, and James Bullard. A year later, Paschal R. Smith, of Deming, and General Frank Marshall, of Denver, purchased the property and organized the Valverde Copper Company. A fifty-ton smelter was built, launching the life of Paschal camp. By mid-1882 Paschal had grown into a community of a thousand persons. Businesses listed in December of that year were the Paschal Hotel and Gem Restaurant, Foote & Booth Store, another store run by Mr. H. Hood, a boardinghouse, two saloons, and a corral.

The smelter ran successfully until the plummeting cost of copper, high-priced labor, and exorbitant freight costs caused the management to close down. Contracts were let on the St. Louis Mine for a while, but when these expired, the population began to drain from Paschal. By March, 1883, three hundred persons remained. The camp gradually became depopulated except for one man retained as watchman for the property. Then the smelter was dismantled, the buildings torn down, and Paschal vanished.

Perryville

COUNTY: *Colfax*
LOCATION: *3 mi. southeast of Eagle Nest*
MAP: *page 239*
P.O. est. 1894; discont. 1895.

Perryville, established in 1877, functioned for some years as a small community at the head of Cimarron Canyon. Named for a Mr. Perry who operated a blacksmith shop and worked as a machinist for the placer mines in Moreno Valley, the town had a hotel, store, school, and a number of log cabins.

The town is gone, but the site of it is on U.S. 64, just below the present Eagle Nest dam.

Pinos Altos

COUNTY: *Grant*
LOCATION: *7 mi. northeast of Silver City*
MAP: *page 255*
P.O. est. 1867; discont. 1964.

Gold gave birth to Pinos Altos. In May of 1860 a group of forty-niners composed of Colonel Snively, Hicks, and Birch stopped at Bear Creek. While taking a drink from the stream, Birch discovered gold. News of the discovery quickly leaked out, and a month later the area was teeming with prospectors, who formed a settlement named Birchville. So infectious was the cry of gold that by December, fifteen hundred Argonauts had arrived at the treasure site from California, Texas, and Mexico. Men were making $10 to $15 a day scraping the gulches and stream beds. That month Thomas Mastin discovered and located the first quartz lode, naming it the Pacific Mine. The following spring he sold it to his brother Virgil, who later became a prominent citizen of Pinos Altos. In 1861 Birchville's business life included Samuel and Roy Bean's merchandise store on Main Street and a hotel run by Buhl and Gross.

The gold was there, but miners worked warily. Apache Indians were everywhere, and there was always the constant threat of attack. On September 27, 1861, all the Apache petty harassments climaxed in a major raid on the settlement. Five hundred warriors under the famous leaders Mangas Colorados and Cochise swept down on Birchville. During the battle Thomas Mastin was killed. Most of the miners, fearful of future attacks, decided to abandon the area. However, a few chose to remain. One of these was Virgil Mastin. For the next few years, until 1864, Birchville quietly slumbered. During this interval some of the remaining Mexicans renamed the camp Pinos Altos. Inhabitants and mining activity started to rejuvenate Pinos Altos at the end of 1864, but again the Apaches forced suspension of work until 1866. That year Virgil Mastin, Samuel J. Jones, Joseph Reynolds, J. Edgar Griggs, and Jacob Amberg organized the Pinos Altos Mining Company. The following year Pinos Altos town was laid out and platted by the Pinos Altos Town Company, headed by Samuel J. Jones. Virgil Mastin was one of the town's leading merchants until murdered by Apaches in 1868.

Conditions were still so unsafe that people hesitated to venture beyond the confines of the town, fearful of lurking Apaches. Finally an agreement was made between the settlers and the Indians. As part of the agreement a large cross was placed on a hillside north of Pinos Altos. As long as it remained, there were no killings.

Gold mines at Pinos Altos continued to be productive until the early 1920's. High-grade silver was accidentally discovered two miles from Pinos Altos on June 18, 1891, by the Dimmick brothers, who had taken up a homestead in the area. While driving a cow, one of the brothers picked up a heavy rock to throw at the grazing beast, only to discover that the hefty chunk was silver. Their mine, called the Silver Cell, was among the celebrated properties of the district. Copper, lead, and zinc also played roles in the town's mining history.

Pinos Altos functions today as a sleepy little village with a store, a restaurant, and a population greatly reduced from its palmy mining days of yesteryear.

Pyramid

COUNTY: *Hidalgo*
LOCATION: *about 9 mi. south of Lordsburg*
MAP: *page 257*
P.O. est. 1882; discont. 1897.

Scattered among desert creosote bushes are the remnants of Pyramid—a few concrete posts, a couple of headframes, mine dumps, some rock walls, faint traces of mill ruins, and the inevitable sprinkling of rusty cans.

Before the existence of minerals became known and Pyramid burst into a mining camp, the site was used as a water station on the southern overland route to California. It was also used extensively by the Butterfield Stage Company on their long, hot run between Mesilla and Tucson. Pyramid Peak, rising several thousand feet above the area and visible for several days' travel, became a welcome landmark for the weary traveler because it hailed the approach to a fresh-water spring.

About 1870, attention started to be focused on the ore bodies and mining potential of the area. Prospectors began flocking to the site from California, Nevada, and Colorado. At first, work was carried on in a somewhat haphazard manner. Then several individuals from St. Louis acquired several properties, and under the management of Colonel Amos Green, a prominent railroad promoter, organized work was began on the Viola Mine. Also known as the Leidendorf or the Venus, the Viola Mine was the chief mine and largest producer in the area. The Last Chance and the Robert E. Lee were two other important mines. Silver was the sought-after treasure, but later copper and some lead were also mined in the district.

The camp of Pyramid started in the early 1880's. In 1891 Pyramid Mining and Milling Company employed fifty-five men. There was a company-owned store, a boardinghouse run by Mrs. J. M. Costello, and a twenty-stamp mill which operated for over ten years, until the fall in the price of silver. Pyramid camp died sometime in the late 1890's.

One of the employees at the Pyramid mines was David McComas, son of Judge H. C. McComas. David worked at Pyramid while living in Lordsburg, and it was during this time, in March, 1883, that his father, step-mother, and their young son, four-year-old Charlie, decided to make the trip from Silver City to Lordsburg to visit David. The McComases never arrived at their destination. They were attacked by a band of Chiricahua Apaches near Nights Ranch, and both Judge Mc-Comas and his wife were killed. No trace of little Charlie was ever found. It was often speculated that he was probably raised by the Indians and eventually became one of them. His father's death was too much for David, who never recovered from the shock and died two years later. The Mc-Comas tragedy was one of the last Indian massacres in New Mexico.

Above—Wooden headframe at the site of Pyramid.

Bonito, Chiricahua Apache. ". . . Bonito and Natchez were in the raiding party that killed Judge McComas. Bonito states that he was not present at the killing but came up afterwards. He found two of the bucks quarreling as to which would have Charley, and says the quarrel would have resulted in the boy's death, had it not been for his arrival. He told them he would settle the dispute by taking the child himself, and says he took him to Mexico and kept him in his wickeeup. . . ." from the *Silver City Enterprise*, November 30, 1883. *Photograph courtesy Rose Collection, University of Oklahoma Library.*

Rabenton, deserted home.

Rabenton

COUNTY: *Lincoln*
LOCATION: *19 mi. northeast of Carrizozo*
MAP: *page 249*
P.O. est. as Raventon 1896; discont. 1900. Re-est. as Rabenton 1910; discont. 1928.

Rabenton's livelihood was farming and ranching. For many years rock houses dotted the valley, and prosperous crops of beans, corn, and cane and herds of sheep, cattle, and hogs attested to Rabenton's prosperity. The community once had three stores, four saloons, a post office, livery stable, and a schoolhouse. In later years there was a church, but before it was built mass was celebrated in a store.

The little that is left of the town is scattered throughout the valley. People drifted away after World War II, and only a few buildings and ruins remain. A "new" schoolhouse built in 1933 and used into the forties is standing. There are black-boards on the walls and debris clutters the wood floor. Next to it is the one-room school teacher's cottage, compactly designed with kitchen and living-room areas and a fireplace. In what was once the center of town are the rock ruins of the old school, similar ruins of the post office, and the adobe ruins of a store.

Rabenton had its tragedies. There was apparently a good deal of family feuding, and as a result, some killings. Juan Martinez, owner of one of Rabenton's stores, answered a knock at his door one night and upon opening it, he was shot and killed. The unidentified murderer fled into the night and was never apprehended.

Angelito Luceros, returning home drunk from a saloon, fell from his horse and tragically died. Every time the Spaniards passed the place of Angelito's death they blessed a rock and put it on the spot where he fell. Today the pile of rocks is still there.

Rabenton's "new" school, discontinued during the 1940's.

Cornerstone of Rabenton's "new" school.

Rock ruins of post office at Rabenton.

Red River

COUNTY: *Taos*
LOCATION: *11 mi. east of Questa*
MAP: *page 239*
P.O. est. 1895 to present.

Gold turned Red River into a booming mining camp. Today the place booms as a tourist mecca and a recreational paradise.

During the 1869–70 gold excitement at Elizabethtown, prospectors explored the Red River area with varying degrees of success. Both lode and placer gold deposits were discovered. The Waterbury Company built a smelter at the site of Red River in 1879, but it proved a failure and operated only a short time. Then, in 1889, it burned down.

The first permanent settlers of Red River were the Mallette brothers; Orin, Vet, and George. Other homesteaders, prospectors, and drifters gradually filtered into the valley. About 1894, E. I. Jones, a promoter from Colorado Springs, arrived at Red River, bought the rights to the claims that had been homesteaded by the Mallette brothers, and began the task of organizing a townsite. A meeting was held in a large tent, town officials were selected, and plans were commenced on the proposed townsite of Red River.

Soon frame buildings and businesses began to mushroom. Within a year and a half the town had attracted several thousand residents. There were about a dozen saloons, two general stores, boardinghouses, several hotels, livery stable, barber-shop, blacksmith shop, dance hall, a short-lived hospital that was torn down after the doctor died, and a log schoolhouse that was also used for church services. At various times the town supported one or more newspapers. There was the *Red River Record*, the *Red River Prospector*, the *Red River News*, and the *Red River Sun*.

The gold mining boom only lasted a few years, but during that time many valuable properties were located and worked. Some of the noted mines were the Golden Treasure, the Jay Hawk, and the Black Copper. One experienced prospector, Ed Westoby, claimed that a piece of pure gold the size of both fists came from the Black Copper Mine.

Practical jokes were often the order of the day. When the Taos sheriff visited Red River, he was cordially lodged in a barn used as a jail. So, when the Red River sheriff went to Taos, naturally the joke was reciprocated, and he found himself promptly housed in the Taos jail. Once a few men entered a saloon that was built on piles over Bitter Creek and told the proprietor that he had better leave, because a wall of water was coming down the creek bed and would probably wash away the saloon. The proprietor hastily retreated as the men calmly sat down, drank their fill, and then carried away his remaining liquor stock.

One of the hazards of reaching Red River in the early days was the dangerous, steep mountain grade that had to be descended in order to reach the valley floor. Cut trees were often chained to the backs of wagons to help hold them on steep grades that in some places were as much as 27 per cent. In 1916 the Forest Service built a new road considered to be one of the most amazing road engineering feats of its time.

Important molybdenum deposits were recognized about 1917. They had been discovered years earlier, but samples sent to be assayed were mistaken for graphite. When World War I started, and molybdenum was being used in hardening steel, ore samples sent again from Red River were finally correctly identified. The deposits were developed and worked, but the gold mining that had triggered Red River's growth had died, and with it died Red River's gaudy, prosperous years. Gradually the town, decreasing in population, became a sleepy mountain hamlet. In the 1930's Red River reawakened to become one of the most famous summer resorts of the Southwest.

Red River, date unknown.—*Courtesy Museum of New Mexico.*

Riley

COUNTY: *Socorro*
LOCATION: *20 mi. north of Magdalena*
MAP: *page 247*
P.O. est. 1890 interm. to 1931.

On the bank of the Río Salado opposite Spear's Ranch rests abandoned Riley. About half a dozen deserted, gradually melting adobes, a large one-room stone school building still boasting blackboards on its walls, a few stucco buildings, sheds, and outhouses dot the townsite. A small cemetery nestles beside the only building at Riley that is still maintained and used, the little church of Santa Rita. Once a year on the feast day of Santa Rita, May 22, mass is celebrated at the church by a priest from Magdelena. The rest of the year Riley slumbers undisturbed.

Originally called Santa Rita, the community was an early Spanish settlement that later acquired its Anglo name from a local sheep rancher. Farming, ranching, and mining supplied the livelihood of Riley. In 1897 the settlement of 150 reported mining as its principal resource, with four producing mines. Gold, silver, and lead were sent to Denver for treatment and miners wages were $1.75 a day. The Riley school ran five months of the year, and mass was held at the church once every four months. There were two general merchandise stores, run respectively by Anastacio Baca and C. Nelson. A. R. Cordova was postmaster, and Potfitio Sanchez the justice of the peace.

For many years Riley lived, but gradually the whims of Nature and the march of progress contributed to the town's death. The water table dropped below the level of the irrigation ditches, making it difficult to raise crops. Then more promising opportunities of making a living elsewhere lured people away.

Riley, looking south over Río Salado. St. Rita Catholic Church at right.

Stone school and other buildings at Riley.

Robinson

COUNTY: *Socorro*
LOCATION: *about 4 mi. northwest of Winston*
MAP: *page 251*
P.O. est. 1882; discont. 1883.

In anticipation of a proposed Santa Fe railroad branch, in 1882 the townsite of Robinson was laid out at the intended terminal point. Town lots were sold at twenty-five to two hundred dollars, and about three hundred people soon settled in Robinson, hoping to become rich from the promising mines in the area. Fabulous prices were offered for mining claims, and big fortunes changed hands or were refused for some of the choicest properties.

For a while the town enjoyed success. It even had a newspaper, *The Black Range*, which was first published at Robinson before it was moved to Chloride. Even after it moved, local bits of news from Robinson found their way into a couple of the June, 1884, issues. J. D. Perkins of Robinson constructed a chicken incubator out of a box that was heated with oil lamps. A party of intoxicated cowboys passing through Robinson caused considerable damage by shooting out the windows and perforating with bullets the mill company's two-story house and the printing office building.

When the railroad branch failed to materialize, and it was realized that without systematic development work the mines would not yield sizable profits, Robinson's high hopes were shattered. People began leaving faster than they had arrived. Less than a decade after the birth of Robinson not a house or foundation remained to mark the site of the former town.

THE BLACK RANGE.

DEVOTED TO THE MINING INTERESTS OF THE BLACK RANGE COUNTRY.

ROBINSON, SOCORRO COUNTY, N. M., FRIDAY, OCTOBER 6, 1882.

| SIZE. | MEN TO PATRONIZE. | NEW MEXICO AT DENVER. | some interesting features, among which | sends a chloride and gray copper ore in | achite, and |

Title block and advertisements from *The Black Range*, first printed at Robinson.—*Courtesy Highlands University Library*.

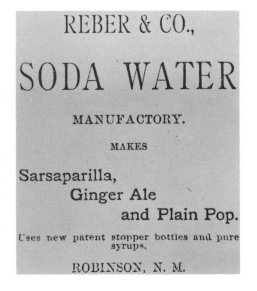

HILL & BECKETT

Keep everything a Miner wants.

Groceries and Colorado Flour

A SPECIALTY.

Best Brands of Smoking and Chewing Tobaccos

ALWAYS ON HAND.

PICKS, HAMMERS, AND HANDLES

Of all kinds, and all kinds of

BLASTING POWDER and FUSE,

In fact, we aim to keep everything a person can call for. We buy all our goods from the large wholesale houses of the east, and can sell goods as cheap as any other house in the Range.

ROBINSON, N. M.

REBER & CO.,

SODA WATER

MANUFACTORY.

MAKES

Sarsaparilla,
Ginger Ale
and Plain Pop.

Uses new patent stopper bottles and pure syrups.

ROBINSON, N. M.

Rosedale

COUNTY: *Socorro*
LOCATION: *about 24 mi. southwest of Magda-lena*
MAP: *page 247*
P.O. est. 1899; discont. 1928.

J. W. (Jack) Richardson discovered gold in the north end of the San Mateo Mountains on December 15, 1882. The find quickly precipitated a rush to the district. For several years, however, frequent Apache raids culminating in several massacres managed to drive most of the prospectors from the region. When the Indian trouble lessened, the camp of Rosedale began to grow.

The principal mine was called the Rosedale.

Mrs. J. W. Richardson apparently found the first float, and it was through her urging that her husband had the piece assayed and found it rich with gold.

Some of the other mines in the area were the Baking Powder, Alabama, Graham, Seal Package, Noonday, Red Wave, and Amy B.

In 1905, Rosedale listed a population of a hundred, a saloon, and a general store. Mining continued until about 1937.

Today the remnants of Rosedale consist of an adobe one-room building, remains of a wooden flume on the mill tailings pile, concrete mill ruins, a corrugated mine building on the hill, and various other foundations and walls. A cemetery is just east of the townsite.

Rosedale, 1905. Mill and cyanide plant of the Rosedale gold mine.—*Courtesy C. H. Gorden, U.S. Geological Survey.*

Above—View of mill launder, looking west toward the Rosedale Mine.

Below—Present mill ruins at Rosedale.

Sacramento City

COUNTY: *Otero*
LOCATION: *about 14 mi. south of Alamogordo*
MAP: *page 241*
P.O. *none*

Sacramento City was a short-lived promotional town laid out just east of the El Paso and Northeastern Railroad, fourteen miles south of Alamogordo. The Sacramento Valley Irrigation Company sponsored the enterprise and on July 8, 1907, filed the town plot in the Otero County Clerk's office at Alamogordo.

To assure the growth of the town, a cement and plaster manufacturing company was established at Sacramento City but, for some unknown reason, soon folded.

Lots were auctioned, and extensive advertising brought buyers from as far away as Kansas, Nebraska, and Iowa. Although lots were sold, generating a certain amount of promise that Sacramento City would achieve metropolitan proportions, the expected town never became much of a reality. A few tents and shacks were all that were erected. After these were removed, natural elements took over the site, obliterating all traces.

San Antonio

COUNTY: *Socorro*
LOCATION: *11 mi. south of Socorro*
MAP: *page 247*
P.O. est. 1870 to present.

San Antonio has had three periods or individual townsites. The first San Antonio dates back to 1629, when Fray Garcia de Francisco de Zuniga and Fray Antonio de Arteaga founded the Mission of San Antonio. More than two centuries later the second townsite of San Antonio was established near the old mission. The village was on the Atchison, Topeka and Santa Fe Railroad and, until the branch line tracks from the coal mines at Carthage were torn up in the early 1890's, made a junction with the main line at San Antonio. Coal was brought to the coke ovens at San Antonio from Carthage to be converted into coke, thus supplying San Antonio with a flourishing industry.

Sometime, probably in the late 1880's, A. H. Hilton arrived at San Antonio and established the Hilton Mercantile Co., which also sufficed as the local bank, and the Hilton Hotel. It was here that the fabulous Hilton Hotel got its start and claimed for San Antonio a famous son. Conrad Hilton, born December 25, 1887, started his career at a young age by carrying luggage from the train station to his father's hotel. In 1915 Conrad became business partners with his father and four years later bought his first hotel in Cisco, Texas.

In 1897 San Antonio contained, in addition to the usual assortment of businesses, a public school with an enrollment of eighty-four pupils, Wells Fargo & Co. Express, Western Union, two stage lines running to White Oaks and Lincoln, and a Catholic church. Fruit and wheat raising, wine making, bee-keeping, livestock raising, and farming were listed as the principal industries. The precinct claimed about 1,250 inhabitants. The stages running between San Antonio and White Oaks seem to have been frequent targets for stage robbers. In a two-week period in October, 1896, the outgoing and incoming coaches both were twice held up and robbed.

The Hilton Store was eventually converted into a night club about 1932 and in the mid-1940's was destroyed by fire. Today the once prosperous Hilton section of San Antonio is reduced to an old post office building, a few other deserted buildings, and ruins. Present-day San Antonio, a functioning community, lies just north of this older section.

Stage timetable from *The Socorro Chieftain*, May 29, 1884.— *Courtesy Highlands University Library.*

SOUTHWESTERN
STAGE COMPANY
RUNNING BETWEEN.
San Antonio,
White Oaks
—AND— Ft. Stanton

TIME TABLE

SAN ANTONIO.
Arrive.............................11:30 a. m.
Depart.............................7 a. m.
WHITE OAKS.
Arrive from San Antonio........4 a. m.
Depart for " " ......2:30 p. m.
Arrive for Ft. Stanton.........2:30 p. m.
Depart for " ....4 a. m.
FORT STANTON
Arrive.............................7 p. m.
Depart.............................8 a. m.

R. H. HILL'S, Sup't,

Above—San Antonio, Crystal
Palace.

Right—Railroad station.

Right—Open area beside adobe
building once occupied by the Hilton store and bank and the boy-
hood home of Conrad Hilton of
hotel fame. Building at center is
the old post office.

San Augustine

COUNTY: *Doña Ana*
LOCATION: *about 3 mi. south of Organ*
MAP: *page 253*
P.O. est. 1876; discont. 1888.

A silver lode was discovered by a Mexican in 1849 on the west flank of the Organ Mountains. Hugh Stephenson, a prospector in the vicinity, joined in partnership with the Mexican and in a few years became sole owner of the mine. The small camp located at the mine workings was continually on the lookout for Apaches. Raids were so numerous that strong adobe fortifications were constructed on the heights overlooking the mine. In the 1850's, Mr. Stephenson sold the mine to an army officer named Bennett at Fort Fillmore for $12,500. The mine was worked intermittently by the new owner and was a good producer of silver and lead.

In 1884 the small community of San Augustine consisted of Davis Lesinsky & Co. general merchandise, a hotel operated by H. M. Forster, a couple of cattle companies, and a population of a hundred people. A stagecoach made daily runs to Las Cruces, twenty-four miles away, and mail arrived three times a week.

By 1889 the Stephenson-Bennett Mine was worked out, the population of miners scattered, and the camp of San Augustine disintegrated.

San Augustine, date unknown. View of the Stevenson-Bennett Mine, which produced about $1,200,000 of silver and lead.—*Courtesy Museum of New Mexico.*

San Geronimo

COUNTY: *San Miguel*
LOCATION: *19 mi. west of Las Vegas*
MAP: *page 243*
P.O. est. 1922; discont. 1923. Re-est. 1942; discont. 1944.

The history of San Geronimo dates back to about 1835, when a Spanish justice, Jose de Jesús Ulibarri y Duran, granted some 400,000 acres of land to a group of settlers. San Geronimo was founded within the western boundary of this land grant, and, as the justice stipulated, non-landowners who resided there were given the same privileges as the petitioning settlers.

During the early years, frequent Indian raids gave the pioneers reason for building their homes close together to serve as fortress protection. In the 1870's, several sheepherder boys were reported kidnapped by the Indians. However, years later, a few of them are said to have escaped and returned to their families.

About 1879 the Atchison, Topeka and Santa Fe Railroad laid track west, and the new industry of tie hacking came to San Geronimo. Eugenio Romero built a sawmill at the village and secured a contract from the Santa Fe to supply all the ties to be used from Raton to El Paso.

As the Spanish village grew, the lands were taken over by a wealthy Spanish gentleman whose name has been forgotten. As owner of the local store he became a generous benefactor, paying bills at baptisms, weddings, and funerals. Every settler who had a small farm worked for the highly respected Spanish don and looked to him for security and advice. About 1917, when the town's patriarch died, his adopted son took over the lands, but lost possession of them during the Great Depression.

A Catholic church was built in 1906 in the central plaza, and a school was constructed about 1907.

In 1937 the town consisted of about forty families and fifty-eight houses of stone, mud, and adobe. A small store was operated in a private home, the town had one telephone that belonged to the forest service, and mail was collected and delivered three times a week.

San Geronimo celebrated the feast days of Saint

Jerome and Saint Paul. In preparation for the occasion the church would be whitewashed inside and freshly plastered outside. On the festive day everyone arrived in their brightest and best clothes to participate in the dancing and merrymaking.

Today, San Geronimo, a quiet little cluster of buildings, looks much as it probably did fifty years ago. The young people have all moved away from the valley and most of the old ones have died. Only a few families remain. The buildings of the once prosperous community are guarded by a lonely cemetery that overlooks it from the east.

San Geronimo, adobe home.

San Geronimo, looking north toward church.

Overlooking San Geronimo from the cemetery. Looking west toward the Sangre de Cristo Mountains.

San Marcial

COUNTY: *Socorro*
LOCATION: *about 32 mi. south of Socorro*
MAP: *page 247*
P.O. est. 1869; discont. 1944.

In the early 1850's a farmer, Pascual Joyla, moved his family to an adobe shack that he built on the east bank of the Río Grande a few miles south of recently constructed Fort Conrad. Joyla cut and sold firewood and hay to the military post. Soon others moved to join him, and the little community of La Mesa de San Marcial began to grow. Fort Conrad relocated south of La Mesa on the west side of the Río Grande in 1854 and became Fort Craig; and, in 1866, La Mesa de San Marcial was wiped away by a flood. The people lost no time in moving their surviving possessions to the Río Grande's west bank, re-establishing the village on the old Pedro Armendaris land grant.

When the Atchison, Topeka and Santa Fe Railroad extended south to San Marcial in 1880, there were about a hundred adobe dwellings. Wilson Waddingham, owner of the land grant property on which the townsite was located, controlled the San Marcial Land and Improvement Company and was eager to do business with the railroad. Rather than construct the railroad's division terminus facilities at San Marcial, the roundhouse, freight depot telegraph building, and a Harvey House restaurant were built about a mile north and served as a nucleus for a new town of San Marcial. No sooner had the new town begun to grow than, in July of 1881, it was nearly wiped out by fire. Bouncing back rapidly, the community thrived quickly and soon boasted of a thousand residents, along with every describable business. Mr. Waddingham donated lots for a school and two churches, and Martin Zimmerman, a New York businessman, bought 4,000 acres of land, 250 acres of which he divided into 2,500 lots at the site of the new town. The river front and principal streets were planted with cottonwood trees which, in due time, afforded grateful shade for beautiful walks and drives.

San Marcial had typical growing pains. Frontier flotsam and jetsam filtered in and out, sometimes peaceably and other times causing much trouble. Charles Walker, the city marshal, was shot to death by Paddy Ryan, an escaped convict on the dodge from El Paso. Ryan was beating his wife when Walker arrived at the ruckus and tried to stop them. After a brief argument, Ryan fired six shots at the marshal, with five finding their mark. Ryan fled to the mountains and, although pursued by an angry posse, escaped.

Bill White and Bill Johnson, both well-known toughs from Socorro, arrived in San Marcial one day, proceeded to get violently drunk, and decided to push a few people around. Throughout the morning they were armed to the teeth and threatened to shoot anyone who came too close. By the middle of the afternoon, with bottle in hand, they bullied a man with a wagon into driving them to Old Town. On the way, one of the drunks dropped his hat in the dust and ordered the driver to fetch it. The other drunk commanded the driver to stay where he was or he would be shot. After sporadic laughing and arguing the two passengers began to shoot at the driver's head to see how close they could aim without hitting him. Finally, tired of their game, much to the relief of the frightened driver, they retrieved the hat and continued on their way. On reaching their destination—another saloon—they continued drinking and threatening lives and limbs until they stumbled into a vacant room and succumbed to unconsciousness. A group of townspeople hastily gathered to guard the room and prevent further trouble. During the night a mob of men, armed and masked, entered the room. Finding the two troublemakers asleep, the intruders deliberately shot them. An inquest was immediately held, and in the presence of the bullet-riddled bodies the coroner rendered a verdict of killed by unknown parties.

By 1897, San Marcial had a two-room school with 120 pupils, and two teachers conducted classes for six months a year. Its people attended services at the Catholic, Methodist, and Episcopal churches, and in addition to the usual saloons, stores, and restaurants, the residents patronized the San Marcial Skating Rink, an ice and soda water company, a bicycle repair shop, insurance agent, and the Columbia Building and Loan Association. The *San Marcial Bee*, the official Socorro County newspaper, was published every Saturday. The Rosedale Mines in the San Mateo Mountains to the west had their headquarters at San Marcial, and the community became the center for agricultural and irrigation projects.

During the course of its life San Marcial had three newspapers at different times; the *San Marcial Reporter*, *San Marcial Bee*, and the *San Marcial Standard*.

For the next fifteen years the town's population remained constant, but new enterprises such as the Bank of San Marcial, Southwestern Milling and Electric Company, the Santa Fe Eating House and Dining Car System, the Royal Dye Works, and several other flour mills and mining companies were established there.

By 1929 the population peaked at fourteen hundred. Then on the night of August 13, the waters of the mighty Río Grande began to rise and soon reached the flood stage. Hundreds of people began to panic as water entered their homes and adobe walls began melting away. The men gathered to sandbag and reinforce the dikes, since San Marcial was directly on the flood plain. Women and children grabbed what belongings they could and fled for high ground to the west. Padre Emil Barrat watched the Catholic church crumble and all of the furnishings, his vestments, and the chalice box wash down the great river. Red Cross food and clothing were brought in, a large force of workmen was rushed in by special train to aid in strengthening the levees, and the railroad supplied fresh water, but still the crest of the flood was to come. By the next morning the town was submerged up to the second floor of the buildings, while some three hundred people camped on the banks overlooking the disaster. Fortunately no one was killed, and gradually the waters receded, but silt many feet in depth covered the town. Most of the people, seeing their homes a total loss, left.

By 1938 a reported two hundred persons lived in San Marcial, and the second floor of the Harvey House served as a waiting room and telegraph office for the railroad.

Gradually throughout the years the remaining ruins have eroded away or been covered by silt and water from the Río Grande. The only visual evidence remaining is a lonely cemetery hidden in the mesquite.

185
s

Advertisement from the *San Marcial Reporter*, July 28, 1888.—*Courtesy Highlands University Library*.

-

Featherston & Keith.

GROCERS!

Keep the Finest Assortment of Staple and Fancy Groceries to be found anywhere in the West.

Provisions, Fresh Butter, Eggs, Vegetables and Fruits always on hand.

San Marcial,   New Mexico.

The Largest and Best Assortment
——OF——

Dry Goods, Clothing, Etc.
——AT——

JOSEPH FREUDENSTEIN'S,
SAN MARCIAL, NEW MEXICO.

SAN PEDRO SMELTER.

NG CO TOPEKA KANSAS.   Photos. by Bass, Santa Fe.

Above—Ruins of stone ovens where coal was coked for use in the smelter.

Left—Charcoal sketch of San Pedro copper smelter, *circa 1882.—Courtesy New Mexico Record Center and Archives.*

San Pedro

COUNTY: *Santa Fe*
LOCATION: *32 mi. northeast of Albuquerque*
MAP: *page 243*
P.O. est. 1881; discont. 1918.

When Lieutenant J. W. Abert of the United States Army visited San Pedro in October, 1846, he reported an active gold placer strike in progress. Men, women, and children were mining gravels out of vertical shafts with windlasses and piling them nearby, while other workers separated the gold on wooden platters in small pools of water. Mining continued spasmodically in this primitive fashion until 1880, when the San Pedro and Canon del Agua Company attempted full-scale hydraulic mining operations. Large dams constructed in the Sandia Mountains some twenty-five miles to the west supplied water to the placer deposits through fourteen-inch pipelines, giving San Pedro the boost it needed to develop into a full-fledged mining

camp. A formal townsite was laid out, providing locations for a general merchandise store, a good hotel operated by Callaway & Patterson, three saloons, and dwellings for about four hundred residents. Once the camp began to flourish, the San Pedro and Canon del Agua Company opened a large copper mine two miles east of the village. Stamp mills, crushers, a smelter, and a reverbatory furnace were constructed, and soon the company employed forty men to operate the equipment and extract the copper from the rich sulfide ore.

About the time that San Pedro was at its peak, litigation problems over mineral rights on the San Pedro Land Grant developed between small mine owners and the large company. Prominent citizens, including Miguel A. Otero, William A. Vincent, and Golden's newspaper man, Colonel R. W. Webb, attempted to seize some property of the San Pedro Company and were promptly jailed. Another attempt to fight the large company erupted when miners erected a bastion and christened it Fort Otero. They hoisted a Mexican flag on one side and an American flag on the other. A small-scale revolution was avoided, however, when the lack of drinking water caused the entrenched miners to give up their plans.

After several years of water shortages and litigation the pipeline was abandoned and the smelter was shut down. Then, in 1887, a new gold strike rekindled the mining fever and San Pedro went into a new era of prosperity. Thomas Wright opened the famous Lucky Mine, and the Golden Hydraulic Company repaired the San Pedro Smelter, the pipelines, and reservoirs. Ordinary labor was paid $2.00 a day and miners received $2.50. About fifteen buildings and many new businesses sprang up in San Pedro, including the San Pedro Hotel, Delmonico's restaurant, the *Golden 9* newspaper, a stage line to Albuquerque, a drug store, a barbershop, and a "well-stocked" bar.

In 1888 the territorial supreme court ruled against the San Pedro and Canon del Agua Company, denying their mineral rights to several thousand acres. A year later the Lewisohn family acquired the San Pedro property and for many years operated the Santa Fe Gold and Copper Company.

Gold and copper mining continued in spurts until after World War I, when the price of copper dropped. The Lewisohns closed the mines and sold the property to a Denver company, who razed the buildings and shipped away the equipment.

W. S. Carnahan operated the Anaconda, Lucky, and Amazon mines at San Pedro during the late 1920's. He built a store on a hill east of San Pedro and acquired post office service between 1927 and 1930 under the name of Carnahan.

The mines at San Pedro have long since closed, leaving only a small battery of beehive coke ovens, a few shattered foundations, and a run-down cemetery.

187
s

Advertisement from *The Cerrillos Rustler*, September 5, 1890.—*Courtesy Highlands University Library.*

San Pedro cemetery.

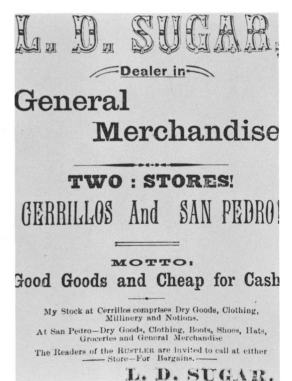

L. D. SUGAR.
Dealer in

General Merchandise

TWO : STORES!

CERRILLOS And SAN PEDRO!

MOTTO:
Good Goods and Cheap for Cash

My Stock at Cerrillos comprises Dry Goods, Clothing, Millinery and Notions.

At San Pedro—Dry Goods, Clothing, Boots, Shoes, Hats, Groceries and General Merchandise

The Readers of the RUSTLER are invited to call at either Store—For Bargains.

L. D. SUGAR.

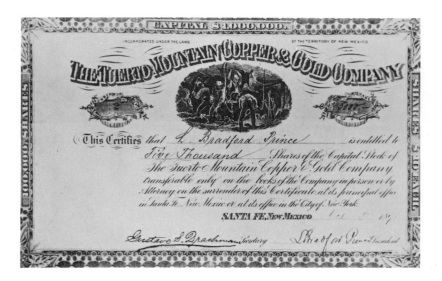

Above—Stock certificate once worth $50,000, owned by L. Bradford Prince. Right—L. Bradford Prince (1840–1922), New Mexico Territorial governor (1889–93). He held extensive mining and land interests around San Pedro.—*Courtesy New Mexico Record Center and Archives.*

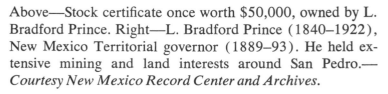

Santa Rita, 1915. Relics of a Spanish mine found in the open-pit copper mine of Santa Rita.—*Courtesy Museum of New Mexico.*

Santa Rita

COUNTY: *Grant*
LOCATION: *15 mi. east of Silver City*
MAP: *page 255*
P.O. est. 1881 to present.

Discovery of the rich copper deposits at Santa Rita date back to 1800, when Lieutenant Colonel Manuel Carrasco, Spanish commandant, was in charge of a military fort in that locality. Legend claims that Carrasco cared for an Apache Indian who was suffering from a rattlesnake bite, and in return for his kindness the Indian guided the

Colonel to a rich deposit of native copper. Carrasco immediately recognized the potential for mining, but was unable to provide adequate finances for proper development of the deposits. In 1804 he sold his interest in the property to a Chihuahua banker, Don Francisco Manuel Elguea, who moved to Santa Rita del Cobre. There he operated a penal colony under a Spanish crown grant and mined the rich copper. Elguea built a triangular-shaped fort-prison with large round towers at the corners and thick adobe walls between. From this stronghold his Indian slaves and convict labor supplied the Spanish government in Mexico City with high-quality coinage copper, transported by burro train across the rugged Sierra Madres.

Mining methods were crude, with narrow, winding shafts and tunnels driven from one rich copper vein to another. The slaves worked in dark, cramped openings and lifted the ore in baskets and leather sacks up notched poles to the surface. Collapse of the workings and live burial of the laborers were undoubtedly frequent, as suggested by the artifacts and skeletons found some hundred years later in the open pit mine.

After Elguea's death in 1809, his widow leased the workings to various parties for about thirteen years.

When Sylvester Pattie and his son James were trapping in the southwest in 1812 they were stranded at Santa Rita after the Indians ran off their horses and stole their supplies. The Patties leased the mine for several years, until a trusted clerk absconded with thirty thousand dollars in gold that was to have been used to buy equipment.

In 1837, during the time there was a lull in Indian attacks, a man named James Johnson, a part-time scalp hunter, conceived a treacherous plan to eliminate the Apaches. Braves, women, and children were enticed to a feast at the Santa Rita Presidio. After they had filled themselves with food and liquor they were invited to the courtyard to help themselves to all of the "harina" and ground corn that they could carry. In the middle of the excitement a large number of Apaches were at the food pile frantically grasping for their share. A cannon hidden in a pile of rubbish was touched off, blasting bullets, nails, and metal shot into the Indians. Those who could, scattered, while the Spaniards leaped from their hiding places and opened fire with muskets, leaving more than three hundred blood soaked bodies dead or dying among the shattered bowls of corn meal.

Mangas Coloradas, one of the Apaches who escaped the Santa Rita massacre, assumed the role of chief of the Mimbres Apaches and led them on vengeful expeditions against the Spaniards. The raids against Santa Rita were so intense that the Spaniards abandoned the mine and fled south in a caravan. Before they reached the safety of the southern missions about two hundred of them were believed to have been killed by the Apaches.

After being abandoned for three years the mine was taken over by a Spaniard named Siqueiros who kept it until the outbreak of the Civil War, when the Confederate Army occupied the old adobe fort at Santa Rita. When the Confederates were chased out of New Mexico the mines were taken over and intermittently operated by Messrs. Sweet, LaCosta, Brand, and Flesh until 1870.

In 1873, Martin B. Hayes acquired clear title to the property. There followed a series of leases, options, and extensive underground mining activity. The property finally came under the ownership of the Chino Copper Company, and in 1910 steam shovels began open pit operations.

The little village of Santa Rita acquired a post office in 1881 and gradually grew from a population of five hundred persons in 1884 to twenty-five hundred residents in 1915. The prosperous town added a fifty-two bed hospital, with Dr. F. W. Carrier as physician surgeon and with three trained nurses. A Catholic church was erected, and other denominations held occasional services in a hall belonging to the Ladies' Guild of Santa Rita. The Orpheum Theatre held weekly movies and presented live dramatic and musical entertainment several times a year. A few businesses of 1915 included the Santa Rita Store, Celestina Carrillo's Saloon, Santa Rita Steam Laundry, Mountain States Telephone Co., Mrs. C. G. Messenis' boardinghouse, a bakery, blacksmith, two shoemakers, Owen Bros.' Billiards, a restaurant, meat market, barber, and ice company. The population increased to about six thousand persons and remained there until the 1950's, when the expanding pit began to force the abandonment of the town. The buildings have all been razed and the Santa Rita pit, the third-largest open pit in the United States, covers the area once occupied by the town.

Above—Winter view of Santa Rita with the open-pit copper mine in background, looking south, date unknown.—*Courtesy Museum of New Mexico.*

Right—Steam shovel loading train cars with copper ore in the Santa Rita pit, date unknown.—*Courtesy Museum of New Mexico.*

Below—Santa Rita, *circa* 1920, looking northeast.—*Courtesy L. C. Graton, U.S. Geological Survey.*

Above—Santa Rita, looking northeast, 1967.

Left—Santa Rita Casino, 1967.

Destroyed hotel at Santa Rita, 1967.

Sawyer

COUNTY: *Valencia*
LOCATION: *about 28 mi. southwest of Prewitt*
MAP: *page 245*
P.O. est. 1909; discont. 1916.

In the early 1900's the small lumbering camp of Sawyer was founded high in a timbered valley of the Zuni Mountains. The American Lumber Company ran the operation, shipping lumber to Albuquerque along the Zuni Mountain Railroad as far as Grants and then on Atlantic & Pacific tracks the remaining distance.

In the years when lumbering operations were at full swing, Sawyer had approximately thirty families, a saloon and large mercantile store, a two-room school in session during the winter months, and a village constable. Mail arrived by horseback and a priest visited Sawyer once a month to celebrate mass in one of the homes.

The trees disappeared, the sawmills closed, and by 1919 Sawyer had become a ghost town. A handful of sturdy log buildings and a few dilapidated shacks remain at the townsite high in the peaceful grasslands.

Sawyer, log buildings.

Sawyer, looking northeast.

Cliff Mine and crew at Senorito, *circa* 1900.—*Courtesy Schmit Collection, University of New Mexico Library.*

Senorito

COUNTY: *Sandoval*
LOCATION: *about 4 mi. southeast of Cuba*
MAP: *page 243*
P.O. est. 1901; discont. 1924.

As a small copper mining camp established in 1893, Senorito served a population of about a hundred people. It contained a store, sawmill, post office, several houses, a crusher, and smelter. The post office remained active for several years after the mining operation ceased.

Today it is difficult to pinpoint the exact site of Senorito, because only the ruins of one building and an ore chute mark the approximate location.

Senorito post office, *circa* 1900.—*Courtesy Schmit Collection, University of New Mexico Library.*

Below—Senorito and the Tierra Trias copper smelter, *circa* 1900. *Courtesy Schmit Collection, University of New Mexico.*

Shakespeare, looking from the General Merchandise Store across Avon Avenue. Left, Roxy Jay Saloon; center, Grant House; right, Stratford Hotel.

Shakespeare

COUNTY: *Hidalgo*
LOCATION: *2 mi. south of Lordsburg*
MAP: *page 257*
P.O. est. as Ralston 1870; discont. 1871. Reest. as Shakespeare 1879; discont. 1885.

In the late 1850's the Butterfield Overland Stage Company established an alternate route south of its main line that passed the site of Shakespeare, at that time known as Mexican Springs. When the stagecoach service discontinued during the Civil War, Confederate soldiers briefly encamped at an old rock fort at Mexican Springs. About three years after the war ended the National Mail and Transportation Company pioneered its way through the southwest, sending John Evensen and Jack Frost to locate stations. At Mexican Springs, where good water was abundant, they established a mail stop, renaming it Grant in honor of the popular general. Of the many travelers who passed by, only a few stayed for any length of time. One of these was W. D. Brown, a surveyor for the United States government, who was helping to lay out a proposed western overland route along the thirty-second parallel. Along with his government work, Brown did some prospecting in the Pyramid Mountains, pocketed several samples, and eventually landed in San Francisco with silver specimens that assayed twelve thousand ounces of silver per ton. Through either careful planning or blind luck he ended up in the office of William C. Ralston, founder of the Bank of California, and interested the financier in a mining venture.

In 1870, Harpending and Company, under the direction of William Ralston, staked claims and invested heavily in the newly formed Ralston mining district, thereby spearheading the overnight growth of Grant. The town was laid out in blocks, with three parallel streets and cross streets, the desert was cleared, tents were erected, wells were dug, and the name was changed to Ralston. During the next few weeks William Ralston posted a general claim to the entire district and formed the New Mexico Mining Company in London, selling stock worth 500,000 pounds. On arrival of his representatives to Ralston, now a community of about two hundred persons, they found the best properties to be claimed by Ralston employees of an earlier expedition.

The Ralston mining venture was short-lived. Mining claims had been hastily staked and improperly recorded, leaving the land open for other companies to refile claims. Further exploration for the rich silver bonanza resulted in a few isolated pockets of ore, and Ralston's mining empire was on thin ice. The mining stock dropped in value, and people left the freshly formed camp.

The time appeared ripe, and it was reported that diamonds were found someplace in the southwest. A story is told that two prospectors, Philip Arnold and John Slack, found the precious gems and brought them to Ralston's bank in San Francisco. William Ralston immediately became excited over the discovery, had the diamonds appraised by Tiffany's as worth $150,000, and began plans for a diamond empire. Henry Janin, a highly respected consulting engineer, was taken to the prospect blindfolded by the two prospectors, inspected the diamond fields, and confirmed their discovery.

The location of the diamond deposits was speculated to be somewhere in the southwest. Several diamonds were reported found on Lee's Peak near Ralston. People were skeptical and confused by all the reports, but still they invested heavily in new diamond stocks, and important notables such as Horace Greeley, Baron Rothschild, and Asbury Harpending became involved. A large number of gem seekers supported the Ralston camp until late in 1872, when Clarence King, a government geologist, uncovered the hoax. Based on scanty information supplied him by Henry Janin, King found a location in the Unita Mountains in northeastern Utah that revealed planted diamonds. It was therefore assumed that the diamond discoveries at Lee's Peak were also a fraud.

William Ralston gradually recovered from the blow, paying from his own pocket all who had invested in the scheme. Nearly everyone left Ralston by 1873 except a handful of people who served the stage station and did some prospecting. William Ralston suffered through several years of hardship until finally, during the depression of 1875, the Bank of California collapsed, leaving him in financial ruin. On August 27 of that year Ralston went for a swim in San Francisco Bay and drowned.

During the late 1870's Colonel John Boyle of St. Louis staked some silver claims for the Shakespeare Mining Company. It was believed that a

Shakespeare, looking down Avon Avenue, *circa* 1900.—*Courtesy Glen H. Dorsett.*

name change from Ralston would improve the town's mining reputation, and it was formally renamed Shakespeare in 1879. The principal mines were the Henry Clay, Atwood, Eighty-Five, and Yellow Jacket. Colonel Boyle bought and remodeled an adobe building, tacking unbleached muslin between the walls for partitions, and placed a sign outside identifying it as the Stratford Hotel.

Shakespeare had a smaller population than Ralston in its prime and only one well-defined street, named Avon. The buildings were constructed of adobe and the town had one section in the northwest called Poverty Flat, where the red-light district was located. During the 1880's a group of about seventy armed citizens, the Shakespeare Guard, was organized to protect the village from Apaches. When Judge and Mrs. McComas were killed by Indians in 1883 the Guard offered a reward for the return of kidnaped Charlie McComas and attempted to track down the hostiles, but were unsuccessful.

The Grant House, a stage station and eating house, during the early 1880's was the site of a tragedy. The story is related that while Sandy King, a well-known desperado, was making his home in Shakespeare he engaged in an argument with a storekeeper at Smyth's Mercantile Store and shot off the clerk's index finger. The shot attracted a crowd, and after a brief struggle King was held in custody. At about the same time Russian Bill, a companion of King's, stole a horse and headed east. Two of Shakespeare's men took after Bill and trailed him about sixty miles to Deming, where they captured him in an abandoned boxcar. After returning Russian Bill to Shakespeare that evening, local vigilantes decided to hang the two roughnecks. Selecting the Grant House as the place of execution, a mob of men dragged the victims into the dining room. They threw ropes over the heavy ceiling timbers and lynched the two. The dead men were left hanging where they died that night. The next morning when the stagecoach pulled up to the Grant House the passengers unloaded and rushed into the dining room for breakfast. Stopping short, the travelers gasped at the gruesome sight. Finally they helped cut down the corpses and buried them before sitting down to eat.

In 1884 Shakespeare claimed two hundred citizens, and among its businesses were three saloons, two hotels, two blacksmiths and liveries, a meat market, mercantile store, a lawyer, deputy sheriff, express agent, and surveyor.

Gradually the silver mines closed, and by the 1890's only a few buildings were occupied, and the surrounding country was being used for grazing cattle. About 1907 some of the old mines began operating again, and the Stratford Hotel reopened to furnish rooms for the miners. The Eighty-Five mine, Henry Clay, and Atwood were rejuvenated, and about 1914 the Southern Pacific Railroad laid a spur line down Avon Avenue to connect the new village of Valedon, about two miles south, to the main line at Lordsburg. While miners operated at Valedon, Shakespeare was booming again. This streak of good fortune lasted until the Depression, when most of the mining was discontinued.

In 1935 the Frank Hill family took over the abandoned townsite of Shakespeare and established a ranch. They have maintained the old buildings, fighting wind, rain, and erosion to preserve the last surviving vestige of a real frontier town.

Above—William C. Ralston (1826–75), founder of Bank of California and mining promotor.—*Courtesy California Historical Society*.

197
s

View of Shakespeare, now a private ranch.

Shandon

COUNTY: *Sierra*
LOCATION: *14 mi. south of Truth or Consequences*
MAP: *page 251*
P.O. est. 1904; discont. 1906.

About two years before the placer gold fields in the Caballos Mountains were made known to the public, Bernardo Silva made visits to Hillsboro to cash in gold nuggets. One Sunday evening, November 22, 1903, Silva became intoxicated and told of a rich deposit of placer gold. Several persons overheard the story in the saloon and started traveling at once the eighteen miles to the Caballos Mountains in order to stake claims. The next morning the news of the rich Eldorado became known in Hillsboro, and in a din of wild excitement a general exodus took place. Men left their jobs and families and hitched a ride on any means of transportation available. The district court in session adjourned, and Judge Parker, District Attorney Turner, District Court Clerk Mitchell, Attorney H. B. Holt, and Court Interpreter Eugene Van Patten left in a frenzy.

News of the old-fashioned mining boom traveled throughout the neighboring territories as trains brought newcomers from Colorado, New Mexico, Arizona, and Texas to the train station at Rincon, on the Río Grande twenty-five miles south of the strike. Within twenty-four hours after the news leaked out, some five hundred prospectors armed with rifles and revolvers guarded their individual twenty-acre claims. Gradually the excitement quieted, the weapons were laid aside, and the miners busied themselves with picks, shovels, gold pans, and dry washers. The placers were confined to Silva and Trujillo gulches, where gold was found on the bedrock beneath a covering of alluvium.

After a time, when the pay streaks were found and surveyors established claim boundaries, the overflow population left and a small camp was formed. In 1905 it claimed 150 persons, a general merchandise store, saloon, and three placer-mining companies. The camp lasted only a couple of years. An occasional few ounces of gold were still being mined from the detrital washes as late as 1942.

Steins

COUNTY: *Hidalgo*
LOCATION: *19 mi. southwest of Lordsburg*
MAP: *page 257*
P.O. est. as Doubtful Canyon 1888; discont. 1905. Re-est. as Steins 1905; discont. 1944.

There are several names associated with the history of Steins that have been interchanged throughout the years. Doubtful Canyon was the name given to a pass in the north end of the Peloncillo Mountains. It received the name because emigrant travelers passing through the canyon were under constant threat from Indian attacks. The Butterfield Overland Stage route passed through the canyon in the late 1850's. In 1873 a skirmish between Apache renegades and a small detachment of cavalry occurred at the pass in Doubtful Canyon, resulting in the death of a Captain Stein. From that time on, the location of the engagement was called Steins Pass.

A few years later, prospectors searched the Peloncillo Mountains north of Steins Pass and discovered mixed deposits of gold, silver, lead, and copper. The area of the strikes was labeled the Kimball mining district, and soon several small but busy camps sprang up along the Peloncillo range for a distance of six or seven miles. A post office was established as Doubtful Canyon on the main wagon road in Steins Pass in 1888 and served the little camps of Kimball, Pocahontas, and Beck. Tents and frame cabins covered the hillsides, and John D. Weems started a store and hotel at the Beck camp, with buckboard service to the newly established Southern Pacific station at Steins Pass. Water had to be hauled for six or seven miles at a price of $1 a barrel, and wood was scarce. Only one saloon was reported in the district, and the camps were supplied with beef by Scott White's ranch in the Chiricahuas.

On December 9, 1897, the Southern Pacific Sunset Limited was held up at Steins Pass by the Black Jack Ketchem gang. Edward Cullen, a trainman, was killed, and the robbers escaped, but without any money.

The Fourth of July, 1902, was eagerly anticipated by the camps, because James Gordon Henry of New York's Empire State Society Sons of the American Revolution had presented Steins Pass with a magnificent American flag measuring six feet wide and ten feet long. ". . . the Occasion will be honored in due and ancient form by the citizens of Steins Pass. It is needless to remark that the donor's health will not be forgotten. In the absence of music we will be favored with the trained voices of our coyote band and several other variety of dogs, now nightly practicing for the event"—*Silver City Enterprise*, June 27, 1902. During the same year Steins Pass reported thirty-five registered voters and the arrival of Miss Caddis, the new resident school teacher.

Early in the 1900's a new camp called Steins began to take shape as a station on the Southern Pacific Railroad a few miles east of the older station. By 1905 it had a post office, a population of a hundred citizens, a mercantile store operated by William Charles, a saloon run by Bob Williams, Law Huen's restaurant, and it was the headquarters for a couple of mining companies. The maximum population was probably no more than two hundred, as reported in 1919. The small railroad community lasted until World War II, when the bulk of the populace moved away, leaving only a handful of railroad service personnel.

Steins is hardly noticed today as speeding traffic passes along Interstate 10. Deserted adobe buildings, several with advertisements still fastened to the walls, stand among the creosote bushes and mesquite of the gradually encroaching desert.

Buildings at Steins.

Below—Steins Main Street, looking west.

Sugarite

COUNTY: *Colfax*
LOCATION: *about 9 mi. northeast of Raton*
MAP: *page 239*
P.O. est. 1912; discont. 1944.

Chicorica Canyon was active with cattle ranches long before the coal mining camp of Sugarite was settled in 1909. The property was developed by the Chicorica Coal Company and later taken over by the St. Louis, Rocky Mountain and Pacific Company. In the beginning, coal was hauled by wagon to Raton for domestic and steam use. The Rocky Mountain Company expanded its operation in 1912, importing about fifty Japanese workers to the mines. The school was opened that year in a four-room house with Catherine McLaughlin as the first teacher. Later a new two-room school was constructed containing a large auditorium upstairs which was used for dances, motion pictures, and other social events. The population increased to five hundred residents in 1915; Mr. and Mrs. Barbont operated a boardinghouse; and M. M. Evans was postmaster and sold ice cream. The camp contained the Blossburg Mercantile Company, the Bell Telephone Co., an opera house, physician, justice of the peace, and a music teacher.

The town grew with the construction of concrete, stone, and hollow-tile buildings in neatly arranged terraces along the sides of the canyon. Soccor, football, and baseball were enjoyed in the summer, and a clubhouse was erected to serve as the center of activity during the cold winter months. Movies were shown there twice a week, cultural programs were sponsored by the Goldenrod Club, and the center had a soft drink bar and a pool room. Christmas time was always special, and the children provided the townspeople with an elaborate Christmas program. Costumes were made by the sewing class, and every child participated in some part of the pageantry. Catholics attended mass in the community center, and the Reverend McKean often brought a choir from Raton for the Presbyterian Easter services.

Sugarite's population fluctuated by one or two hundred residents from season to season and year to year, and was reported at 450 in 1941, when the Rocky Mountain Company announced that the mines were closing. The shutdown affected about fifty-six men; all families were given plenty of time to relocate. Homes were moved to Raton, the population scattered, and Sugarite was deserted.

Today rock foundations sprinkle the sides of Chicorica (Sugarite) Canyon. At the north of the company site the thick stone walls of the mule barns overlook the road. The remaining ruins are covered by vegetation, and a person could drive past the townsite never realizing that a thriving community once existed there.

Sugarite, building foundations on the east side of Sugarite Canyon, looking south.

Above—Sugarite powerhouse looking east, *circa* 1915. —*Courtesy Evelyn Shuler.*

Above—Ruins of powerhouse at Sugarite.

Right—Building the Sugarite school, 1912.—*Courtesy John Southwell.*

Sugarite, looking east, *circa* 1915.—*Courtesy Evelyn Shuler.*

Swastika

COUNTY: *Colfax*
LOCATION: *6 mi. northwest of Raton*
MAP: *page 239*
P.O. est. 1919; discont. 1940. Name changed to Brilliant 1940; discont. 1954.

At the end of World War I the Swastika Fuel Company, owned and operated by the St. Louis, Rocky Mountain and Pacific Company, was organized to open new coal deposits south of Brilliant. Soon the camp of Swastika began to take shape with neatly laid out plots of brick and concrete homes. To the local townsfolk the good fortune of Swastika meant a regular pay check, warm comfortable company houses, education for the children, and company-sponsored events and activities for their entertainment. The local mine union donated thirty-six dollars for purple and gold basketball uniforms for the school. The children sponsored plays, recitals, and pantomimes for the P.T.A. benefit to raise funds for their library. The camp consisted of families with strong Italian emigrant blood, with a great enthusiasm for soccer. When Swastika challenged opponents, generally two neighboring camps would join together to play the game against them.

As increased oil exploration stimulated Texas and Oklahoma, more coal was supplied from the camps of northeastern New Mexico for conversion into steam power to drive the rotary drills. This business aided Swastika, and its population reached five hundred residents in 1929.

The old town of Brilliant, located about a mile north, had closed its doors, hence at the beginning of World War II, when the name Swastika was no longer appropriate, the name was logically changed to Brilliant.

The site of Swastika (New Brilliant) today is reduced to rows of concrete foundation outlines and black mine dumps extending about half a mile along Dillon Canyon.

Swastika Fuel Company building in Raton, with company salesmen standing by their autos, 1923.—*Courtesy Evelyn Shuler.*

Swastika and coal dry cleaning plant, *circa* 1925.—*Courtesy Evelyn Shuler.*

Swastika foundations, looking south, all that remains.

Company homes at Swastika, *circa* 1925.—*Courtesy Evelyn Shuler.*

Sylvanite

COUNTY: *Hidalgo*
LOCATION: *about 20 mi. southeast of Animas*
MAP: *page 257*
P.O. est. 1908; discont. 1913.

In February of 1908, "Doc" Clark discovered placer gold along the southwest flank of the Little Hatchet Mountains and triggered a boom that started Sylvanite. Prospectors immediately moved to the strike and began to search for the lode deposits that supplied the placers. Within a matter of months a tent camp of five hundred people sprang to life, providing business for the Sylvanite Mercantile store and post office. The population rose to nearly a thousand before the tent camp folded away. By June of 1909 only seventy residents remained. The total estimated placer production amounted to $1 million.

Today only traces of rock foundations, broken glass, and rusting cans mark the site of Sylvanite's past activities.

Sylvanite, General Merchandise Store, *circa* 1910.—*Courtesy George Pendleton.*

Sylvanite, looking northeast, 1909.—*Courtesy J. M. Hill, U.S. Geological Survey.*

Above—Sylvanite as a tent camp, 1908.—*Courtesy New Mexico Magazine.*

Right—Wagon ruins near Sylvanite.

Site of Sylvanite, looking northeast.

Telegraph

COUNTY: *Grant*
LOCATION: *about 27 mi. west of Silver City*
MAP: *page 255*
P.O. none

A. J. Kirby, a Texan, located the first silver lode claim in the Telegraph district. It was called the Tecumseh lode and served as the initiating force behind the founding of Telegraph camp. Del Potter and the Dorsey brothers were among the first arrivals, and within the next few months an embryo village of log cabins began to form a short distance west of the Gila River. By 1884 the camp probably consisted of a hundred or so persons, the minimum of a store and saloon, and, as reported in an article of the *Silver City Enterprise*, was confident of a brilliant future. The mines were progressing under the management of John T. Mitchell, a road over the mountains connecting the mines with the Gila River was completed, and it was predicted that a new reduction works for the silver ore would be finished later that summer.

On June 22, 1884, Telegraph's society wildly celebrated the camp's first marriage. The "dashing and popular" Charley Dun was wed to the "graceful and attractive" Miss Maggie Cox. The ceremony was performed at the home of the bride, with W. H. Crawford, justice of the peace, officiating. "Toothsome dishes of every description loaded the board, the grateful juice of the grape flowed abundantly and sparkling wit and happy toasts were the order of the day"—*Silver City Enterprise*, June 27, 1884.

Within the year, the Tecumseh closed down its operations, forcing people to leave Telegraph.

Tererro

COUNTY: *San Miguel*
LOCATION: *16 mi. north of Pecos*
MAP: *page 243*
P.O. est. 1927 to present.

Tererro's livelihood was dependent entirely upon the operations of the American Metal Company of New Mexico at the Pecos Mine. The deposits were located in 1882 and at that time were known as the Hamilton or Cowles Mine. Limited copper ore was mined and hauled by wagon to Glorieta where it was shipped to El Paso for smelting. The unprofitable mining efforts were shortly terminated, and for about three decades the property was worked only intermittently. The Goodrich-Lockhart Company acquired the mine in 1916 and did extensive developing of the property. Then, in 1926, the American Metal Company became the owners. From January, 1927, until May 29, 1939, the Pecos Mine produced large quantities of lead, zinc, copper, gold, and silver amounting to about $40 million. The company built a twelve-mile aerial tramway to transport the ore from the mine to the mill at Alamitos. In its day it was the longest aerial tramway on the North American continent.

Tererro, rock chimney.

At its peak the mine camp of Tererro had about three thousand residents and a twelve-bed, white-frame hospital run by a Dr. Smith. John Earickson was postmaster and ran, in connection with the post office, a soft drink and confectionary shop. Walt Anderson had a restaurant, there was an elementary school, a jail, several boarding-houses, a two-chair barbershop, a red-light district known as "Chihuahua," and two general stores run respectively by H. S. Farley and the Pick brothers, Henry and Emil.

One summer day in 1934, Henry Pick left Tererro to drive to Santa Fe in order to deposit some cash. About seven miles south of Tererro, Pick was held up, shot, and killed. Strangely enough, the money was not taken. Pick's murderer was never apprehended.

· Tererro boasted one of the best baseball teams in the state. The camp sent out notices to entice players to try out for their team. If accepted, a player would be hired as a mucker by the mining company. Jobs were in demand, and miners failing to fill a daily ore quota were fired and immediately replaced by a waiting miner. The baseball players hired as muckers, however, did not have to fill their ore quota and never feared being replaced.

The miners, mostly Spanish-speaking, often gave each other nicknames because of certain feats or characteristics. There was "El Toro" (the bull), "El Muneco" (the doll), "El Leon" (the lion), "El Burro," and many others. "El Torro" earned his name by taking a 250-pound Liner steam drill and climbing a 100-foot ladder. "El Burro" was a tough fellow whom no one cared to cross. One day Little Mike, the barber, was cutting "El Burro's" hair and accidentally nicked one of his ears. "El Burro" never moved a muscle but demanded Little Mike to cut the other ear so that they would match. Little Mike was so terrified that he collapsed and the other barber had to finish "El Burro's" haircut.

On February 12, 1936, mine laborers struck for higher wages, more sanitary camp conditions, abolishment of the scrip system good only at the Pick store, and reinstatement of two discharged strike leaders. After some difficulty and trouble instigated by the strike leaders, work finally resumed again after three months. Operations continued undisturbed until May, 1939, when the mine closed permanently, and Tererro became a ghost town.

Not much is left of old Tererro, because the buildings were all torn down. Extensive mine tailings piles, mine ruins, an old wooden ore chute, and a single stone chimney seem to be the only obvious remaining relics. A store and post office function today at the site of the mining camp.

Concrete foundations of
the Pecos Mine at Tererro.

Tierra Blanca

COUNTY: *Sierra*
LOCATION: *about 10 mi. southwest of Hillsboro*
MAP: *page 251*
P.O. est. 1892; discont. 1903.

Tierra Blanca, a small group of prospects and mines at the head of Trujillo Creek, was given its name because of the white rhyolite that capped the mountain slopes. Rich pockets of gold and silver chloride were taken at grass-roots depths from mines named the Log Cabin and Lookout. In 1897 the population was reported at thirty-five, and the camp consisted of only a clustering of miner's shacks with a postmaster. A teacher instructed a handful of children six months of the year, and mail arrived twice a week from Lake Valley.

Tokay

COUNTY: *Socorro*
LOCATION: *19 mi. southeast of Socorro*
MAP: *page 247*
P.O. est. 1919; discont. 1932.

Bartley H. Kinney, a former mining official at the Carthage mines, organized the San Antonio Coal Company about 1918 and began mining operations. The settlement that soon sprang up on the New Mexico Midland Railroad two miles west of Carthage was named Tokay. During its prime, Tokay catered to about five hundred residents and supported several establishments, including the Kinney store, a church, and a miners' boardinghouse. A two-story building handled a pool hall on the lower floor and a schoolroom on the upper, with movies shown in the evening when the students' seats were unoccupied.

In the late 1940's the mining operation shut down, and most of the frame buildings were moved to Socorro.

Today the townsite is occupied by a private ranch, with the former Kinney home converted into the main ranch house. The other remaining building is a bunkhouse, formerly used as a boardinghouse during the coal mining days. Aside from these buildings only scant rubble and black waste dumps suggest that a bustling coal mining camp once lived here.

Trementina

COUNTY: *San Migual*
LOCATION: *about 46 mi. east of Las Vegas*
MAP: *page 241*
P.O. est. 1901 to present.

One of the most ghostly of towns, Trementina's vacant structures stand pitted against the elements on a lonely bluff overlooking Trementina Creek. The ruins consist of at least two dozen rock buildings; most are roofless, doorless, and windowless. Some contain the rusty remains of stoves, bedsprings, and other scraps and pieces of man's inhabitancy. On the north side of the road near the creek bank is a walled cemetery. Here slabs of stones are etched with crosses, stars, and various religious symbols. The names and dates of death, varying between 1894 and 1907, are written in Spanish.

The town was named for the creek, which in turn probably derived its name from the piñon trees, which contain the properties of gum and turpentine.

No doubt people had been living along Trementina Creek for many generations, farming the river banks, but the actual townsite was chosen about the turn of the century. Miss Alice Blake, a Presbyterian medical missionary, was apparently the leading cohesive force of the community. She settled in Trementina as a missionary, adopting the roles of postmistress and principal of the Presbyterian Mission School. In 1901, when a diphtheria epidemic swept through the village, it was Miss Blake who saved all the afflicted children by administering a new remedy, antitoxin. In addition to the post office and school and its thirty or forty homes, Trementina claimed a store, a church, hospital, a community house, and a population of several hundred residents.

The dissolution of Trementina was attributed to various adverse events. The 1929 depression, Miss Blake's forced retirement because of illness in 1930, a severe drought, and enlistment for World War II forced people to leave their homes and farms and move on.

Trementina, dry rock masonry.

Trementina, view of deserted town, looking west.

Twining mill and smelter, abandoned, *circa* 1910.—*Courtesy Holder Collection, Kit Carson Museum.*

Twining

COUNTY: *Colfax*
LOCATION: *15 mi. northeast of Taos*
MAP: *page 239*
P.O. est. 1902; discont. 1910.

William Fraser discovered copper mineralization high on a mountain slope above the camp of Amizette. He interested Albert C. Twining, a New Jersey banker, in the venture, and soon Twining's money was being absorbed into the camp on the Río Hondo which honored his name. A deep tunnel driven into Fraser Mountain started the development, with the later addition of narrow gauge tracks, drills, ventilation fans, pumps, and a cable tram extending down the mountain to a newly constructed mill. When the first ore bucket was sent on its way down the cable tram the brakes of the cable drum failed, causing the heavy bucket to sail into the mill and crash through the opposite wall to the creek bed below. After a fire-clay seam was opened in the mountainside, kilns were constructed and fire brick sold, providing additional economy to the town.

Jesse Young, a son of Brigham Young, established a sawmill near the mine and supplied timbers for mine support, cord wood for the power plants, and logs for resident construction. By 1903 the camp included a concentrator, mill, smelter, charcoal furnace, lime kiln, hotel, store, and saloon, and thirty men were employed by the Fraser Mountain Copper Company. In the evening the cabins and hotel were illuminated by electric lights provided by small Delco light plants installed by A. J. Graham. Single miners lived in bunkhouses and earned $3 per nine-hour day. Out of this amount one dollar a day paid his board and room. On payday Gerson Gusdorf drove a wagon from his store in Amizette loaded with clothes, shoes, cigars, liquor, and other delights to capture his share of the trade. In 1903 the Kit Carson Cornet Band rode to Twining from Taos for the Fourth of July celebration. After a morning of speeches, music, and patriotic toasts, the fourteen-member band enjoyed an exhilarating ride in a tram car.

The reasons for the demise of Twining are not clear. Although there is no official record of any copper or gold production from this district, there are some claims that copper concentrate was shipped to El Paso until the Twining smelter was completed. The story is told that when the smelter was used for the first time it melted the copper concentrate, but because of poor-quality charcoal the

Log cabins at Twining, *circa* 1910.
—*Courtesy Holder Collection, Kit Carson Museum.*

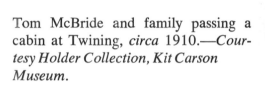

Tom McBride and family passing a cabin at Twining, *circa* 1910.—*Courtesy Holder Collection, Kit Carson Museum.*

melt solidified in the furnace, preventing it from being used again. Another opinion expressed is that the smelter was successful before the incident of the frozen matte, and that it was poor mill concentration of the copper ore that forced the mine to close. Regardless of the reasons, mining operations ceased in 1903, and the camp was abandoned. Those who made the camp were charged with its failure. Albert Twining was convicted of embezzling the New Jersey bank funds and served a term in prison.

William Fraser formed a partnership with Jack Bidwell and Clarence Probert of the Taos Bank and attempted to restore the mine to its original status. Progress was slow, because a rift developed between Bidwell and Fraser. Bidwell accused Fraser of transferring financier investment cash into his own pocket. When word of this accusation reached Fraser, he quickly drove a team and wagon up the Río Hondo to Jack Bidwell's cabin, where the two confronted each other in a heated argument. Fraser threateningly withdrew a revolver from a pack on the wagon seat beside him, and Bidwell disappeared into his cabin and returned with a rifle. Fraser took aim, but before he had time to fire he was knocked from the wagon seat by a slug from Bidwell's rifle. Tom Holder, a nine-year-old boy, witnessed the killing and, although accidentally wounded by the ricocheted slug that killed Fraser, Tom testified on Bidwell's behalf and cleared him of all charges.

After the mine closed, the cabins of Twining were moved to Taos. The hotel remained where it was for many years, with furnishings cluttering the rooms and dishes stacked in the kitchen. In 1924 a wrecker tore down the combination hotel, store, and post office, along with the smelter. The mill burned in 1932, removing the last trace of Twining.

The former site of Twining is now an active ski resort.

Looking through the archway of the Tyrone Trading Post, 1967.

Tyrone, looking west, *circa* 1918: (1) railroad station and warehouse. (2) department store, (3) Tyrone Union Church, (4) trading post, (5) mining offices.—
Courtesy Phelps Dodge Corporation.

Tyrone

COUNTY: *Grant*
LOCATION: *13 mi. southwest of Silver City*
MAP: *page 255*
P.O. est. 1906 to present.

Probably the most luxurious mining camp to exist was Tyrone. Unlike the typical helter-skelter camp of its day, Tyrone was envisioned as a well-planned, ultimately modern mining city. At a cost of a million dollars, Phelps Dodge made this dream city come true.

Copper was the sought-after treasure. It made Tyrone, but it also broke Tyrone. The first recorded mining locations of copper and turquoise in the area date to 1871 and to the brothers Robert and John Metcalf. Times were uncertain due to the ever-present Apaches, so the Metcalfs were

forced to abandon their claims. A few years later, about 1875, John E. Coleman, better known as "Turquoise John," rediscovered turquoise in some of the old pits and immediately staked a number of copper and turquoise claims. With interest revived in the area, considerable activity occurred and many properties were developed during the ensuing years. In the early years of the present century a small mining camp named Tyrone sprang up in the Burro Mountains. It was named by a Mr. Honeky from Tyrone, Ireland.

In 1909, Phelps Dodge began buying up many of the claims around Tyrone and the nearby camp of Leopold. Phelps Dodge established its local headquarters at Tyrone and began directing efforts toward developing the underground ore bodies and erecting the necessary mine equipment. A new townsite and a new town of Tyrone seemed in keeping with the elaborate mining expansion taking place. The new site chosen was about a mile and a half northeast of the original camp, and Bertram G. Goodhue, designer of the San Diego Exposition of 1915, was called in to be the architect for the new mining camp.

On April 13, 1915, plans were officially announced for the construction of new Tyrone. It was to be a deluxe model mining town and an innovation in modern townsite planning. Using Spanish mission style architecture, Goodhue designed the business portion of Tyrone around a large plaza crossed with walks and planted with trees, grass, and shrubs. The largest building facing the plaza was the imposing company store, which contained everything from ready-to-wear clothing to groceries and furniture. Behind the store was a warehouse, and next to the store the post office and the $100,000 colonnaded railroad station with a marble drinking fountain. There was also a six-hundred-pupil school. Opposite the company store on the other side of the plaza was a restaurant, garage, Burro Mountain mining office, the trading post, bank, and library. Beyond the plaza was the Tyrone Union Church, the three-cell jail, and a court for the justice of the peace. On the ridge behind the plaza were the homes, and between the homes and the mine was the T. S. Parker Hospital, equipped with two operating rooms, air-conditioned X-ray laboratory, and an intercom system allowing patients to talk with one another.

Tyrone seemed to have everything; but despite its beauty and convenience, it was doomed. In April, 1921, mining operations were suspended. A sharp drop in copper prices following World War I and Tyrone's lowering ore grades made it necessary for Phelps Dodge to close down. When Cleland Dodge arrived at Tyrone to inspect the situation he was met by the workers, who volunteered a 25 per cent decrease in their wages if only the camp would remain open. Cleland Dodge would not agree; Tyrone had to close, and it did. The town that once claimed seven thousand residents, died.

For about forty-five years Tyrone slumbered. Its plaza became choked with weeds, but a few people still lived there, renting houses for very little. In July, 1969, after twenty years of exploratory drilling by Phelps Dodge, the new open pit copper mine at Tyrone went into production; but the old town had been sacrificed when stripping operations had begun two years before. Nothing is left of the million-dollar city but the chapel and justice of the peace court. The present town of Tyrone, with a Phelps Dodge Merchantile, garage, and new homes, has been built in Pipe Line Draw, a few miles north of the copper pit and the site of old Tyrone.

Tyrone plaza, looking west. Department store on left and the Tyrone Union Church in the right background, *circa* 1918.—*Courtesy Phelps Dodge Corporation.*

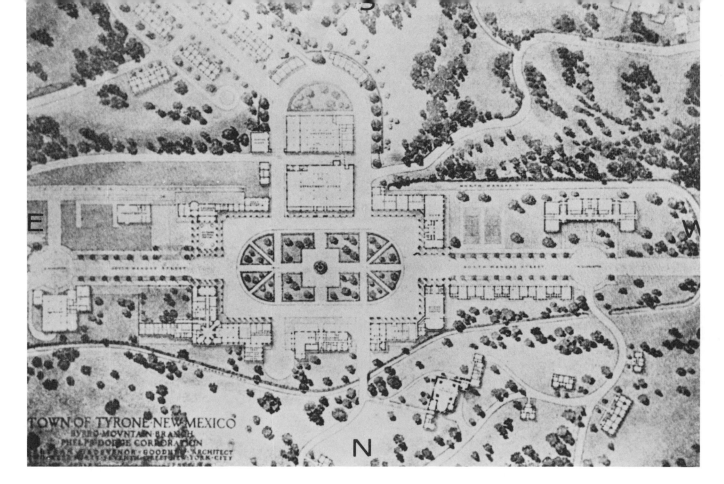

Above—Tyrone, town plan conceived by a New York architectural firm.—*Courtesy George Eckhart.*

Tyrone, company homes, date unknown.—*Courtesy Library of Congress.*

T. S. Parker Hospital at Tyrone, *circa* 1918.—*Courtesy Phelps Dodge Corporation.*

T. S. Parker Hospital in 1967, before it was torn down.

Tyrone, view of the Tyrone Union Church, 1967.

Tyrone–Phelps Dodge Company building, 1967.

Valedon

COUNTY: *Hidalgo*
LOCATION: *3 mi. southwest of Lordsburg*
MAP: *page 257*
P.O. est. 1917; discont. 1932.

The Eighty-Five claims were located by W. P. Griffith, Sam Ransom, and Victor Van Hall in 1885. After it had passed through several owners, the Eighty-Five Mining Company took over this property and sank a shaft about 1913. Nearby, the camp of Valedon began to grow, and a railroad spur from the Southern Pacific line at Lordsburg was extended to the mines. As the Henry Clay, Atwood, and other mines came into production, a mill was constructed to handle the gold, silver, and copper ores. Two years later the entire operation was taken over by the Calumet and Arizona Mining Company.

As the camp grew into a company town, land was leased to the people, and the workers built their own homes. Anglos clustered in frame houses on a hill to the south, and the Mexicans built their adobe and rock homes elsewhere. By 1926, two thousand people were dependent upon the mines and several businesses including the 85 Store, the Victoria Theatre, Winslow & Sons Meat Market, several boardinghouses, and a blacksmith served the community. A two-room school, the best in southwestern New Mexico, handled Valedon's youngsters along with those who were bused from Lordsburg.

Lyman Garrett, who claimed to be a distant cousin of Pat Garrett, slayer of Billy the Kid, served as deputy sheriff at Valedon. One morning he was found in the jail, beaten to death. Two men were later captured and convicted of the murder.

Phelps Dodge Company bought the property in 1931 and a year later, with a warning of only a few days, discontinued the mining operation. In the face of the Great Depression people were shocked with the announcement. Company orders were given for them to vacate the property, and almost immediately many of the buildings were torn down or moved away.

At present, the Banner Mining Company has operations in the vicinity, and the Valedon mines are intermittently improved and occasionally worked. The townsite, which is private property, consists of an extensive assortment of building foundations and partially collapsed walls. Although the mines have officially been abandoned for years, the Henry Clay headframe stands well-preserved and ready for use.

View of Valedon as it looks today, looking north.

Panorama of Valedon, looking southeast, 1920.—
Courtesy Glen H. Dorsett.

Below—Valedon, building ruins.

Above—Headframe of the Henry
Clay Mine at Valedon.

Left—Present skyline of Valedon site, with Henry Clay Mine
at right.

Below—Ruins at Valedon,
looking northwest.

Valmont

COUNTY: *Otero*
LOCATION: *11 mi. south of Alamogordo*
MAP: *page 241*
P.O. est. as Camp 1908; discont. 1910. Name changed to Shamrock 1910; discont. 1916. Name changed to Valmont 1917; discont. 1922.

In 1859 a detachment of mounted riflemen of the Eighth Infantry from Fort Bliss, Texas, pursued a band of Apaches into Dog Canyon on the west flank of the Sacramento Mountains. High in a rocky chine an engagement ensued, and three soldiers and nine Indians were killed.

Early in the 1900's a railroad station was named for Dog Canyon five miles to the east. A post office at the Dog Canyon Station was named Camp for the first postmaster. In 1910 the name of the post office was changed to Shamrock, and in 1917 it became Valmont, from the combination of the words vale and mountain. Soon a community of about forty persons developed in the vicinity of the station, established a grade school, and prospered for several years.

Shortly before World War I, drought and other factors caused the families to leave, and Valmont slumped into a state of depression.

Nothing remains to mark the site of the station or the former community.

Van Houten

COUNTY: *Colfax*
LOCATION: *18 mi. southwest of Raton*
MAP: *page 239*
P.O. est. as Willow 1902; discont. 1902. Name changed to Van Houten 1902; discont. 1952.

The St. Louis, Rocky Mountain and Pacific Company revived mining activities at the coal mining camp of Willow late in 1902. The village name was changed to Van Houten for S. Van Houten, the company president, and soon the mines were producing at full capacity. Two hundred and seventy-nine miners and five boys worked underground, with twenty men and five boys working at the tipple. By 1910 the Atchison, Topeka and Santa Fe Railroad had extended a branch line to Van Houten, and the mine efficiently operated with the latest electrical haulage and ventilation equipment. Some of the bituminous product was shipped to coke ovens at nearby Gardiner, and some was sold to railroad companies such as the Colorado and Southern, Chicago and Rock Island, and the El Paso and Southwestern.

The camp gradually increased in size to a peak of about fifteen hundred residents in 1915, when the town businesses included two hotels, the Blossburg Mercantile Co., a barber, billiard hall, and a stage line. The community, consisting primarily of Germans, Austrians, and Italians, was fond of gala affairs and celebrations. The local twenty-two-member band entertained with concerts and at Saturday night dances. Movies were shown Monday and Wednesday at the amusement hall, and baseball games were a popular pastime. The town sponsored an active Red Cross chapter and during World War I sold $111,000 worth of Liberty War Bond subscriptions. This was the largest per capita investment in the war effort of any town in the nation.

A favorite picnic spot for young people about a mile and a half from Van Houten was called the Devil's Kitchen. At this spot a slow-glowing fire supplied by natural gas seepage had been burning for several years. When the fire was low and visitors wished to do a bit of cooking they would vigorously scratch the charred ground surface and the flames would burst through. The local old-timers told how early pioneers scared off attacking Indians when a discharging rifle ignited the gases, causing a large explosion and a mass of flame which scattered the frightened savages in every direction.

As the years wore on, telltale signs of the declining coal economy brought uncertainty to Van Houten. A series of railroad strikes temporarily slowed coal production, and development of new oil and gas deposits competed strongly with the mines. In 1940 the mine closed, but it was reopened a year later with the crisis of World War II. In 1948 a twenty-four-day strike critically damaged the St. Louis, Rocky Mountain Company, forcing them to increase the employees' pay. The fatal blow was dealt with the loss of contracts from the A.T. & S.F. Railroad and the Colorado Fuel and Iron Corporation. The drastic reduction in coal demand affected all the coal camps in the region, forcing many mines to discontinue operations. On May 27, 1954, all mining activity ceased at Van Houten, putting about a hundred men out of work. Families moved, buildings were torn down, and the company records closed.

All of the buildings of Van Houten have disappeared. Today the property is privately owned by Kaiser Steel Corporation.

Number 5 mine tipple at Van Houten, *circa* 1915.—*Courtesy Evelyn Shuler.*

View of upper tipple and a portion of Van Houten, *circa* 1910.—*Courtesy Evelyn Shuler.*

221
v

Vera Cruz

COUNTY: *Lincoln*
LOCATION: *about 10 mi. southeast of Carrizozo*
MAP: *page 249*
P.O. est. 1881; discont. 1883.

A small gold mining camp was founded about 1880 on the west side of the Tucson Mountains. The miners who lived there worked at the Vera Cruz gold mine, and although an organized townsite was proposed, it seems only to have reached the post office stage. It was soon discontinued because the anticipated gold deposits were of too low a grade.

About 1893, M. D. Gaylord of Nogal represented a company of Denver capitalists with intentions to reopen the Vera Cruz Mine. Plans were advertised that the company intended to install a hundred-stamp mill and haul sixty tons of machinery to the mine. These hopes failed to materialize, and the mine idled away.

Only the dump of the Vera Cruz Mine is seen today, high in the Tucson Mountains as one drives the highway between Carrizozo and Lincoln.

Virginia City

COUNTY: *Colfax*
LOCATION: *about 4 mi. north of Eagle Nest*
MAP: *page 239*
P.O. est. 1868; discont. 1869.

Some dredging dumps from placer deposits along Willow Creek and an obscure cemetery situated on a prominent hill in the vicinity mark the site of long forgotten, short-lived Virginia City.

Virginia City's birth was initiated from the same frenzied gold boom that spawned Elizabethtown and Baldy; however, Virginia City preceded both of these towns.

In October of 1866, three men sent to do assessment work on a previously located copper property near the top of Baldy Mountain camped one night on Willow Creek, where they accidentally discovered rich gold placers. News of the find quickly circulated, and in the following years scores of ruddy-faced gold seekers flocked to Willow Creek to stake claims. The site was on the Maxwell Land Grant, so when a sprawling little camp began to form, Lucien B. Maxwell named it for his daughter, Virginia. By naming the hastily and crudely constructed array of shanties a "city," Maxwell must have had high hopes for the camp.

Virginia City fell far short of Maxwell's dream of a booming metropolis. In the spring of 1868 the community consisted of a haphazardly organized grid of streets dotted with about fifteen houses, many of which were still roofless. The businesses amounted to one store and a post office.

Before Virginia City had a chance to show any prosperity, the populace began drifting to the newly established and more promising camp of Elizabethtown, five miles to the northwest.

Advertisement from the *Golden Era*, November 2, 1882.—*Courtesy Highlands University Library.*

Waldo

Henry L. Waldo, appointed chief justice of the New Mexico Supreme Court in 1881, for whom the town was named. —*Courtesy Museum of New Mexico.*

Building at Waldo.

COUNTY: *Santa Fe*
LOCATION: *about 4 mi. northwest of Cerrillos*
MAP: *page 243*
P.O. est. 1920; discont. 1926.

About 1879, the Santa Fe Railroad was pushing its way westward across central New Mexico. Company geologists examined coal seams in Miller Gulch, Waldo Gulch, and Madrid Canyon as potential locomotive fuel, and a year later the Santa Fe tracks were laid past the town of Waldo. The coal, however, was anthracite rather than bituminous and not suited for locomotive fuel.

The small community of Waldo got its start before the arrival of the Atchison, Topeka and Santa Fe Railroad and took its name from Judge Henry L. Waldo, who was at one time chief justice of the Supreme Court of the Territory of New Mexico. The little village received an economic boost in 1892, when the Cerrillos Coal Railroad Company constructed a spur line from Waldo to the coal mines at Madrid. A few years later the Colorado Fuel and Iron Company acquired coal leases from the Santa Fe Railroad and built fifteen coke ovens at Waldo which processed a high-quality smelting coke. In 1906 the C. F. & I. Company gave up their mining rights and closed the mines. However, Waldo continued to serve the new and booming coal mining town of Madrid, about six miles to the south. All of Madrid's water, some 150,000 gallons a day, had to be hauled from the wells at Waldo in large tank cars, which made four trips a day.

In 1921 the town claimed a population of 125 and a general merchandise store operated by T. DeLallo. Waldo's life depended upon the coal mines at Madrid, and when they closed in 1954, Waldo died.

At the site of Waldo today, a few shacks, the usual broken glass, rusty tin cans, and debris are scattered amid several large cottonwood trees beside the railroad tracks.

223
w

White Oaks, looking southwest, *circa* 1890.—*Courtesy Museum of New Mexico.*

White Oaks

COUNTY: *Lincoln*
LOCATION: *11 mi. northeast of Carrizozo*
MAP: *page 249*
P.O. est. 1880; discont. 1954.

The Homestake gold lode was first discovered in 1879, when George Wilson, Jack Winters, and George Baxter were prospecting in the Jicarilla Mountains. A version of the story relates that while the three prospectors were lunching one day, Wilson climbed up the mountain with rock pick in hand. Resting by a massive quartz outcrop he chipped away on the rock and, on examination, was much surprised to find that it contained gold. He reported his find to those below and, for reasons unknown, sold his share of the find to his partners for the price, some say, of forty dollars, a pony, and a bottle of whisky. Wilson left the vicinity for no explainable reason; however, old-timers believe he was running from the law. The rich gold outcrop soon became the heart of the North Homestake Mine, and word spread of the gold on Baxter Mountain.

The mining camp of White Oaks, named for nearby White Oaks Spring, soon sprouted in a disheveled arrangement of tents and haphazardly erected businesses. By the end of 1880 the South Homestake, Little Mack, Old Abe, Comstock, Rip Van Winkle, and other properties were located, and the camp exploded into life. A townsite was surveyed, with streets called White Oaks Avenue, Livingstone, Placer, and Jicarilla, and the crude log cabins and shabby tents were replaced by buildings of stone and brick.

Shortly after Will Huddgens was appointed deputy sheriff, "Billy the Kid," on the run from the law, tried to find sanctuary in White Oaks. Although the saloons and gambling halls were deemed essential, most of the new citizens of White Oaks came from a respectable eastern environment and were law-abiding and sensible. At the first suggestion that the Kid was arriving in White Oaks a posse was formed and rode out to discourage him from entering the town. On one occasion Deputy Huddgens and his men trapped "Billy the Kid" and his gang at the Greathouse and Kuch Ranch on the road between White Oaks and Las Vegas. The subsequent gunfight resulted in the death of Jimmie Carlyle, a young blacksmith from White Oaks.

As mining increased to a large-scale operation, a twenty-stamp mill supplied with water from White Oaks Spring was built below the new town. A deposit of coal was conveniently discovered nearby and provided steam power for the mines and mill.

Stagecoach service connected White Oaks to Carthage and Fort Stanton for fees of fifteen dollars and five dollars respectively, and a water line was installed along the main street. The first newspaper, *The Golden Era*, was established in 1881 and lasted three years. Other weekly newspapers, the *Lincoln County Leader* (1882–94), *New Mexico Interpreter* (1885–91), and the *Old Abe Eagle* (1885–91), also played important roles in White Oaks history. The population in 1884 was reported to be a thousand residents, with businesses including Anderson & Fredericks Saloon; Joseph Biggs, blacksmith; Bond & Stewart, general store; J. A. Brothers Hotel; Gantan Frenchie, blacksmith; Hewett and Fergusson, lawyers; B. A.

Shapley, dentist; M. Wardell, physician; The Boss Store, and the Bonnell Opera House. The Hewett Block Building housed the Exchange Bank on the first floor and several law offices upstairs which belonged to men who later became important politicians. Among these notable lawyers were W. C. McDonald, first governor of the state of New Mexico, and H. B. Fergusson, later a delegate to Congress and father of writers Harvey and Erna Fergusson. Emerson Hough, novelist who used White Oaks as a setting for his book *Heart's Desire*, worked as a reporter for *The Golden Era* newspaper.

One of the most colorful ladies to set foot in White Oaks was called Madam Varnish. Madam arrived in town one day with three lovely daughters. Soon afterward a man claiming to be the treasurer of the adjoining county arrived in White Oaks and fell in love with the fair widow. After a brief courtship she promised to marry him if he would provide for her family. Shortly thereafter

White Oaks, present ruins of the Exchange Bank building on Main Street.

the five of them left by stage for Roswell, where the wedding ceremony was performed. Two days later Madam and her girls returned to White Oaks without the bridegroom. The following day he arrived by stage and immediately contacted the sheriff. The infuriated bridegroom swore out a warrant for the arrest of his bride, charging her with robbing him of thirty-five hundred dollars that was hidden under his pillow on their wedding night. Madam Varnish was arrested and then released on her own good word until the day of the trial. Madam and her girls then visited the treasurer in his hotel room and informed him that if he pressed charges she would accuse him of absconding with thirty-five hundred dollars of county funds. Madam Varnish was never brought to trial and later established her family in business at the Little Casino.

A staunch church-going merchant who ran a general store on White Oaks Avenue invented an unusual scheme to sell liquor. He cut a door in the side of his store and built a small shed on the adjoining lot. A patron would enter the shed from the store, take a cup hanging on the wall and tap his drink from a whisky barrel. After placing ten cents on top of the keg and finishing his pleasure he would walk back into the store and out the door, unobserved as having indulged.

On the south side of White Oaks is a Victorian mansion called Hoyle Castle. A tale is told that Andy Hoyle, superintendent of one of the mines, built it for his bride-to-be. The mansion was masterfully constructed of brick and stone, with stained-glass windows, hand-carved pine and redwood paneling, and a lead pipe water system. It was decorated with the most expensive furniture of the period. When the prospective bride arrived at White Oaks she rejected Hoyle and his castle, for reasons unknown, and returned to her home. Hoyle's dream crumbled. After residing in his masterpiece for a short while, he faded out of the history of White Oaks.

In the late 1890's, White Oaks' residents anticipated the coming of the railroad. Newspapers speculated that, without a doubt, either the Atchison, Topeka and Santa Fe or the El Paso and Northeastern Railroad would soon be laying tracks to the community. The town's businessmen were so sure of the pending railroad connection that they held out for high right-of-way prices. The El Paso and Northeastern had other alternatives. They extended a branch line from Carrizozo to Capitan, bypassing White Oaks by ten miles.

The peak of White Oaks' prosperity had been reached. Families gradually left, as one by one the mines ran out of ore. The population of White Oaks, reported as four hundred in 1907, decreased to two hundred in 1938.

Today a few ranch families occupy homes scattered across the townsite. The three most prominent buildings in White Oaks are the Exchange Bank building on White Oaks Avenue, the ten-thousand-dollar abandoned brick school on a hill overlooking the town, and Hoyle's Castle south of town, standing as solidly as when it was built.

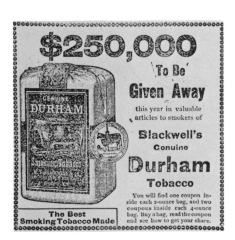

Advertisement from the *White Oaks Eagle,* July 2, 1896.— *Courtesy Lincoln County Courthouse Library.*

Advertisement from *The Socorro Sun,* February 21, 1881.—*Courtesy Highlands University Library.*

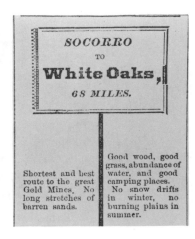

Above—Bond and Stewart Store, White Oaks, *circa* 1887.—*Courtesy Jackie S. Silvers.*

Left—Advertisement from the *Golden Era*, May 1, 1884.—*Courtesy Highlands University Library.*

Left—Advertisement from *The Old Abe Eagle*, February 23, 1893.—*Courtesy Lincoln County Courthouse Library.*

Right—Advertisement from the *Golden Era*, April 24, 1884.—*Courtesy Highlands University Library.*

Left—Advertisement from the *Golden Era*, October 8, 1885.—*Courtesy Highlands University Library.*

White Oaks, 1917. Center, Exchange Bank building, also known as the Hewett building; right,
Little Casino.—*Courtesy Jackie S. Silvers.*

Victorian mansion at White Oaks.

View of present-day White Oaks, looking south.
Left, school; left background, Hoyle Castle;
right, Exchange Bank building.

Winston, present view of Main Street. The center building was Blun's store.

Winston

COUNTY: *Sierra*

LOCATION: *28 mi. northwest of Truth or Consequences*

MAP: *page 251*

P.O. est. as Fairview 1881; discont. 1930. Name changed to Winston 1930 to present.

Winston was originally named Fairview. Today people still live in the town. It is a quiet little community including a combination store and post office, an old deserted school building at one end of town and the new successor at the other end, and several other interesting old buildings.

The town got its start back in 1881. Following Harry Pye's discovery of the Pye lode, the town of Chloride sprang to life and at about the same time Fairview also took root as a mining camp a few miles to the northeast. In spite of menacing Indians, Fairview rose quickly. By June, 1881, twenty-five buildings were reported to be under way, preparations were being made to dig a well, and the imminent construction of a hotel was announced. In 1892 the Black Range mining district

newspaper stated that up until 1883, Fairview had a population of five hundred. A population of a hundred residents was claimed at the beginning of 1884. Various merchants opened their respective businesses. Jacob and Henry Blun ran a mercantile store, William Cloudman had a meat market, J. W. Sansom owned a grocery store, and M. G. Levy & Co. a mercantile store. Mrs. Mayers operated the Continental Hotel and Charles Russell the Black Range Hotel. Charles Buckner was Fairview's druggist and S. S. Porter the town's physician.

Fairview celebrated the Fourth of July, 1884. One of the amusements planned for the day was a three-hour go-as-you-please foot race. The competition was open to any able-bodied soul in Sierra County who could plunk down a twenty-five-dollar entry fee and survive three monotonous hours on a circular track. The event obviously had limited appeal, since a week before the Fourth only two hardy contestants had signed up for the race.

September of 1884 saw a killing at Fairview. George G. Quarles, on a round-up camping near Fairview, went to the Blun Brothers store to ask Jacob Blun for a loan of five dollars. Blun refused.

The next day, Quarles went to Levy's store, bought a revolver, and returned to Blun's. There he confronted Jacob again, with harsh words and threats. Refusing to be intimidated, Jacob calmly started for the rear room of the store to get his gun, with Quarles closely following him. Jacob's brother, Henry, standing behind the counter watching the affray, shouted to Quarles that he had no right to enter the rear room. Quarles turned on Henry, and both fired simultaneously. Quarles's bullet burrowed harmlessly into the floor, but Henry's bullet hit Quarles squarely in the mouth, causing instant death. George G. Quarles was buried at Chloride. No one knew his birthplace or whether or not he had any family or relatives. The verdict of the jury claimed that the killing was justifiable.

A cry of "Fire!" set off frantic behavior on the evening of March 2, 1886. Everyone rushed about grabbing buckets and throwing water. Havoc reigned. Some threw their buckets with the water, others threw buckets without water. In the excitement a man rescued a dry goods box but left the forty-dollar saddle the box was resting on. Another individual saved a sack of hay worth twenty cents but discarded a valuable gun. Then someone pushed a table into the doorway of the burning building so that no one could get inside to save any more valuables. Cartridges began exploding inside the house, adding to the confusion. No one was hurt, but everyone was scared. Despite heroic efforts and lots of irrational commotion, the one building burned down. The occupants of the house, James and Will E. Taylor, were in Grafton at the time, so the origin of the blaze remained a mystery.

A new school building opened its doors to thirty-two pupils in September, 1886. Fairview organized a literary club. Horse races were held on Christmas, 1886. In 1889 it was reported that Fairview, with a population of 125, traded with ranchers, farmers, and miners; had one school, a smelter, and a hotel; and ran a daily stage from Engle Station, fifty miles away on the Atchison, Topeka and Santa Fe Railroad. Only thirty people were listed at Fairview for 1897. Frank H. Winston operated a general merchandise store and was postmaster. Cattle and mining were the town's principal resources. By 1905 the population was back up to a hundred. Frank Winston still had his general store and was president of the Fairview Cattle Company. A 1915 business directory lists Frank H. Winston Company general store, Frank H. Winston, president of Fairview Cattle Company, and Frank H. Winston, proprietor of the Fairview garage. Needless to say, Frank Winston was a prominent and popular citizen of Fairview. Originally from Wisconsin, Winston settled in Grafton, New Mexico, at the age of thirty. In 1886 he moved to Fairview, where he opened his general store. When times were hard he gave extensive credit at his store, knowing that there was little chance of being paid back. His generous and helpful nature was enough to convince people that in some way Frank H. Winston should be honored. He died November 10, 1929, and the next year Fairview was officially renamed Winston.

Advertisement from *The Black Range*, September 24, 1886.—*Courtesy Highlands University Library.*

Opposite page—View of Fairview (later called Winston), looking south, *circa* 1890.—*Courtesy Schmit Collection, University of New Mexico Library.*

Above—Fairview (changed to Winston, 1930) *circa* 1915. Blun's store at left, Frank Winston in black suit at right.— *Courtesy Schmit Collection, University of New Mexico Library.*

Right—The Black Range Hotel at Fairview, *circa* 1900.— *Courtesy Schmit Collection, University of New Mexico Library.*

Above—Home of Frank Winston, *circa* 1915.—
*Courtesy Schmit Collection, University of New
Mexico Library.*

Left—Frank H. Winston (1856–1929), long-
time resident of Fairview and later a New
Mexico legislator.—*Courtesy Schmit Collection, University of New Mexico Library.*

SOMETHING NEW!

STRAWBERRY
and
LEMON BEER.

The STRAWBERRY and LEMON
BEER is a Temperance Drink and of
Home Manufacture. It is a new thing
and is prepared by

H. MORGAN,

FAIRVIEW, - - N. MEX

Christmas race advertisement from *The
Black Range*, November 26, 1886.—*Courtesy Highlands University Library.*

Left—Advertisement from *The Black
Range*, July 4, 1886.—*Courtesy Highlands University Library.*

Below—Winston. Home of Tom Scales, mining engineer,
date unknown.—*Courtesy Schmit Collection, University of
New Mexico Library.*

CHRISTMAS SPORTS!
GRAND RACE,
800 yards for
$1,000!
At Fairview, N. Mex.,
ON
Saturday, December 25, '86.

PROGRAME:

One o'clock. Eight hundred yards
race between A. Rush Bowe's brown
gelding, Dude, and James Moore's bay
gelding, Perico. Stakes, $500 aside.

Purse race for 800 yards open to all;
entrance money added. Frst prize
$50.00. Second prize, $40.00. Third
prize, $30.00. Entrace fee $20.00.

Many entertaining features will be
added to the programme not here
mentioned.

Racing every day until New Years.
On New Years there will be a

GRAND TOURNAMENT
for gold medal valued at $100. En-
trance $5.00, open to all.

All races to be governed by the
Fairview Jockey Club rules.

Above—Tenth Cavalry during the Apache campaign at Silver Monument south of Fairview, *circa 1882.—Courtesy Schmit Collection, University of New Mexico Library.*

Above—Group photo of the Fairview school class, *circa 1900.—Courtesy Schmit Collection, University of New Mexico Library.*

Winston, deserted school.

Yankee

COUNTY: *Colfax*
LOCATION: *about 8 mi. northeast of Raton*
MAP: *page 239*
P.O. est. 1906; discont. 1922.

For many years prior to the development of the Yankee camp, farmers from nearby Johnson Mesa dug coal on the slopes of the mesa for their own domestic use. In 1904 a dual investment venture was launched to develop the bituminous coal beds in Johnson and Barela mesas, and a branch line of the A.T. & S.F. Railroad was extended from Raton up the east fork of Sugarite Canyon, connecting the new mines to the main line. The Chicorica Coal Company, backed by the Wall Street brokerage firm of E. D. Sheppard and Co., and the Santa Fe, Raton & Eastern Railroad, promoted by A. D. Ensign, went forward with their development, and a small tent camp of Yankee began to grow. As eastern investors of the railroad poured money into the town and the Yankee mines continued to develop, frame houses and neatly painted business establishments stabilized the town. In 1907 the population of Yankee and immediate vicinity claimed two thousand residents. Several businesses, including a post office, three boardinghouses, a bakery, the Yankee Amusement Hall, Yankee Mercantile Co., Yankee Fuel Co., a justice of the peace, and a grade school, provided for the needs of the miners and their families.

A. D. Ensign built a beautiful two-story, two-fireplace, green-roofed home in Sugarite Canyon about three miles west of Yankee. "The Ensign Ranch" was a show place of solid mahogany and velvet furniture, oriental rugs, and marble statues. It overlooked spacious grounds of apple and cherry orchards. Major R. Lawrence acquired the guest ranch shortly after it was built, using it as a residence and center of entertainment until the beginning of World War I. The Ensign estate changed hands several more times, and by 1923 its treasures had been sold and the mansion fell into a state of ruin.

The peak of Yankee's prosperity lasted until World War I. The good years were highlighted with victories of the Yankee baseball team, excursion train rides to Raton, the Amusement Hall with its bowling alley and billiard tables, and Fourth of July picnics, contests, and dances. In February, 1912, the camp was snowbound. It took the train two days to travel the nine miles from Raton.

In 1914 the Llewellyn, Sperry, Honeyfield, and Turner coal mines closed down, and by 1915 the population was recorded as three hundred. In 1917 the Superior Coal Co. obtained operating leases on several of the mines, rebuilt several inclined shafts, and began supplying coal to the railroads. This rebirth of Yankee was greatly welcomed, but the few prosperous years that followed never compared to the pre-war days.

Yankee began to close its mines during the early 1920's, but the ideal location for living and the proximity to other producing coal mines encouraged many families to remain. In 1940 the population was stated at 148, as a few residents still hung on.

All traces of the Yankee coal mining camp have vanished, and the site is now occupied by a cattle ranch. A short distance up Sugarite Canyon on a low knoll, the abandoned ruins of the Ensign mansion overlook the valley.

Ruins of the Ensign house at the mouth of Sugarite Canyon. This house was once a fashionable show place.

Yankee baseball team, 1907.—*Courtesy John Southwell.*

Snowbound at the Yankee station, 1912.—*Courtesy John Southwell.*

Maps

Township, range, and section co-ordinates are included for each map, enabling the serious ghost town explorer to locate the towns on standard base maps.

238
MAPS

MAP 1

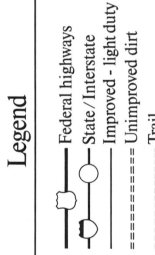

Legend

━🏠━ Federal highways

━◯━ State / Interstate

━━━ Improved - light duty

======= Unimproved dirt

------- Trail

Co-ordinates

Amizette: NW¼, T.27N., R.14E.
Anchor: NW¼, T.29N., R.15E.
Baldy: SE¼, T.28N., R.16E.
Blossburg: SW¼, T.31N., R.23E.
Brilliant: SW¼, T.32N., R.23E.
Catskill: SW¼, T.32N., R.20E.
Colfax: SW¼, Sec.5, T.27N., R.21E.
Dawson: NE¼, T.28N., R.20E.
Elizabethtown: NW¼, T.27N., R.16E.
Gardiner: SE¼, T.31N., R.23E.
Hematite: NE¼, T.28N., R.15E.
Johnson Mesa: NW¼, T.31N., R.26E.
Koehler: NW¼, T.29N., R.22E.
La Belle: NW¼, T.29N., R.15E.
Midnight: NW¼, T.29N., R.15E.
Otero: NE¼, T.30N., R.23E.
Perryville: SE¼, T.27N., R.16E.
Red River: SE¼, T.29N., R.14E.
Sugarite: NW¼, T.31N., R.24E.
Swastika: SW¼, T.31N., R.23E.
Twining: NW¼, T.27N., R.14E.
Van Houten: SE¼, T.30N., R.22E.
Virginia City: NE¼, T.27N., R.16E.
Yankee: SW¼, Sec. 6, T.31N., R.25E.

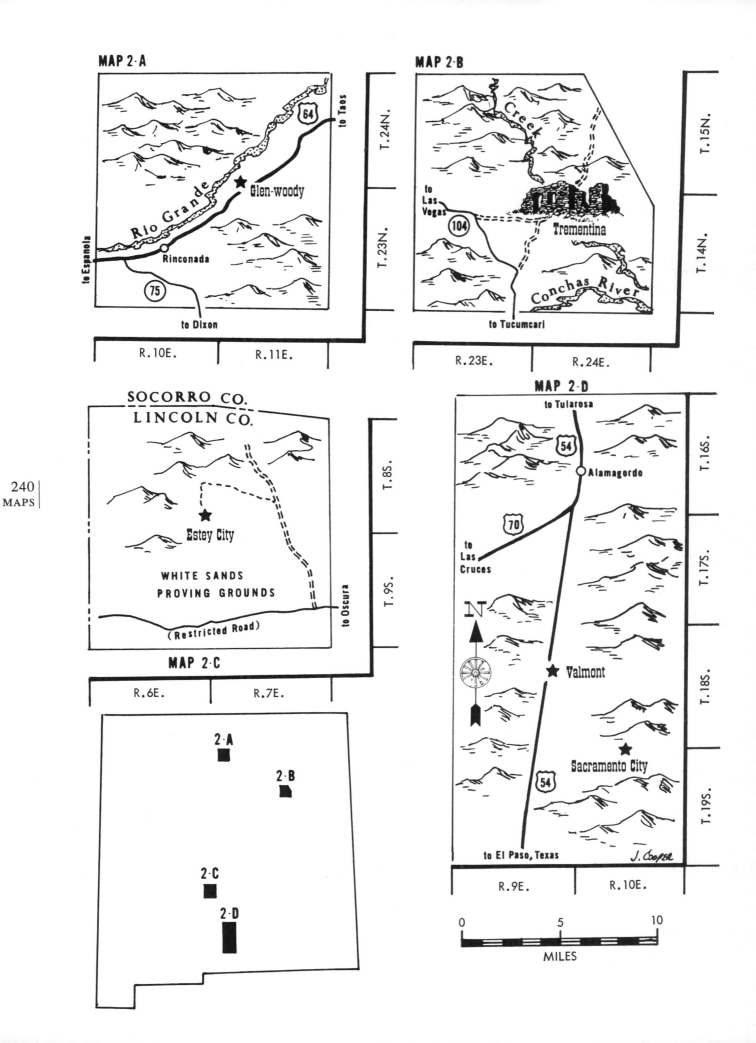

MAP 2-A

to Taos

64

Glen-woody

Rio Grande

Rinconada

to Espanola

75

to Dixon

T.24N.

T.23N.

R.10E.   R.11E.

MAP 2-B

Creek

to Las Vegas

104

Trementina

Conchas River

to Tucumcari

T.15N.

T.14N.

R.23E.   R.24E.

SOCORRO CO.

LINCOLN CO.

Estey City

WHITE SANDS
PROVING GROUNDS

to Oscura

(Restricted Road)

MAP 2-C

T.8S.

T.9S.

R.6E.   R.7E.

MAP 2-D

to Tularosa

54

Alamagordo

70

to Las Cruces

N

Valmont

54

Sacramento City

to El Paso, Texas

J. Cooper

T.16S.

T.17S.

T.18S.

T.19S.

R.9E.   R.10E.

2-A

2-B

2-C

2-D

0   5   10

MILES

Legend

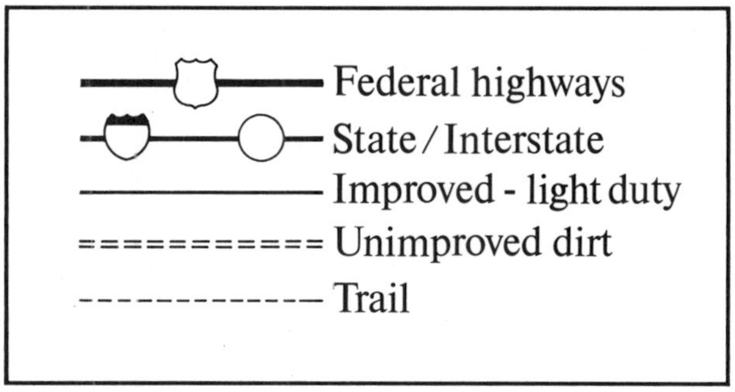

──⬡──	Federal highways
─⬤──○─	State / Interstate
─────	Improved - light duty
==========	Unimproved dirt
------------	Trail

MAP 2a

Glen-Woody: SW¼ , T.24N., R.11E.

MAP 2b

Trementina: NW¼ , T.14N., R.24E.

MAP 2c

Estey City: SE¼ , Sec. 36, T.8S., R.6E.

MAP 2d

Sacramento City: SW¼ , T.18S., R.10E.
Valmont: NE¼ , T.18S., R.9E.

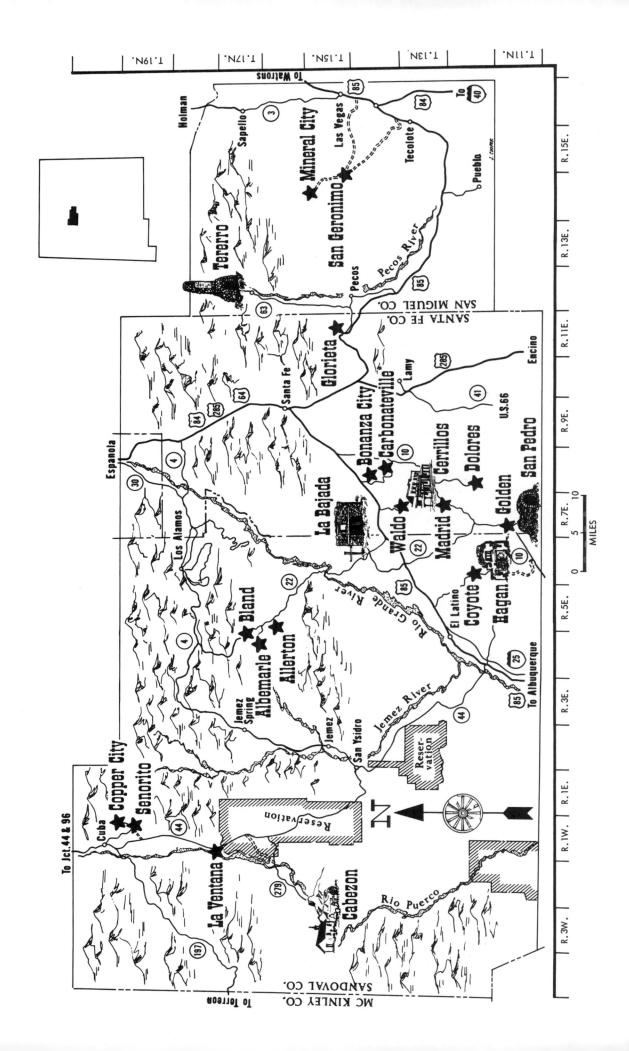

MAP 3

Legend

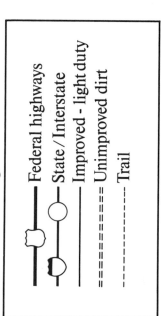

—■— Federal highways

—◯— State / Interstate

——— Improved - light duty

=========== Unimproved dirt

------------ Trail

Albemarle: SE¼, T.18N., R.4E.
Allerton: NW¼, T.17N., R.5E.
Bland: SE¼, Sec.25, T.18N., R.4E.
Bonanza City: SE¼, Sec.8, T.15N., R.8E.
Cabezon: SE¼, Sec.12, T.16N., R.3W.
Carbonateville: SE¼, Sec. 21, T.15N., R.8E.
Cerrillos: SE¼, Sec. 18, T.14N., R.8E.
Copper City: NW¼, Sec.2, T.20N., R.1W.
Coyote: SW¼, T.13N., R.6E.
Dolores: SW¼, T.13N., R.8E.
Golden: NW¼, T.12N., R.7E.
Glorieta: SW¼, Sec.27, T.16N., R.11E.
Hagan: SW¼, T.13N., R.6E.
La Bajada: SW¼, Sec.6, T.15N., R.7E.
La Ventana: SE¼, Sec.31, T.19N., R.1W.
Madrid: SE¼, T.14N., R.7E.
Mineral City: NE¼, T.16N., R.14E.
San Geronimo: SW¼, T.16N., R.15E.
San Pedro: N½, Sec.29, T.12N., R.7E.
Senorito: SW¼, Sec.11, T.20N., R.1W.
Tererro: NE¼, T.18N., R.12E.
Waldo: NE¼, Sec.13, T.14N., T.7E.

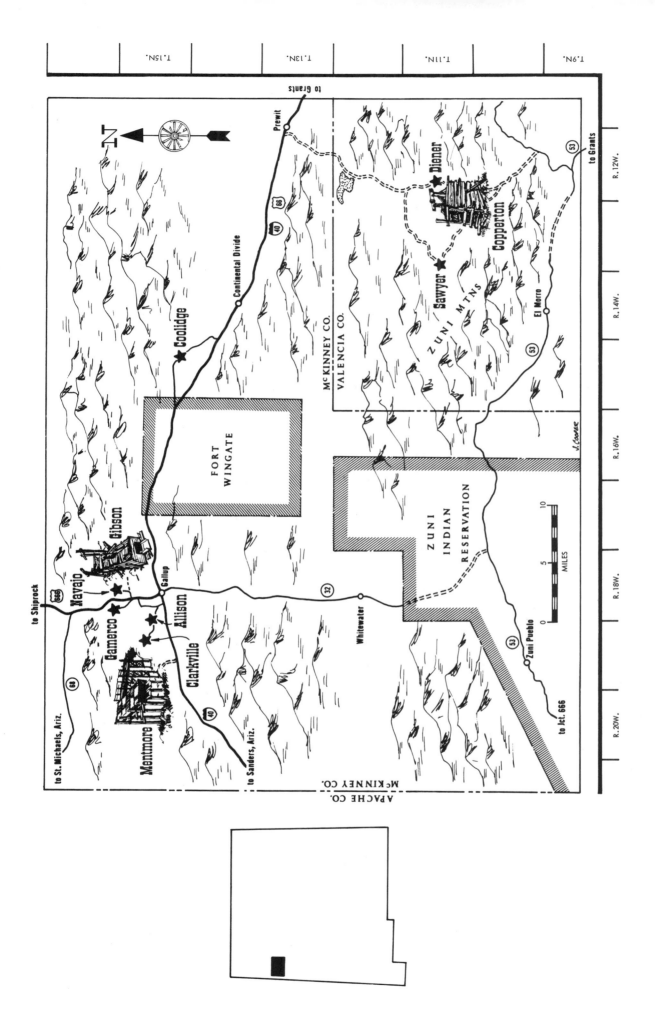

MAP 4

Legend

Federal highways	
State / Interstate	
Improved - light duty	
=========	Unimproved dirt
- - - - - - - -	Trail

Allison: SE¼, Sec.18, T.15N., R.18W.
Clarkville: SW¼, Sec.11, T.15N., R.19W.
Coolidge: SE¼, T.15N., R.15W.
Copperton: SW¼, T.11N., R.12W.
Diener: SW¼, T.11N., R.12W.
Gamerco: SE¼, Sec.32, T.16N., R.18W.
Gibson: NW¼, Sec.3, T.15N., R.18W.
Mentmore: NW¼, Sec.22, T.15N., R.19W.
Navajo: SE¼, Sec. 33, T.16N., R.18W.
Sawyer: SW¼, T.11N., R.13W.

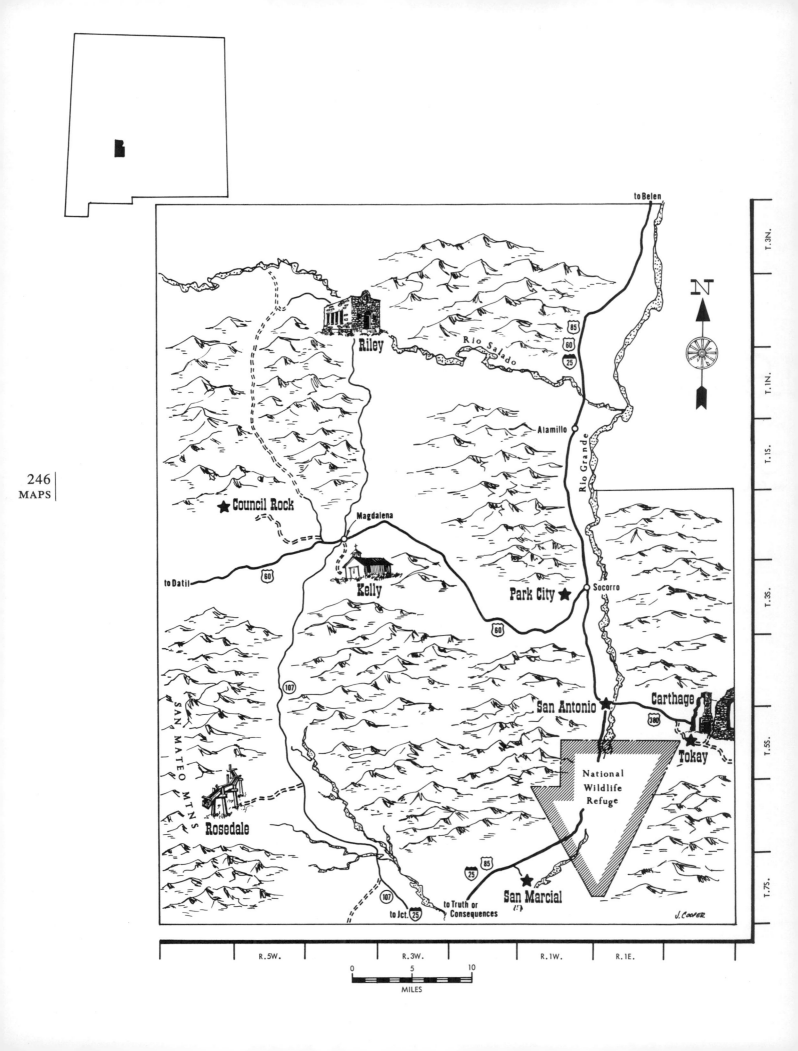

to Belen

T.3N.

T.1N.

T.1S.

Riley

Rio Salado

85
60
25

N

Alamillo

Council Rock

Magdalena

Rio Grande

T.3S.

to Datil

60

Kelly

Park City

Socorro

60

107

San Antonio

Carthage

380

SAN MATEO MTNS

Rosedale

National
Wildlife
Refuge

Tokay

25
85

to Truth or
Consequences

San Marcial

J. COOPER

107

to Jct.
25

R.5W.   R.3W.   R.1W.   R.1E.

0   5   10

MILES

T.5S.

T.7S.

MAP 5

Legend

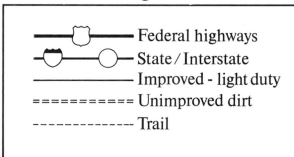

Federal highways
State / Interstate
Improved - light duty
Unimproved dirt
Trail

Carthage: NW¼ , Sec.15, T.5S., R.2E.
Council Rock: approx. NE¼ , T.2S., R.6W.
Kelly: NE¼ , Sec.1, T.3S., R.4W.
Park City: NE¼ , T.3S., R.1W.
Riley: S½ , Sec.23, T.2N., R.4W.
Rosedale: NE¼ , T.6S., R.6W.
San Antonio: SW¼ , Sec. 32, T.4S., R.1E.
San Marcial: NW¼ , T.7S., R.1W.
Tokay: SW¼ , Sec.16, T.5S., R.2E.

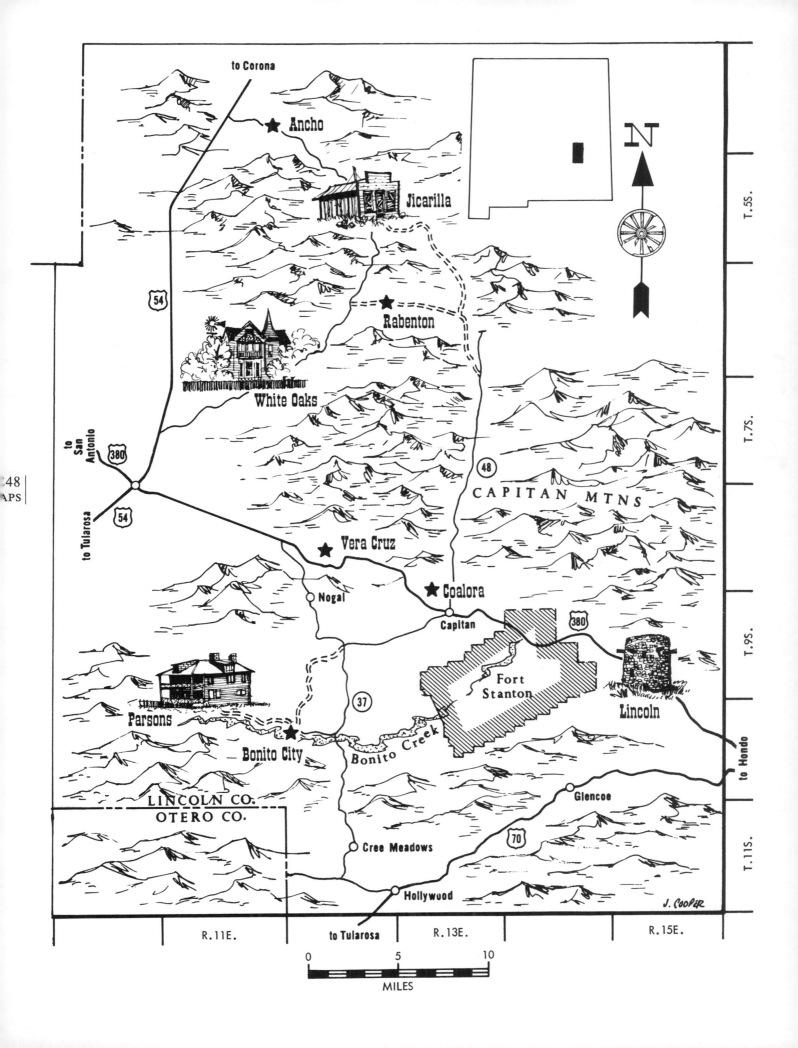

to Corona

Ancho

Jicarilla

N

T.5S.

54

Rabenton

White Oaks

to San Antonio

380

48

CAPITAN MTNS

T.7S.

348
APS

54

Vera Cruz

Nogal

Coalora

Capitan

380

T.9S.

to Tularosa

Fort Stanton

Lincoln

Parsons

37

Bonito City

Bonito Creek

to Hondo

LINCOLN CO.
OTERO CO.

Glencoe

70

T.11S.

Cree Meadows

Hollywood

J. COOPER

R. 11E.

to Tularosa

R. 13E.

R. 15E.

0   5   10

MILES

MAP 6

Legend

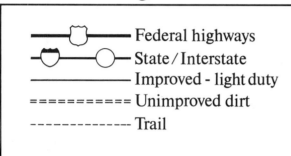

Federal highways
State / Interstate
Improved - light duty
Unimproved dirt
Trail

Ancho: SE¼ , T.4S., R.11E.
Bonito City: N½ , T.10S., R.12E.
Coalora: SE¼ , Sec.32, T.8S., R.14E.
Jicarilla: NE¼ , T.5S., R.12E.
Lincoln: SE¼ , Sec.29, T.9S., R.16E.
Parsons: NE¼ , Sec.34, T.9S., R.11E.
Rabenton: NE¼ , T.6S., R.12E.
Vera Cruz: NW¼ , Sec.20, T.8S., R.13E.
White Oaks: N½ , Sec.36, T.6S., R.12E.

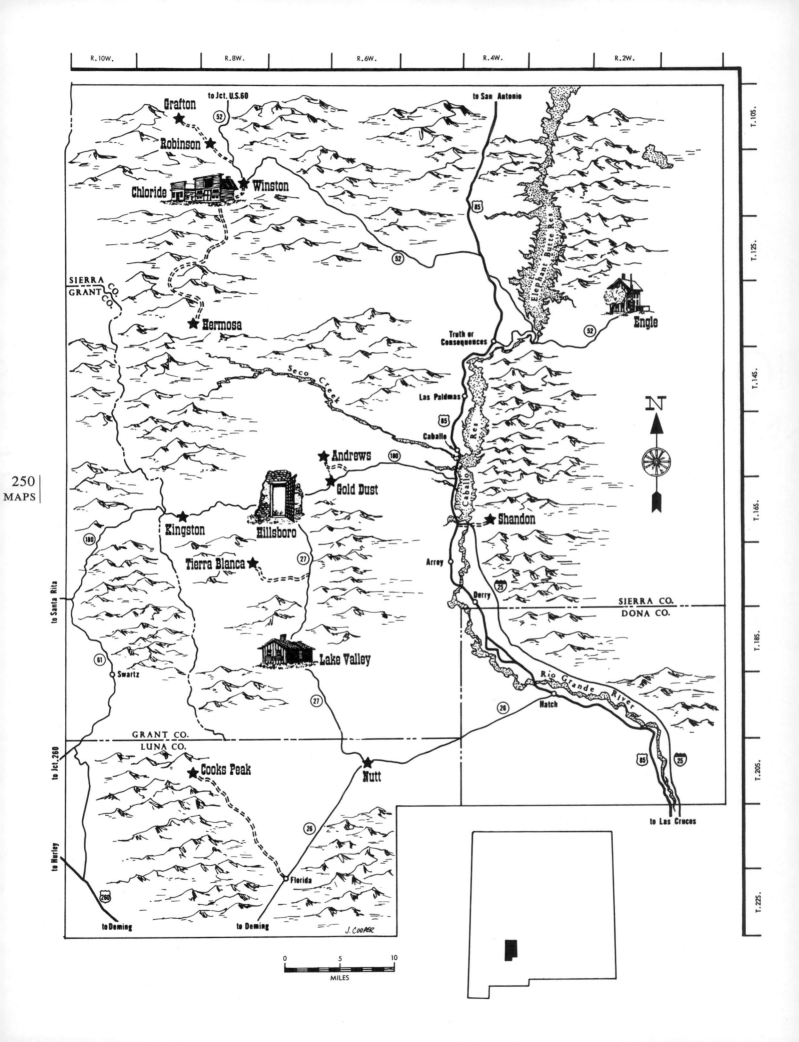

R.10W. R.8W. R.6W. R.4W. R.2W.

T.10S.
T.12S.
T.14S.
T.16S.
T.18S.
T.20S.
T.22S.

Grafton
to Jct. U.S.60
52
to San Antonio
Robinson
Chloride Winston
85
SIERRA CO.
GRANT CO.
52
Elephant Butte Res.
Hermosa
Engle
52
Truth or Consequences
Seco Creek
Las Palomas
85
Caballo
Andrews
190
Caballo Res.
Gold Dust
250
MAPS
Kingston
Hillsboro
Shandon
180
Tierra Blanca
27
Arrey
25
Derry
to Santa Rita
SIERRA CO.
DONA CO.
61
Lake Valley
Swartz
27
Rio Grande River
26
Hatch
85 25
GRANT CO.
LUNA CO.
to Jct. 260
Cooks Peak
Nutt
to Las Cruces
to Hurley
26
27
Florida
260
to Deming
to Deming
J. COOPER

0   5   10
MILES

MAP 7

Legend

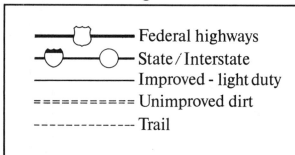

———🛡——— Federal highways
—◖——◯— State / Interstate
——————— Improved - light duty
=========== Unimproved dirt
------------- Trail

Andrews: approx. NW¼ , Sec.25, T.15S., R.7W.
Chloride: NE¼ , Sec. 20, T.11S., R.8W.
Cooks Peak: NE¼ , Sec.24, T.20S., R.9W.
Engle: NE¼ , T.13S., R.2W.
Gold Dust: NW¼ , Sec. 6, T.16S., R.6W.
Grafton: NE¼ , Sec.22, T.10S., R.9W.
Hermosa: SE¼ , Sec.23, T.13S., R.9W.
Hillsboro: NW¼ , Sec.16, T.16S., R.7W.
Kingston: NW¼ , Sec.18, T.16S., R.8W.
Lake Valley: NW¼ , Sec.28, T.18S., R.7W.
Nutt: NE¼ , T.20S., R.6W.
Robinson: NE¼ , Sec.31, T.10S., R.8W.
Shandon: approx. SW¼ , T.16S., R.4W.
Tierra Blanca: SW¼ , Sec.10, T.17S., R.8W.
Winston: SE¼ , Sec.15, T.11S., R.8W.

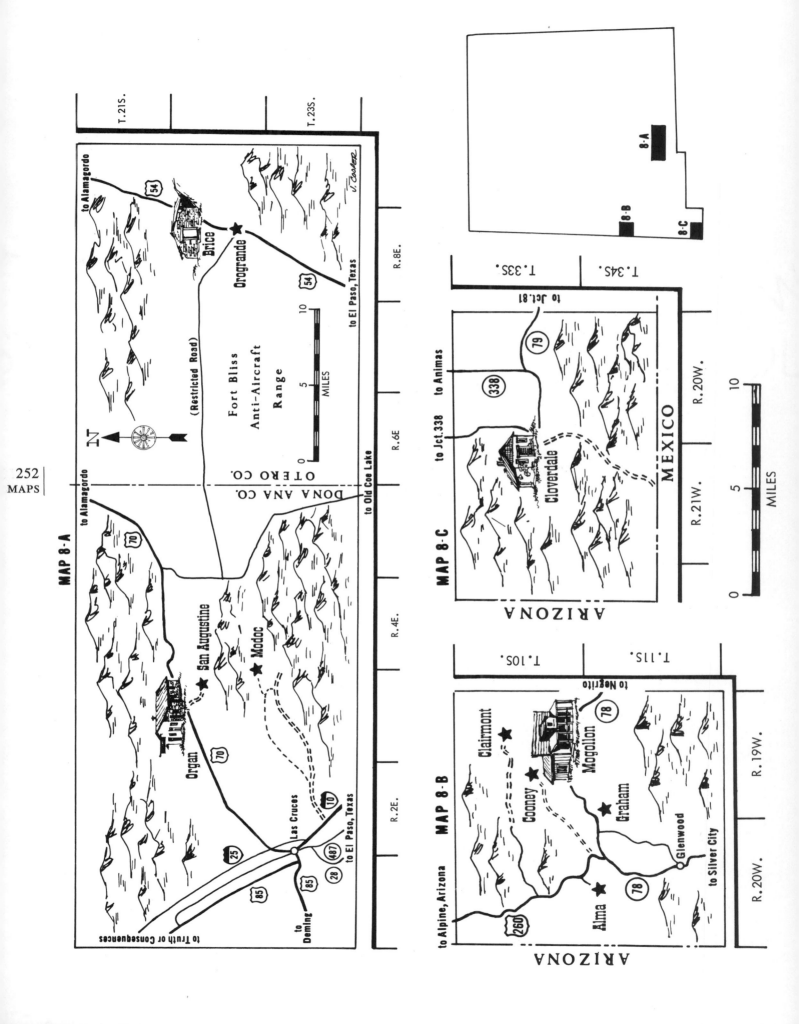

MAP 8-A

to Alamagordo

54

Brice

Orogrande

54

to El Paso, Texas

R.8E.

T.21S.

T.23S.

J. Cooler

Fort Bliss
Anti-Aircraft
Range

(Restricted Road)

OTERO CO.
DONA ANA CO.

to Alamagordo

to Old Coe Lake

N

70

R.6E.

0   5   10
MILES

R.4E.

San Augustine

Modoc

Organ

70

10

R.2E.

Las Cruces

to El Paso, Texas

487

25

28

85

85

to Deming

to Truth or Consequences

MAP 8-B

to Alpine, Arizona

Clairmont

Cooney

Mogollon

78

to Negrito

Graham

Glenwood

78

to Silver City

Alma

260

R.19W.

R.20W.

T.10S.

T.11S.

ARIZONA

MAP 8-C

to Jct.338

338

to Animas

79

to Jct.81

Cloverdale

MEXICO

R.20W.

R.21W.

0   5   10
MILES

T.33S.

T.34S.

ARIZONA

8-A

8-B

8-C

MAP 8a

Brice: SE¼, Sec.10, T.22S., R.8E.
Modoc: SE¼, Sec.36, T.22S., R.3E.
Organ: NE¼, Sec.2, T.22S., R.3E.
Orogrande: N½, Sec.23, T.22S., R.8E.
San Augustine: SE¼, Sec.11, T.22S., R.3E.

MAP 8b

Alma: NE¼, Sec.4, T.11S., R.20W.
Clairmont: SE¼, Sec. 15, T.10S., R.19W.
Cooney: SW¼, Sec.21, T.10S., R.19W.
Graham: S½, Sec.6, T.11S., R.19W.
Mogollon: E½, Sec.33, T.10S., R.19W.

MAP 8c

Cloverdale: S½, Sec. 24, T.33S., R.21W.

Legend

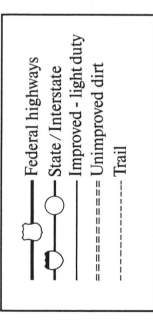

— Federal highways
—◯— State / Interstate
— Improved - light duty
========= Unimproved dirt
--------- Trail

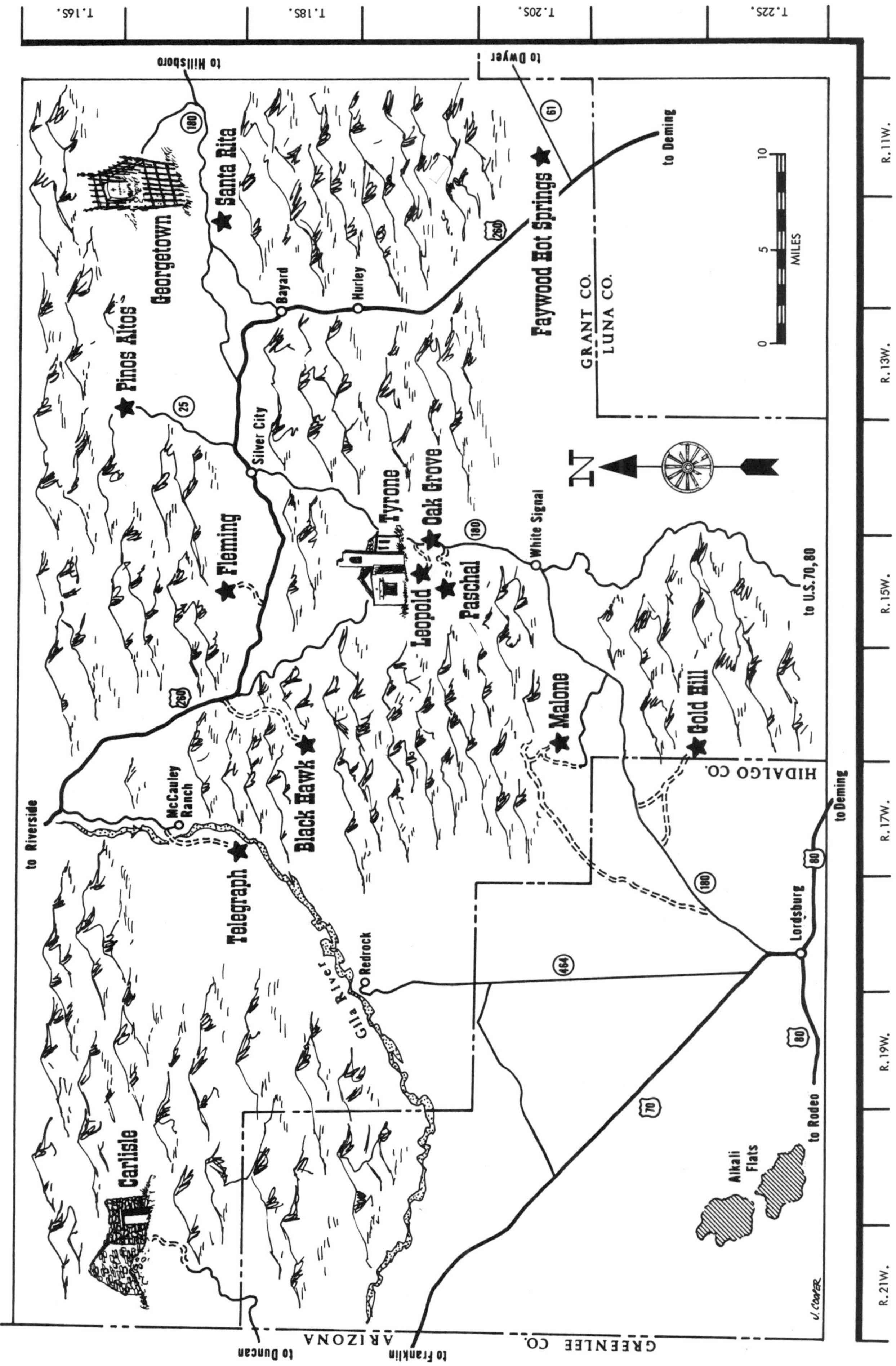
to Hillsboro
to Dwyer
Santa Rita
Georgetown
Pinos Altos
Bayard
Hurley
Silver City
Fleming
Tyrone
Oak Grove
Leopold
Paschal
White Signal
Faywood Hot Springs
to Deming
GRANT CO.
LUNA CO.
MILES
0
5
10
N
to U.S. 70,80
Malone
Gold Hill
Black Hawk
HIDALGO CO.
McCauley Ranch
to Riverside
Telegraph
to Deming
Lordsburg
Redrock
Gila River
Carlisle
to Rodeo
Alkali Flats
to Duncan
ARIZONA
to Franklin
GREENLEE CO.
J. COOPER
T.16S.
T.18S.
T.20S.
T.22S.
R.11W.
R.13W.
R.15W.
R.17W.
R.19W.
R.21W.

MAP 9

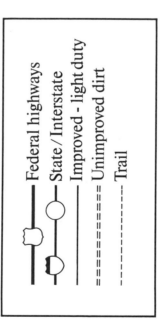

Legend

——— Federal highways

——O— State / Interstate

——— Improved – light duty

========== Unimproved dirt

---------- Trail

Black Hawk: E½, Sec.21, T.18S., R.16W.
Carlisle: S½, Sec.1, T.17S., R.21W.
Faywood Hot Springs: NE¼, Sec.20, T.20S., R.11W.
Fleming: Sec.34, T.17S., R.15W.
Georgetown: NW¼, Sec.7, T.17S., R.11W.
Gold Hill: Sec.31, T.21S., R.16W.
Leopold: SW¼, Sec.22, T.19S., R.15W.
Malone: NW¼, Sec.29, T.20S., R.16W.
Oak Grove: NE¼, Sec.25, T.19S., R.15W.
Paschal: approx. SE¼, Sec.21, T.19S., R.15W.
Pinos Altos: NE¼, Sec.6, T.17S., R.13W.
Santa Rita: NW¼, Sec.26, T.17S., R.12W.
Telegraph: SW¼, Sec.32, T.17S., R.17W.
Tyrone: NE¼, Sec.14, T.19S., R.15W.

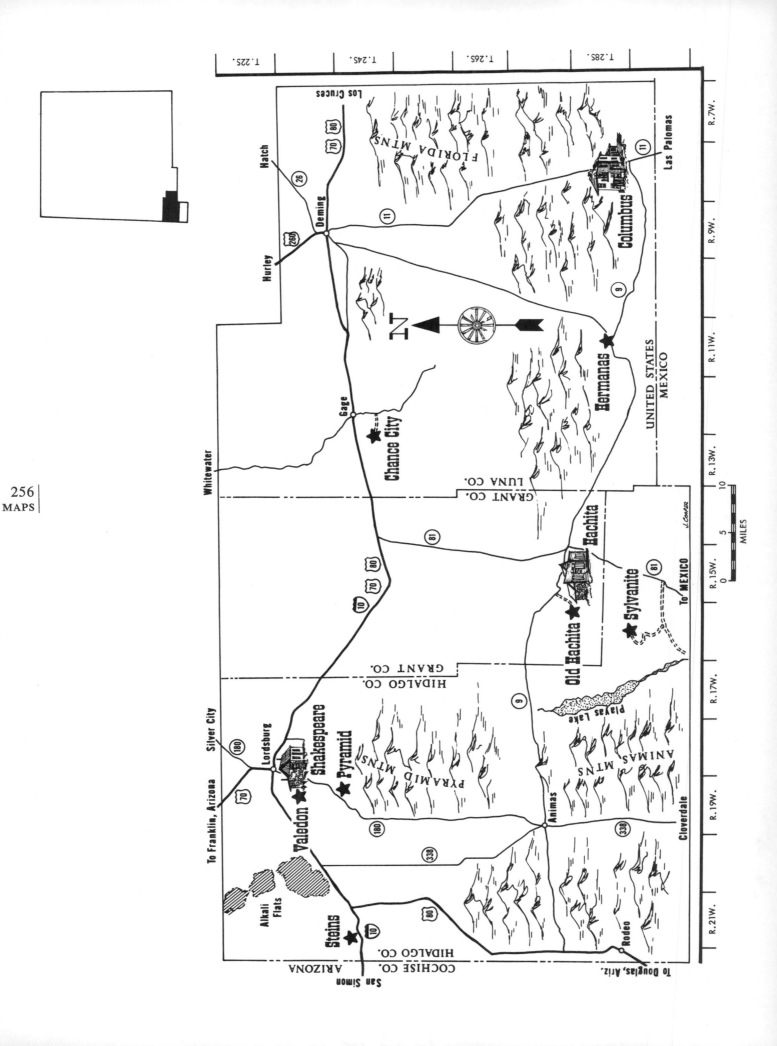

MAP 10

Legend

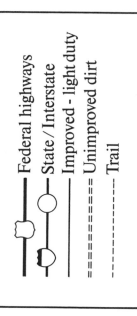

Federal highways

State / Interstate

Improved - light duty

Unimproved dirt

Trail

Chance City: W½, Sec.29, T.24S., R.12W.
Columbus: SE¼, T.28S., R.8W.
Hachita: NE¼, Sec.36, T.27S., R.15W.
Old Hachita: W½, Sec.36, T.27S., R.16W.
Hermanas: SE¼, T.28S., R.11W.
Pyramid: N½, Sec.1, T.24S., R.19W.
Shakespeare: NW¼, Sec.7, T.23S., R.18W.
Steins: NE¼, T.24S., R.21W.
Sylvanite: SW¼, Sec.34, T.28S., R.16W.
Valedon: SE¼, Sec.12, T.23S., R.19W.

Selected Bibliography

Anderson, Eugene Carter. *The Metal Resources of New Mexico and Their Economic Features Through 1954.* State Bureau of Mines and Mineral Resources *Bulletin No. 39.* Socorro, N.M., 1957.

Anderson, George B. *History of New Mexico: Its Resources and People.* Vols. I–II. Los Angeles, Pacific States Publishing Co., 1907.

Brevoort, Elias. *New Mexico: Her Natural Resources and Attractions.* Santa Fe, 1874.

Carruth, J. A., ed. *Business Directory Arizona and New Mexico for 1897.* Las Vegas, N.M., Daily Examiner Printing and Binding Est., 1897.

Charles, Mrs. Tom. *Tales of the Tularosa.* Alamogordo, Private printing, 1954.

———. *More Tales of the Tularosa.* Alamogordo, Bennett Printing Co., 1966.

Christiansen, Paige W., and Frank E. Kottlowski. *Mosaic of New Mexico's Scenery, Rocks, and History.* State Bureau of Mines and Mineral Resources *Scenic Trips to the Geologic Past No. 8.* Socorro, N.M., 1967.

Clendenen, Clarence C. *Blood on the Border.* Toronto, Macmillan Co., 1969.

Coan, Charles F. *A History of New Mexico.* Vols. I–II. Chicago, The American Historical Society, Inc., 1925.

Colorado, New Mexico, Utah, Nevada, Wyoming and Arizona Gazetteer and Business Directory 1884–5. Vol. I. Chicago, R. L. Polk & Co. and A. C. Danser, Publishing Co., 1884.

Cooke, Philip St. George. *The Conquest of New Mexico and California.* New York, G. P. Putnam's Sons, 1878.

Cremony, John C. *Life Among the Apaches.* San Francisco, A. Roman & Company, 1868.

Cutts, James Madison. *The Conquest of California and New Mexico.* Philadelphia, Carey & Hart, 1847.

Delgado, N. & D. *Guide to Historical Markers in New Mexico.* Albuquerque, Ward Anderson Printing Co., 1968.

Dunbar, Alexander R., ed. *International Mining Manual.* Denver, Western Mining Directory Co., 1907.

File, Lucien A. *Directory of Mines of New Mexico.* State Bureau of Mines and Mineral Resources *Circulars No. 77.* Socorro, N.M., 1965.

———, and Stuart A. Northrop. *County, Township, and Range Locations of New Mexico's Mining Districts.* State Bureau of Mines and Mineral Resources *Circulars No. 84.* Socorro, N.M., 1966.

Flint, Timothy, ed. *The Personal Narrative of James O. Pattie of Kentucky.* Chicago, The Lakeside Press, 1930.

Frost, Max, and Paul A. F. Walter. *To The Land of Sunshine.* Santa Fe, New Mexican Printing Co., 1906.

Fulton, Maurice G. *Lincoln County War.* Tucson, University of Arizona Press, 1968.

Gibson, A. M. *The Life and Death of Colonel Albert Jennings Fountain.* Norman, University of Oklahoma Press, 1965.

Grant, Blanche C. *When Old Trails Were New: The Story of Taos.* New York, The Press of the Pioneers, Inc., 1934.

Gregg, Josiah. *Commerce of the Prairies.* Ed. by Max L. Moorhead. Norman, University of Oklahoma Press, 1954.

Hamilton, Winifred Oldham. *Wagon Days in Red River.* Private printing, 1947.

Harris, Larry A. *Pancho Villa and The Columbus Raid.* El Paso, Superior Printing Co., 1949.

Hayward, J. Lyman. *The Los Cerrillos Mines and Their Mineral Resources.* South Farmingham, Mass., J. L. Clark Printing Co., 1880.

Hill, Rita. *Then and Now Here and Around Shakespeare.* Private printing, 1963.

Huber, Joe. *The Story of Madrid, New Mexico.* Private printing, n.d.

Jenkinson, Michael. *Ghost Towns of New Mexico.* Albuquerque, University of New Mexico Press, 1967.

Jones, Fayette Alexander. *New Mexico Mines and Minerals.* The New Mexican Printing Co., 1904.

Kubler, George. *Religious Architecture of New Mexico.* Chicago, The Rio Grande Press, Inc., 1962.

Lindgren, Waldemar, Louis C. Graton, and Charles H. Gordon. *The Ore Deposits of New Mexico.* U.S. Geological Survey *Professional Paper No. 68.* Washington, Government Printing Office, 1910.

Lummis, Charles F. *A Tramp Across the Continent.* New York, Charles Scribner's Sons, 1892.

Mason, Herbert Molloy, Jr. *The Great Pursuit.* New York, Random House, 1970.

McKenna, James A. *Black Range Tales.* New York, Wilson-Erickson Inc., 1936.

McKenney's Business Directory of the Principal Towns of Central and Southern California, Arizona, New Mexico, Southern Colorado and Kansas 1882–3. Oakland and San Francisco, Pacific Press, 1882.

McNitt, Frank. *The Indian Traders*. Norman, University of Oklahoma Press, 1962.

Mills, T. B. *New Mexico*. Las Vegas, N.M., 1889.

Montgomery, Arthur, and Patrick K. Sutherland. *Trail Guide to the Upper Pecos*. State Bureau of Mines and Mineral Resources *Scenic Trips to the Geologic Past No. 6*. Socorro, N.M., 1967.

Muehlberger, William R., Brewster Baldwin, and Roy W. Foster. *High Plains Northeastern New Mexico*. State Bureau of Mines and Mineral Resources *Scenic Trips to the Geologic Past No. 7*. Socorro, N.M., 1967.

Mullane, William H., ed. *This is Silver City 1888, 1889, 1890*. Vol. III. Silver City, N.M., Private printing, 1965.

————. *This is Silver City 1891*. Vol. IV. Silver City, N.M., Private printing, 1967.

————. *Indian Raids*. Silver City, N.M., Private printing, 1968.

Myrick, David F. *New Mexico Railroads*. Golden, Colo., Colorado Railroad Museum, 1970.

New Mexico. (*American Guide Series*) New York, Hastings House, 1940.

New Mexico Bureau of Immigration. *Mines of New Mexico*. Santa Fe, New Mexican Printing Co., 1896.

New Mexico and El Paso, Texas Business Directory. Vol. II. Denver, The Gazetteer Publishing Co., 1905.

New Mexico Business Directory Including El Paso, Texas with Denver and Foreign Classifications 1907–08. Denver, The Gazetteer Publishing Co., 1907.

New Mexico State and El Paso, Texas Business Directory. Denver, The Gazetteer Publishing Co., 1915.

New Mexico State and El Paso, Texas Business Directory. Denver, The Gazetteer Publishing Co., 1919.

New Mexico State and El Paso, Texas Business Directory. Denver, The Gazetteer Publishing and Printing Co., 1921.

New Mexico State and El Paso, Texas Business Directory. Denver, The Gazetteer Publishing and Printing Co., 1923.

New Mexico State and El Paso, Texas Business Directory. Denver, The Gazetteer Publishing and Printing Co., 1926.

New Mexico State and El Paso, Texas Business Directory. Denver, The Gazetteer Publishing and Printing Co., 1930.

New Mexico State Business Directory 1929. Denver, The Gazetteer Publishing and Printing Co., 1929.

New Mexico State Business Directory 1938. Denver, The Gazetteer Publishing and Printing Co., 1938.

New Mexico State Business Directory with El Paso Department. Denver, The Gazetteer Publishing and Printing Co., 1940.

Paul, Rodman Wilson. *Mining Frontiers of The Far West 1848–1880*. New York, Holt, Rinehart and Winston, 1963.

Pearce, T. M., ed. *New Mexico Place Names*. Albuquerque, University of New Mexico Press, 1965.

Reno, Philip. *And Farther on Was Gold*. Denver, Sage Books, 1962.

Ritch, Hon. William G. *Aztlan, The History, Resources and Attractions of New Mexico*. Boston, D. Lothrop & Co., 1885.

Stanley, F. *The Grant That Maxwell Bought*. Denver, World Press, 1952.

————. *The San Marcial, New Mexico Story*. White Deer, Texas, Private printing, 1960.

————. *The Elizabethtown, New Mexico Story*. Dumas, Texas, Private printing, 1961.

————. *The Shakespeare, New Mexico Story*. Pantex, Texas, Private printing, 1961.

————. *The Blossburg, New Mexico Story*. Pantex, Texas, Private printing, 1962.

————. *The Chloride, New Mexico Story*. Pantex, Texas, Private printing, 1962.

————. *The Fairview, New Mexico Story*. Pantex, Texas, Private printing, 1962.

————. *The La Belle, New Mexico Story*. Pantex, Texas, Private printing, 1962.

————. *The Georgetown, New Mexico Story*. Pep, Texas, Private printing, 1963.

————. *The Bland, New Mexico Story*. Pep, Texas, Private printing, 1964.

————. *The Catskill, New Mexico Story*. Pep, Texas, Private printing, 1964.

————. *The Cerrillos, New Mexico Story*. Pep, Texas, Private printing, 1964.

————. *The Dawson Tragedies*. Pep, Texas, Private printing, 1964.

————. *The Golden, New Mexico Story*. Pep, Texas, Private printing, 1964.

————. *The Hillsboro, New Mexico Story*. Pep, Texas, Private printing, 1964.

————. *The Koehler, New Mexico Story*. Pep, Texas, Private printing, 1964.

————. *The Lake Valley, New Mexico Story*. Pep, Texas, Private printing, 1964.

————. *The Sugarite, New Mexico Story*. Pep, Texas, Private printing, 1964.

————. *The Van Houten, New Mexico Story*. Pep, Texas, Private printing, 1964.

————. *The Yankee, New Mexico Story*. Pep, Texas, Private printing, 1964.

————. *The Gardiner, New Mexico Story*. Pep, Texas, Private printing, 1965.

————. *The Glorieta, New Mexico Story*. Pep, Texas, Private printing, 1965.

————. *The Hermosa, New Mexico Story.* Pep, Texas, Private printing, 1965.

————. *The Carbonateville, New Mexico Story.* Pep, Texas, Private printing, 1966.

————. *The Columbus, New Mexico Story.* Pep, Texas, Private printing, 1966.

————. *The Brilliant, New Mexico Story.* Pep, Texas, Private printing, 1967.

Southern Pacific Coast Directory 1888–89. San Francisco, McKenney Directory Co., 1888.

Thrapp, Dan L. *The Conquest of Apacheria.* Norman, University of Oklahoma Press, 1967.

Tice, Henry Allen. *Early Railroad Days in New Mexico.* Santa Fe, Stagecoach Press, 1932.

Tompkins, Col. Frank. *Chasing Villa.* Harrisburg, Pa., Military Service Publishing Co., 1934.

Twitchell, Ralph Emerson. *The Leading Facts of New Mexican History.* Vols. III–IV. Cedar Rapids, The Torch Press, 1917.

Whitford, William Clarke. *Colorado Volunteers in the Civil War.* (The State Historical and Natural History Society of Colorado *Historical Series*) No. I. Boulder, Pruett Press, 1963.

Wolle, Muriel Sibel. *The Bonanza Trail.* Bloomington, Indiana University Press, 1958.

Woods, Betty. *101 Trips in the Land of Enchantment.* Santa Fe, New Mexico Magazine, 1956.

————. *Ghost Towns and How to Get to Them.* Santa Fe, The Press of the Territorian, 1964.

Index

Abbot's Saloon (Carbonateville, N. M.): 27
Abert, Lieutenant J. W.: 186
Abileen Salvage Co.: 8
A-Bomb: 79
Ake, Jesse: 79
Alabama (mine): 178
Alamitos, N. M.: 206
Alamogordo, N. M.: 21, 166, 179, 220
Alaska (mine): 102
Albemarle, N. M.: 2, 13
Albuquerque and Cerrillos Coal Co.: 148
Albuquerque Eastern Railroad: 107
Albuquerque, N. M.: 24, 65, 100, 130, 152, 186, 187
Algodones, N. M.: 107
Alhambra (mine): 12
Allerton, N. M.: 2
Allerton Town Co.: 2
Allison, Fletcher J.: 3
Allison (mine): 3
Allison, N. M.: 3
Alma, N. M.: 3, 58, 155
Amazon (mine): 187
Amberg, Jacob: 170
American Brewing Co.: 129
American Flag (mine): 110
American Fuel Co.: 94, 162
American Lumber Co.: 192
American Metal Co.: 206
American (mine): 105
American Revolution, Sons of the: 198
American Smelting and Refining Co.: 167
Amizette, N. M.: 7, 210
Amy B. (mine): 178
Anaconda (mine): 187
Ancho Brick Plant: 8
Ancho, N. M.: 8
Ancho Peak: 116
Anchor (claim): 153
Anchor, N. M.: 153
Ancho Valley: 8
Anderson and Fredericks Saloon (White Oaks, N. M.): 225
Anderson, Bob: 49
Anderson, John: 156
Anderson, Walt: 207
Andrews, N. M.: 10
Angle (Engle, N. M.): 78
Angle, Judge Frank Warner: 140
Animas, N. M.: 49, 204
Antelope (mine): 110
Antrim, William: 104
Apache Canyon: 97
Apache Indians: 3, 42, 56, 58, 82, 85, 91, 96, 99, 102, 104, 110, 112, 125, 132, 138, 155, 170, 171, 178, 182, 188, 196, 198, 213, 220

Aqua Negro River: 139
Aragon, Ramon: 79
Arizona and New Mexico Railroad: 106
Armstrong Brothers' General Store (Engle, N. M.): 78
Arnold, Philip: 195
Arteaga, Fray Antonio de: 180
Arthur, Chester (President of United States): 27
Atchison, Topeka and Santa Fe Railroad: 21, 38, 78, 82, 97, 121, 133, 162, 166, 180, 182, 184, 220, 226, 230, 234
Athens Mining and Milling Co.: 109
Atlantic and Pacific Railroad: 58, 192
Atwood (mine): 196, 217
Austrians (nationality): 220
Avon Street (Shakespeare, N. M.): 196
Axtell, Governor Samuel B.: 138
Aztec Lode (mine): 10

Baca, Anastacio: 176
Baca, Captain Saturnino: 138
Baca, Elfego (television series): 39
Baca Hotel (Park City, N. M.): 167
Bacon Springs (ranch): 58
Bailey, Colonel Andrew O.: 51
Baker, Frank: 139
Baking Powder (mine): 178
Baldy, N. M.: 10, 222
Bank of California: 195
Bank of San Marcial: 185
Banner Mining Co.: 217
Baptist Church: 51
Barbont, Mr. and Mrs. (identified with Sugarite, N. M.): 200
Bar Cross (ranch): 79
Barela Mesa: 234
Barnaby, A.: 124
Barrat, Padre Emil: 185
Bates, T. M.: 137
Baxter, George: 224
Baxter Mountain: 224
Bean, Roy: 169
Bean, Samuel: 169
Bear Creek: 169
Beavers, W. H.: 3
Beck, N. M.: 198
Beckwith, Bob: 140
Bell (Johnson Mesa, N. M.): 117
Bell, Marion: 117
Bell Telephone Co.: 200
Benét-Mercié (machine gun): 52
Ben Hur (novel): 27
Bennett, Mr. (identified with San Augustine, N. M.): 182
Bentley, L. B.: 164
Bentley's Store (Organ, N. M.): 164
Bernalillo Co.: 60
Bernalillo, N. M.: 107
Berry, Frank: 118
Berry, Mrs. Frank: 118
Berry, Pat: 118
Berry, Squire Charles (Justice of the Peace, Bonito, N. M.): 20
Bidwell, Jack: 211
Biggs, Joseph (blacksmith, White Oaks, N. M.): 225
Billing, Gustav: 120, 167
Billing Smelter: 167

Bill, Russian: 196
Billy the Kid (William S. Bonney): 104, 138, 217, 224
Bils, Dr. J. T.: 87
Birch, Mr. (identified with Pinos Altos, N. M.): 169
Birchville (Pinos Altos, N. M.): 169
Bishop, William: 39
Bitter Creek: 174
Blackbird (mine): 104
Black Copper (mine): 174
Blackhawk (mine): 12
Blackhawk, N. M.: 12
Black, John: 12
Black Range Hotel (Winston, N. M.): 229
Black Range Lodge (Kingston, N. M.): 125
Black Range (mining district): 229
Black Range Mountains: 78, 99, 102, 110
Black Range Museum: 112
Black Range (newspaper): 43, 177
Black Range Tales (book): 125
Black, Robert: 102
Blain Bros. (store in Allerton, N. M.): 2
Blair, Sheriff (identified with Mogollon, N. M.): 155
Blake, Miss Alice: 208
Bland Canyon: 2
Bland Herald (newspaper): 13
Bland, N. M.: 2, 13
Bland, Richard Parks: 13
Blazer, Dr. J. H.: 138
Blazer's Mill: 139
Blithen (lumber mill): 34
Blossburg (coal mine): 16, 117
Blossburg Merchantile Co. (Brilliant, N. M.): 21, 87
Blossburg Mercantile Co. (Koehler, N. M.): 129
Blossburg Mercantile Co.: 200, 220
Blossburg, N. M.: 16, 117
Blossburg No. 4 (mine): 87
Blossburg Pioneer (newspaper): 16
Blotcher, Norman: 2
Bluebell (mine): 12
Bluebird (mine): 104
Blue Canyon: 154
Blue Goose Brothel (Engle, N. M.): 79
Blun, Henry: 229
Blun, Jacob: 229
Bonanza City, N. M.: 19, 27, 38
Bonanza Creek: 19
Bonanza Hill: 19
Bond and Stewart Store (White Oaks, N. M.): 225
Bonito Canyon: 20
Bonito City, N. M.: 20
Bonnell Opera House (White Oaks, N. M.): 225
Bonney, William: 138
Boyle, Colonel John: 195
Bowdre, Charlie: 139
Bowman, Mr. "Cherokee Jim" (identified with Blackhawk, N. M.): 12
Boss Store (White Oaks, N. M.): 225
Brady, Major William: 138
Brand, Mr. (identified with Santa Rita, N. M.): 189
Branson, Colonel David: 78

Brazo's Island: 79
Brett Hotel (Catskill, N. M.): 35
Brewer, Dick: 139
Brice, N. M.: 21
Bridal Chamber (stope): 132
Brilliant Electric Co. (Brilliant, N. M.): 21
Brilliant Hotel (Brilliant, N. M.): 21
Brilliant, N. M.: 16, 21, 202
Brilliant and Raton Stage Line: 21
Brilliant II (Swastika, N. M.): 22
Brooks, George L.: 56
Brothers Hotel (White Oaks, N. M.): 225
Brothers, J. A.: 225
Brown and Company (Leopold, N. M.): 137
Brown, Cory T.: 121
Brown, W. D.: 195
Bruce, Mrs. F. B.: 13
Buckner, Charles: 229
Buhl and Gross Hotel (Pinos Altos, N. M.): 169
Buhlman, Mr. (identified with Cooney, N. M.): 58
Bullard, James: 169
Bullard's Peak (mining district): 12
Burke, Dr. (Coolidge physician): 58
Burns, R. E.: 156
Burro Glee Club (identified with Blackhawk, N. M.): 12
Burro Mountains: 12, 137, 163, 169, 213
Burro Mountain Copper Co.: 137
Burro Mountain Copper Company Hotel (Leopold, N. M.): 137
Burro Mountain General Merchandise (Leopold, N. M.): 137
Butecke, John: 99
Butler, Bill: 34
Butler's Livery (Catskill, N. M.): 34
Butterfield Stage Co.: 170, 195, 198

Caballos Mountains: 198
Cabezon, N. M.: 24
Cabezon Peak: 24
Caddis, Miss. (identified with Steins, N. M.): 199
Calico Guards: 85
Callaway and Patterson Hotel (San Pedro, N. M.): 186
Calumet and Arizona Mining Co.: 217
Camp (Valmont, N. M.): 220
Camp Furlong, N. M.: 51, 53
Canadian River: 34
Canby, Colonel Edward R. S.: 97
Cano, Don: 71
Cantwell, Mr. (Deputy Sheriff identified with Fleming, N. M.): 85
Canyon del Agua Co.: 100
Capitan, N. M.: 50, 226
Carbonate Hill: 42
Carbonateville, N. M.: 26, 38
Caribel (claim): 153
Carlisle (mine): 30
Carlisle (mining district): 30
Carlisle, N. M.: 30
Carlyle, Jimmie: 224
Carnahan (San Pedro, N. M.): 187
Carnahan, W. S.: 187
Carranza, Venustiano (President of Mexico): 51

Carrasco, Lieutenant Colonel Manuel: 188
Carrier, Dr. F. W.: 189
Carrizozo, N. M.: 8, 81, 116, 138, 172, 222, 224, 226
Carson (Blackhawk, N. M.): 12
Carson, J. H.: 12
Carson, Kit: 59
Carthage Fuel Co.: 32
Carthage, N. M.: 32, 180, 208, 225
Casino (Kingston, N. M.): 125
Casna, Andrew: 3
Cassidy, Butch: 4, 104
Catholic Church: 16, 24, 39, 64, 74, 87, 91, 94, 112, 121, 130, 164, 180, 182, 185, 189
Catholics: 200
Catron Co.: 3, 48, 58, 104, 155
Catron, Thomas B.: 138
Catskill, N. M.: 34, 131, 153
Catwalk: 104
Cayplass, Edgar: 27
Celestina Carrillo's Saloon (Santa Rita, N. M.): 189
Cerrillos Coal Railroad: 223
Cerrillos Hills: 38
Cerrillos House (Cerrillos, N. M.): 38
Cerrillos, N. M.: 38, 223
Chalchihuitl (mine): 26
Champion (mine): 155
Chance City, N. M.: 42
Chance (claim): 42
Chapman, Chip: 34
Charles, William: 199
Chaves, Fray Angelico: 100
"Cherokee Jim" (identified with Blackhawk, N. M.): 12
Chicago and Rock Island Railroad: 220
Chicago, Ill.: 10
Chick, William: 58
Chicorica Canyon: 200
Chicorica Coal Co.: 200, 234
Chihuahua, Mexico, city of: 189
Chihuahua, Mexico, state of: 51, 138
Chihuahua (red light district): 207
Chinese (nationality): 30, 64, 84, 92, 133
Chino Copper Co.: 189
Chipman, J. (merchant, Allerton, N. M.): 2
Chiricahua Apaches: 171
Chiricahua Mountains: 198
Chisum, John S.: 138
Chisum (ranch): 140
Chivington, Major John M.: 97
Chloride Creek: 43
Chloride Gulch: 42
Chloride, N. M.: 42, 102, 177, 229
"Choctaw Kelly" (E. M. Kelly): 27
Christmas Celebration: 21, 149, 200, 230
Cimarron Canyon: 169
Cimarron Mountains: 155
Cimarron, N. M.: 50, 63
Civil War: 51, 79, 96, 189, 195
Clairmont, N. M.: 48
Clark, Charles: 163
Clark Coal Co.: 48
Clark, "Doc" (identified with Sylvanite, N. M.): 204
Clarkville Free Library: 49

Clarkville Hospital: 49
Clarkville, N. M.: 48
Clark, W. A.: 48
Clark, William: 156
Clayton, N. M.: 131
Clermont (Clairmont, N. M.): 48
Clipper (newspaper): 124
Cloudman, William: 229
Cloverdale, N. M.: 49
Cloverdale (ranch): 49
Club Hotel (Coalora, N. M.): 50
Coalora, N. M.: 50
Coates and Moore Co.: 155
Coates, Maurice: 3
Cochise (Apache Chief): 170
Cochiti Gold Mining Co.: 2
Cochiti (mining district): 13
Cochiti Reduction and Improvement Co.: 2
Coe, Frank: 139
Coe, George: 139
Coleman, John E.: 213
Colfax City (Colfax, N. M.): 50
Colfax, Co.: 10, 16, 21, 34, 50, 63, 73, 87, 109, 117, 129, 153, 166, 169, 200, 202, 210, 222, 234
Colfax Hotel: 51
Colfax, N. M.: 50, 220
Colla Canyon: 2
Colorado and Southern Railroad: 35, 220
Colorado Fuel and Iron Co.: 94, 220, 223
Colorado Volunteers: 97
Columbia Building and Loan Association: 184
Columbus Courier (newspaper): 51
Columbus Garage (Columbus, N. M.): 51
Columbus Hotel (Columbus, N. M.): 51
Columbus News (newspaper): 51
Columbus, N. M.: 51
Columbus State Bank: 51
Commercial Hotel (Columbus, N. M.): 51
Community Mission: 112
Comstock (mine): 224
Concord (stagecoach): 133
Confederate Army: 79, 97, 189, 195
Confidence (mine): 104
Constitutionalist Army: 51
Continental Hotel (Winston, N. M.): 229
Cooke, Captain Philip Saint George: 56
Cooks Peak, N. M.: 56
Coolidge, N. M.: 58
Coolidge, Thomas Jefferson: 58
Cooney Canyon: 48, 58
Cooney, Captain Michael: 58, 155
Cooney (mine): 4
Cooney, N. M.: 4, 48, 58, 155
Cooney, Sergeant James C.: 48, 58, 155
Copper City, N. M.: 60
Copper Creek: 48
Copperton Canyon: 60
Copperton, N. M.: 60
Cordova, A. R.: 176
Costello, Mrs. J. M.: 170
Cotton, Bill: 34
Council Rock, N. M.: 61
Cowan, W. J.: 16
Cowles (mine): 206

Cox, Miss Maggie: 206
Coyote, N. M.: 107
Crane, Billy: 58
Crane, N. M. (Coolidge, N. M.): 58
Crawford, W. H.: 206
Crescent Coal Co.: 94
"Cripple Creek of New Mexico"
    (Amizette, N. M.): 7
Crook, General George: 102
Cootes Hill: 53
Crystal Theatre (Columbus, N. M.): :51
Cuba, N. M.: 24, 60, 136, 193
Cullen, Edward: 198
Cunn, Colonel Dick (Catskill merchant):
    34

Dabney, T. H.: 51
Daly, George: 132
Daly (Lake Valley, N. M.): 132
Davis, Captain N. S.: 73
Davis Lesinsky and Co. (San Augustine,
    N. M.): 182
Davis, Mr. (prospector identified with
    Council Rock, N. M.): 61
Davy, William: 133
Dawson Fuel Co.: 63
Dawson, John Barkley: 63
Dawson News (newspaper): 63
Dawson, N. M.: 50, 63
Dawson Railroad: 50
Deadwood (mine): 155
Deep Down (mine): 155
Defiance Coal Co.: 152
DeLallo, T.: 223
Delco (light plant): 210
Delmonico's Restaurant (San Pedro,
    N. M.): 187
Del Muerto Spring: 78
Deming, N. M.: 51, 53, 56, 82, 85, 109,
    154, 169, 196
Dennis, Thomas: 56
Denver, Colo.: 2, 153, 169, 176, 187, 222
Devil's Kitchen: 220
Dewey, N. M.: 58
Diamond Coal Co.: 3
"Diamond Queen" (courtesan identified
    with Bland, N. M.): 13
Dienal (mine): 32
Diener, N. M.: 69
Dilco (Mentmore, N. M.): 152
Dilco (mine): 152
DiLisio, Joe: 87
Dillon Canyon: 16, 21, 87, 202
Dimmick Brothers (identified with
    Pinos Altos, N. M.): 170
Dimmitt, Frank: 38
Direct Coal Co.: 152
Disney, Walt: 39
Dividend Mining and Smelting Co.: 81
Dixon, Mrs. Belle: 131
Dodge, Cleland: 214
Dog Canyon: 220
Dog Canyon Station (Valmont, N. M.):
    220
Doheny, Edward: 125
Dolan, James J.: 138
Dolan, J. J. and Co.: 139
Dolan Store (Lincoln, N. M.): 139
Dolores, N. M.: 39, 70
Dona Ana Co.: 154, 163, 182

Dorsey Brothers (identified with Tele-
    graph, N. M.): 206
Doubtful Canyon: 198
Doubtful Canyon (Steins, N. M.): 198
Dougherty, J. L.: 42
Dudley, Colonel (identified with Lincoln,
    N. M.): 140
Dugan, Dan: 112
Dun, Charley: 206
Dupont, Harris: 60
Duran, Jose de Jesus Ulibarri y: 182
Dyer, A. P. and Co.: 102
Dyer, A. P.: 102

Eagle, Nest, N. M.: 10, 73, 169, 222
Earickson, John: 207
East Camp, N. M.: 30
Easter: 149, 200
Eberle, John: 155
Edison (claim): 153
Edison, Thomas A.: 71
Egelston, David: 102
Eighth Infantry: 220
Eighty-Five (claim): 217
Eighty-Five (mine): 196
Eighty-Five Mining Co.: 217
Eighty-Five Store (Valedon, N. M.):
    217
"El Burro" (nickname identified with
    Tererro, N. M.): 207
Eleanor (dredge): 74
Elephant Butte Dam: 79
Eleventh Cavalry: 53
Elizabethtown, N. M.: 10, 73, 174, 222
"El Leon" (nickname identified with
    Tererro, N. M.): 207
Ellis and Co. (Midnight, N. M.): 153
"El Muneco" (nickname identified with
    Tererro, N. M.): 207
El Nido Bar Lounge (La Ventana,
    N. M.): 136
El Nido Hotel (La Ventana, N. M.): 136
El Paso and Northeastern Railroad: 21,
    50, 81, 166, 179, 226
El Paso and Southwestern Railroad: 51,
    106, 109, 220
Elguea, Don Francisco Manuel: 189
El Real de San Francisco (Golden,
    N. M.): 100
"El Toro" (nickname identified with
    Tererro, N. M.): 207
Emporia (mine): 103
Engle, N. M.: 78, 230
Engle, R. L.: 78
Engle Station (Engle, N. M.): 79
Ensign, A.D.: 234
Ensign (ranch): 234
Enterprise Mining Co.: 59
Episcopal Church: 184
Estey City, N. M.: 81
Estey, David M.: 81
Estey Mining and Milling Co.: 81
Eswell, Joseph: 56
E-Town (Elizabethtown, N. M.): 73
Evans, Jesse: 138
Evans, M. M.: 200
Evensen, John: 195
Exchange Bank (White Oaks, N. M.):
    225
Exchange Hotel (La Belle, N. M.): 131

Extension (mine): 91

Fairview Cattle Co.: 230
Fairview Hotel (Mineral City, N. M.):
    154
Fairview (Winston, N. M.): 78, 102, 229
Fall, Albert: 125
Farley, H. S.: 207
Farmer, Mr. (identified with Nutt,
    N. M.): 163
Farr, Sheriff Edward: 131
Faulkner, Herbert: 106
Faulkner, Mrs. E. W.: 110
Faywood Hot Springs Hotel: 82
Faywood Hot Springs, N. M.: 82
Fay, J. C.: 82
Fay, Louis: 48
Fergusson, Erna (writer): 225
Fergusson, Harvey (writer): 225
Fergusson, H. B. (congressman): 225
First Missouri Regiment: 79
First Regiment of Colorado Volunteers:
    97
Fitch, J. B.: 121
Flap Jack Gulch: 99
Fleming, Colonel J. W.: 169
Fleming, Jack: 84
Fleming, N. M.: 84
Fleming, Walter: 21
Flesh, Mr. (identified with Santa Rita,
    N. M.): 189
Florida Station, N. M.: 56
Flynn, C. L.: 58
Folsom, N. M.: 4, 131
Fook, Dong: 30
Foote and Booth Store (Paschal, N. M.):
    169
Forget, George: 105
Fornoff, Captain Fred: 155
Foster, H. M.: 182
Fort Bayard, N. M.: 32, 58, 155
Fort Conrad, N. M.: 184
Fort Cummings, N. M.: 56
Fort Fillmore, N. M.: 182
Fort Otero, N. M.: 186
Fort Selden, N. M.: 32
Fort Stanton, N. M.: 32, 138, 225
Fort Union, N. M.: 10, 73
Fort Wingate, N. M.: 24, 58
Fountain, Henry: 113
Fountain, Judge Albert J.: 113
Fountain murder: 113
Fourth of July Celebration: 35, 102,
    118, 125, 149, 198, 210, 229, 234
Franciscans (religious order): 100
Franks, G. W.: 131
Fraser Mountain Copper Co.: 210
Fraser Mountain: 210
Fraser, William: 210
Freeman, C. A.: 156
Frenchie, Gantan: 225
French, Jim: 140
Frisco, N. M.: 39
Frisco Valley: 3, 58
Fritz, Emil: 138
Froelick, Herman: 74
Frost, Jack: 195
Fowler, Joe: 35
Foxworth-Galbraith Lumber Co.: 51
Fuller Hotel (Catskill, N. M.): 35

264

Gaddis, James: 48
Gage, N. M.: 42
Galisteo River: 38
Gallup American Coal Co.: 86, 94, 162
Gallup (mine): 94
Gallup, N. M.: 3, 48, 58, 86, 94, 152, 162
Galveston Co.: 48
Gamerco, N. M.: 86, 94, 162
Gardiner, James T.: 87
Gardiner Ladies Club: 87
Gardiner, N. M.: 21, 87, 220
Gardiner Reading Circle: 87
Gardiner Saloon (Gardiner, N. M.): 87
Garrett, Lyman: 217
Garrett, Pat: 217
Gavilan Canyon: 99
Gaylord, M. D.: 222
Gem Restaurant (Paschal, N. M.): 169
Georgetown Courier (newspaper): 91
Georgetown, D. C.: 91
Georgetown, N. M.: 91
Germans (nationality): 64, 167, 220
Germany, country of: 3, 167
Geronimo (Apache Chief): 4, 102, 104,
    125
Gibson, John: 94
Gibson, N. M.: 94
Gila River: 206
Gilliland, James: 113
Gillum Hotel (Catskill, N. M.): 35
Givens, Mr. (identified with Fleming,
    N. M.): 85
Glenwood, N. M.: 3, 48, 58, 104, 155
Glen-Woody Mining and Milling Co.: 96
Glen-Woody, N. M.: 96
Glorieta House (Glorieta, N. M.): 98
Glorieta, N. M.: 96, 206
Gold and Copper Deep Tunnel Mining
    and Milling Co.: 10
Gold Bullion Co.: 100
Gold Chief (mine): 102
Gold Dust, N. M.: 99
Golden Era (newspaper): 225
Golden Hydraulic Co.: 187
Golden, N. M.: 39, 199
Golden Nine (newspaper): 187
Goldenrod Club (Sugarite, N. M.): 200
Golden Treasure (mine): 174
Gold Hill: 7, 102
Gold Hill (ranch): 102
Gonzales, Juan: 138
Goodhue, Bertram G.: 214
Goodrich-Lockhart Co.: 206
Gould, Jim: 163
Government (mine): 32
Grafton Hotel (Grafton, N. M.): 102
Grafton, N. M.: 102, 230
Graham, A. J.: 210
Graham, A. R.: 82
Graham, John T.: 104
Graham (mine): 178
Graham, N. M.: 104
Grant Co.: 12, 30, 42, 82, 84, 91, 105,
    137, 163, 169, 188, 206, 213
Grant, General Ulysses S.: 100
Grant House (Shakespeare, N. M.): 196
Grants, N. M.: 192
Grant (Shakespeare, N. M.): 195
Graphic (mine): 120
Graphic (smelter): 121

Great Depression: 87, 182, 217
Greathouse and Kuch (ranch): 224
Greeley, Horace: 195
Greeley, Mr. (saloon keeper identified
    with Elizabethtown, N. M.): 73
Green, Colonel Amos: 170
Green, Richard: 39
Green River (whisky): 164
Greenwood, Chester: 2
Griffin, Frank: 30
Griffin, Private Fred: 51
Griffith, W. P.: 217
Griggs, J. Edgar: 170
Gross, Blackwell and Co. (Carthage,
    N. M.): 32
Guam, N. M.: 58
Guest, Dugan: 65
Gusdorf, Gerson: 7, 210
Guthrie, Dr. (identified with Kingston,
    N. M.): 124
Gypsum Product Co.: 8

Hachita Merchantile Co.: 106
Hachita, N. M.: 105
Hagan Mercantile Co.: 108
Hagan (mine): 107
Hagan, N. M.: 107
Hagan Power and Electric Co.: 108
Haggin, Mr. (identified with Chance
    City, N. M.): 42
Hall, John B.: 58
Hamilton (Cowles Mine): 206
Harkness, D. D.: 38
Harkness, Mrs. D. D.: 38
Harp and Shamrock (saloon): 12
Harpending and Co.: 195
Harpending, Asbury: 195
Hart, Dr. H. M.: 52
Hart, John: 32
Hart, Robert: 38
Harvey, Henry: 163
Harvey House (San Marcial, N. M.):
    184
Hatch, N. M.: 162
Hayes, Martin B.: 189
Hays and Co. (Midnight, N. M.): 153
Head, Mr. (identified with Chance City,
    N. M.): 42
Hearst, Randolph: 42
Heart's Desire (novel): 225
Heaton, N. M.: 86
Hefferman, Festus: 79
Heller, Louis: 51
Heller, Mrs. Richard F.: 24
Heller, Richard F.: 24
Helphinstine, Al: 7
Helphinstine, Amizette: 7
Hematite, N. M.: 109
Henderson, "Wall": 73
Henry Clay (mine): 196, 217
Henry, James Gordon: 198
Herberger, Joseph Antonio: 73
Hermanas, N. M.: 109
Herman, Harry: 155
Hermosa Literary Society: 110
Hermosa, N. M.: 102, 110
Hewett and Fergusson (lawyers, White
    Oaks, N. M.): 225
Hewett Block Building (White Oaks,
    N. M.): 225

Hickcock Saloon (Engle, N. M.): 79
Hicks, Mr. (identified with Pinos Altos,
    N. M.): 169
Hidalgo Co.: 49, 102, 152, 170, 195,
    198, 204, 217
Hill, Frank: 197
Hillsboro, N. M.: 10, 79, 99, 112, 124,
    132, 162, 198, 208
Hillsborough (Hillsboro, N. M.): 112
Hill, Uncle Billy: 61
Hilton, A. H.: 180
Hilton, Conrad: 180
Hilton Hotel (San Antonio, N. M.): 180
Hilton Mercantile Co.: 180
Hilton Store (San Antonio, N. M.): 180
Hilty Brothers (identified with Mineral
    City, N. M.): 154
Hindman, George: 139
Hixenbaugh, Sheriff: 21
Holder, Tom: 211
Holland, J. P. General Store (Mogollon,
    N. M.): 155
Holland, Mr. (saloon proprietor, Bloss-
    burg, N.M.): 16
Holt, Bill: 133
Holt, H. B.: 198
Homestake (mine): 224
Honeky, Mr. (identified with Tyrone,
    N. M.): 213
Honeyfield (mine): 234
Hood, Mr. H.: 169
Hoover, Herbert (President of the United
    States): 30
Hoover Hotel (Columbus, N. M.): 51
Hornet (mine): 105
Hotel Baldy (Baldy, N. M.): 10
Hotel Hachita (Hachita, N. M.): 106
Hot Springs (Truth or Consequences,
    N. M.): 79, 113
Hough, Emerson (writer): 225
Howe, R. T.: 102
Howland, Bob: 102
Hoyle, Andy: 226
Hoyle Castle (White Oaks, N. M.): 226
Hubbard, Dr. (identified with Gardiner,
    N. M.): 87
Huddgens, Will: 224
Hudson Hot Springs (Faywood Hot
    Springs, N. M.): 82
Hudson Hot Springs Hotel: 82
Hudson Hot Springs Sanitarium Co.: 82
Hudson, Richard: 82
Huen's, Restaurant (Steins, N. M.): 199
Hull, Mr. and Mrs. Samuel: 19
Humboldt Hotel (Engle, N. M.): 78
Humboldt Mining Co.: 78
Hunter, James: 85
Hurst, Sheba: 125
Huston, John: 12
Hutchason, J. S.: 120
Hyters, William: 42

Ickes, Harold L. (Secretary of Interior):
    58
Independence, Mo.: 96
Independent Order of Good Templers: 32
Indians: 3, 27, 38, 58, 99, 100, 102, 110,
    112, 125, 138, 155, 170, 171, 178, 182,
    189, 196, 198, 220
Ingersoll, Colonel Robert G.: 103

International Mining and Milling Co.: 152
Iron King (mine): 2
Iron Mountain (mining district): 61
Italians (nationality): 220
Ivanhoe (mine): 102, 103

Jack Canyon: 155
Janin, Henry: 195
Japanese (nationality): 64, 200
Japanese Hotel (Brilliant, N. M.): 21
Jarilla (Brice, N. M.): 21
Jarilla Junction (Orogrande, N. M.):
   21, 166
Jarilla Mountains: 21, 166
Jay Hawk (mine): 174
Jessie (claim): 42
Jicarilla, N. M.: 116
Jicarilla Mountains: 224
Jicarilla Street (White Oaks, N. M.):
   224
Johnson, Bill: 184
Johnson, James: 189
Johnson, Lige: 117
Johnson Mesa, N. M.: 117, 234
Johnson Park: 117
Jones, E. I.: 174
Jones, Jack: 16
Jones, Louis: 4
Jones, Mr. (Catskill teacher): 34
Jones, Myra E.: 60
Jones, Samuel S.: 170
Jones, Walter: 4
Joyla, Pascual: 184
Juanita (mine): 120

Kaiser Steel Co.: 129, 221
Kansas City, Kansas: 120
Kaseman, George: 152
Keefer, Captain (identified with
   Elizabethtown, N. M.): 73
Kellem, Billy: 102
Kelly, Andy: 120
Kelly Canyon: 121
Kelly, E. M.: 27
Kelly, John: 48
Kelly, N. M.: 120, 167
Kendall, Thomas: 84
Kennedy, Charles: 73
Kenney, Henry: 12
Kenney Store (Carthage, N. M.): 208
Kent, William: 42
Kerr and Sullivan (merchants identified
   with Blackhawk, N. M.): 12
Kerr, Barney: 12
Kerr, John: 12
Ketchum, "Black Jack" Tom: 131, 198
Ketchum, Sam: 131
Kezele, Joe: 21
"Kid Allen" (Jim Gould): 163
Kimball (mining district): 198
Kimball, N. M.: 198
King, Clarence: 195
King, Fert: 156
King (mine): 105
King, Sandy: 196
Kingston-Lake Valley Stage Line: 133
Kingston, N. M.: 124, 133, 162
Kinney, Bartley H.: 208
Kirby, A. J.: 206

Kit Carson Cornet Band: 210
Klondike (goldrush): 96
Koehler, Henry: 129
Koehler (mine): 64
Koehler, N. M.: 129
Kroenig, W. H.: 10

La Bajada Hill: 130
La Bajada Mining Co.: 130
La Bajada, N. M.: 130
La Belle Cresset (newspaper): 131
La Belle, N. M.: 131
La Belle Stage Co.: 34
La Costa, Mr. (identified with Santa
   Rita, N. M.): 189
Ladies Guild (Santa Rita, N. M.): 189
La Glorieta Pass: 96
Lake Valley, N. M.: 132, 162, 208
La Luz, N. M.: 113
La Mesa de San Marcial (San Marcial,
   N. M.): 184
Lanagan, Mr. B. E.: 42
Lantern (newspaper): 73
La Placita del Rio Bonito (Lincoln,
   N. M.): 138
La Placita (Lincoln, N. M.): 138
La Posta (Cabezon, N. M.): 24
Largo, Jesus: 138
Las Cruces, N. M.: 113, 163, 182
La Silla Grande Restaurant (Glorieta,
   N. M.): 98
Last Chance (mine): 155, 170
Las Vegas, N. M.: 73, 79, 96, 100, 133,
   154, 182, 208, 224
Laud, Rev. Joseph: 51
La Ventana, N. M.: 136
Lawrence, Major R.: 234
Lay, Elza: 4, 131
Leadville, Colo.: 38
Lee, Oliver: 113
Lee's Peak: 195
Leidendorf (Viola Mine): 170
Lemmon and Romney Store (Columbus,
   N. M.): 52
Leopold, Asa F.: 137
Leopold, N. M.: 137, 213
Levy, M. G. and Co. (Winston, N. M.):
   229
Lewisohn Family (identified with San
   Pedro, N. M.): 187
Liberty War Bonds, sale of: 220
Likes, "Pap": 12
Lincoln Co.: 8, 20, 50, 81, 116, 138,
   168, 172, 222, 224
Lincoln County Bank: 138
Lincoln County Courthouse: 141
Lincoln County Leader (newspaper): 225
Lincoln County War: 138
Lincoln, N. M.: 113, 138, 180, 222
Liner (steam drill): 207
Little Casino (White Oaks, N. M.): 226
Little Fanny (mine): 155
Little Hatchet Mountains: 105, 204
Little Italy (brothel): 156
Little Mack (mine): 224
"Little Mike" (identified with Tererro,
   N. M.): 207
Little Town by the Pretty River (Lincoln,
   N. M.): 138

Livingston Street (White Oaks, N. M.):
   224
Llewellyn (mine): 234
Lobner, Adolf: 116
Lockwood, William: 82
Logan, M. C.: 164
Log Cabin (mine): 208
Long, Joe: 116
Lookout (mine): 208
Lopez, Don Demasio: 71
Lordsburg, N. M.: 30, 102, 105, 152,
   163, 170, 195, 198, 217
Los Alamos, N. M.: 2, 13
Los Cerrillos (Cerrillos, N. M.): 38
Los Cerrillos Hills: 19
Los Cerrillos (mining district): 19
Lothian, Mr. (identified with Blackhawk,
   N. M.): 12
Love, Hugh C.: 43
Lovelady, Earl: 79
Lowe, Jim (Butch Cassidy): 4
Lowery, A. C.: 91
Lucas, Lieutenant John P.: 52
Lucas, Reverend (Catskill parson): 34
Lucero, Angelito: 172
Lucky (mine): 187
Lufkins, George W.: 132
Lukens, J.: 60
Luna Co.: 56, 109, 162
Luna Hotel (Columbus, N. M.): 51
Luna, N. M.: 51

McArthur's Saloon (Blossburg, N. M.):
   16
McBride Canyon: 118
McCain, Lieutenant William A.: 52
McCart, Sheriff (identified with
   Mogollon, N. M.): 155
McCloskey, Mr. (identified with Lincoln,
   N. M.): 139
McComas, Charlie: 171, 196
McComas, David: 170
McComas, Judge H. C.: 170, 196
McComas, Mrs. H. C.: 196
McCoy, W. D. (merchant, Allerton,
   N. M.): 2
McDermott, Mr. T. C.: 82
McDermott, P. H.: 30
McDonald, Platt (Blackhawk Mine
   Superintendent): 12
McDonald, W. C. (Governor, New
   Mexico): 225
McGinnis, William H. (Elza Lay): 4
McGregor (mine): 91
McIntyre, Alex: 10
McIntyre, W. P.: 10
McKean, Rev.: 200
McKenna, James: 125
McKinley Co.: 3, 48, 58, 86, 94, 152,
   162
McKinley (mine): 155
McLaughlin, Catherine: 200
McNue, William: 113
McNulty (mine): 91
McSween, Alexander A.: 138
McSween, Susan: 138
Madden and Maxwell Saloon (Golden,
   N. M.): 100
Maddix, Mr. (magistrate at Carbonate-
   ville, N. M.): 27

266

Madrid Band: 149
Madrid Canyon: 223
Madrid Employees Club: 148
Madrid Miners (baseball team): 149
Madrid, N. M.: 2, 32, 39, 148, 223
Magdelena (mining district): 120
Magdelena Mountains: 120
Magdalena, N. M.: 61, 121, 167, 175, 178
Magruder, George: 91
Mahoney, John J. (U.S. Consul to Algiers): 19
Mallette, George: 174
Mallette, Orin: 174
Mallette, Vet: 174
Malone, John B.: 152
Malone, N. M.: 152
Mammoth Mining Co.: 100
Mangas Colorados (Apache Chief): 170, 189
Marshall, General Frank: 169
Martinez, Dolores: 166
Martinez, Juan: 172
Masonic Lodge: 39
Mastin, Thomas: 169
Mastin, Virgil: 169
"Matt France" (stagecoach): 12
Maud S. (mine): 155
Maxwell Land Grant: 34, 63, 129, 222
Maxwell, Lucien B.: 222
Maxwell, Virginia: 222
Mayberry Hotel (Bonito, N. M.): 20
Mayberry, W. T. (family): 20
Mayers, Mrs. (identified with Winston, N. M.): 229
Memphis (claim): 153
Mentmore, N. M.: 152
Meras, Nica: 138
Mescalero Apache Indians: 21, 138
Mesilla, N. M.: 170
Mes, Jesus: 138
Mes, Juan: 138
Mes, Juanito: 138
Mes, Pas: 138
Messenis, Mrs. C. G.: 189
Metcalf, John: 213
Metcalf, Robert: 213
Methodist Church: 10, 16, 39, 82, 184
Methodist Episcopal Church: 13, 87, 121
Mexicans (nationality): 56, 84, 100, 116, 156, 170, 182, 217
Mexican Springs (Shakespeare, N. M.): 195
Mexico, country of: 51, 64, 70, 169
Mexican War: 100
Middleton, John: 139
Midnight (claim): 153
Midnight (mine): 153
Midnight, N. M.: 153
Midway Theatre (Mogollon, N. M.): 156
Mikesell, M. B.: 84
Miller, Charles DeWitt: 52
Miller Gulch: 223
Miller, Mr. (identified with Blackhawk N. M.): 12
Mimbres Apaches: 189
Mimbres Mining and Reduction Co.: 91
Mimbres Mountains: 112
Mimbres River: 91, 112
Mina-del-Tierra (mine): 26, 38

Mineral City, N. M.: 154
Mineral Creek: 43, 48, 58
Miners Home (Blackhawk, N. M.): 12
Mitchell, John T.: 206
Mitchell, Mr. (identified with Shandon, N. M.): 198
Modoc (mine): 154
Modoc, N. M.: 154
Mogollon, Don Juan Ignacio Flores: 155
Mogollon Mercantile Co.: 156
Mogollon Mountains: 48, 58, 155
Mogollon, N. M.: 155
Mogollon Stage Line: 155
Montoya Grant: 32
Moore, John: 73
Moore, William: 10
Mora Co.: 73
Moreno Creek: 109
Moreno Valley: 73, 169
Moreno Water and Mining Co.: 73
Morgan, Dr. (identified with Johnson Mesa, N. M.): 118
Morgan, Old Man (identified with Albemarle, N. M.): 2
Morris, Harvey: 140
Morris (mine): 152
Morton, George: 139
Mosely, Perrow G.: 51
Mountain States Telephone Co. (Santa Rita, N. M.): 189
Mount Chalchihuitl: 26, 38
Mulholland, Gus: 3
Muralter, Julius: 39
Murphy, Lawrence G.: 138
Murphy, L. G. and Co.: 138
Murphy Store (Lincoln, N. M.): 138
Murphy, Thomas: 113
Mutz Hotel (Elizabethtown, N. M.): 74
"My House of Old Things" (Museum in Ancho, N. M.): 8
Mystic Lode (mine): 10

Nadock, Annie: 131
Nadock Hotel (La Belle, N. M.): 131
Nadock, Mr. and Mrs. (identified with La Belle, N. M.): 131
Naiad Queen (mine): 91
Nana (Apache Chief): 104
Nannie Baird (mine): 21
National Guard: 86
National Hotel (Georgetown, N. M.): 91
National Iron and Metal Co.: 65
National Mail and Transportation Co.: 195
National Miners Union: 86
Navaho Indians: 24, 136
Navajo (mine): 162
Navajo, N. M.: 162
Nelson, C.: 176
Nelson, Martin: 20
New Brilliant (Swastika, N. M.): 202
New Mexico Fuel and Iron Co.: 107
New Mexico Fuel Co.: 50
New Mexico Fuel Company Hospital: 50
New Mexico Interpreter (newspaper): 225
New Mexico Midland Railroad: 32, 208
New Mexico Mining Co.: 71, 195
New Mexico Sales Co.: 50
New Mexico Territorial Legislature: 138

New Mexico Territory: 97
New Organ (Organ, N. M.): 167
New Placer (mines): 100
New Placers (San Pedro, N. M.): 71
News (newspaper): 154
Newton Co. (sawmill): 34
Nicoles, Mrs. (identified with Blackhawk, N. M.): 12
Nights (ranch): 171
Ninth Cavalry: 138
Nogal, N. M.: 168, 222
Noonday (mine): 178
North American (continent): 206
Northern Mexican and Pacific Railroad: 51
North Homestake (mine): 224
Norton, A. H.: 116
Nutt, N. M.: 133, 162
Nutt Station (Nutt, N. M.): 162

Oak Grove, N. M.: 163
Occidental (mine): 102
Ocean Wave (mine): 110
O'Connell, James: 85
O'Folliard, Tom: 140
O'Hara, Ned: 73
Old Abe (mine): 224
Old Abe Eagle (newspaper): 32, 225
Old Boss (mine): 61
Old Coal Mine Museum: 148
Old Gardiner (mine): 87
"Old Hutch" (J. S. Hutchason): 120
Old Man (mine): 84
Old Organ (Organ, N. M.): 163
Old Placers (Dolores, N. M.): 70, 100
Old Taylor (whisky): 164
Old Town (San Marcial, N. M.): 184
"Old Perk" (S. M. Perkins): 21
O'Neil, "Pony": 73
Opera House (Sugarite, N. M.): 200
Opportunity (mine): 112
Orange Hotel (Hagan, N. M.): 108
Orchard, J. W.: 133
Organ Mountains: 79, 154, 182
Organ, N. M.: 154, 163, 182
Oro Dredging Co.: 74
Orogrande, N. M.: 166
Oro Grande Times (newspaper): 166
Orpheum Theatre (Santa Rita, N. M.): 189
Orr, Ed: 56
Ortiz, Jose Francisco: 71
Ortiz (mine): 71
Ortiz Mountain: 70, 81, 100
Oscura Mountains: 81
Oscura Station, N. M.: 81
Otero Co.: 21, 166, 179, 220
Otero County Clerk (office): 179
Otero, Governor Miguel A.: 166, 186
Otero, N. M.: 166
Otero Optic (newspaper): 166
Owasso, Mich.: 81
Owen Bros' Billiards (Santa Rita, N. M.): 189

Pacific (mine): 155, 169
Padilla, Florentino: 136
Page Brothers (identified with College, N. M.): 58
Palace Hotel (Cerrillos, N. M.): 39

Palace Saloon (Park City, N. M.): 167
Palmer, Dr. F.: 39
Palomas Chief (mine): 110
Palomas, Chihuahua: 51
Pancho Villa Museum: 53
Pancho Villa State Park: 53
Park City, N. M.: 120, 167
Park City Saloon: 167
Park City Store: 167
Parker, Judge (identified with Shandon, N. M.): 198
Parker, T. S. (hospital): 214
Parke, Tom: 102
Parlor Saloon (Fleming, N. M.): 85
Parsons Hotel (Parsons, N. M.): 168
Parsons, N. M.: 168
Parsons, R. C.: 168
Paschal Hotel (Paschal, N. M.): 169
Paschal, N. M.: 169
Patching, W. A.: 3
Pattie, James: 189
Pattie, Sylvester: 189
Paxton, Charles: 58
Pecos (mine): 206
Pecos, N. M.: 206
Pecos River: 98, 138
Pedro Armandaris Land Grant: 184
Pelican (mine): 110
Peloncillo Mountains: 198
Penrose (Fleming, N. M.): 84
Peppin, George W.: 140
Percha Bank (Kingston, N. M.): 125
Perea, N. M.: 58
Perkins, J. D.: 177
Perkins, S. M.: 21
Perry, Mr. (identified with Perryville, N. M.): 169
Perryville, N. M.: 169
Pershing, Brigadier General John J.: 53
Pershing's Punitive Expedition: 53
Pflueger, John: 24
Phelps Dodge Co.: 8, 63, 137, 213, 217
Phelps Dodge Merchantile Co.: 214
Phillips, Mr. (merchant identified with Blackhawk, N. M.): 12
Philmont Boy Scout Ranch: 10
Pick, Emil: 207
Pick, Henry: 207
Pick Store (Tererro, N. M.): 207
Pigeon's (ranch): 96
Pilar, N. M.: 96
Pino Canyon: 2
Pinos Altos Mining Co.: 170
Pinos Altos, N. M.: 169
Pinos Altos Town Co.: 170
Pioneer Boarding House (Gold Hill, N. M.): 102
Pioneer Stage Line: 43
Pipe Line Draw: 214
Pitcher, Frank: 112
Pittsburg of the West (Blossburg, N. M.): 16
Placer Street (White Oaks, N. M.): 224
Pleasanton, N. M.: 4
Plemmons, J. C.: 110
Pocahontas, N. M.: 198
Porter, S. S.: 229
Potter, Del: 206
Poverty Flat (Shakespeare, N. M.): 196
Presbyterian Church: 82, 121, 156, 200

Presbyterian Medical Missionary: 208
Presbyterian Mission School: 208
Presbyterians: 34
Prewitt, N. M.: 60, 69, 192
Pridemore and Howe Auto Line: 156
Probert, Clarence: 211
Protestant Union Church: 64
P.T.A. (Parent Teachers Association): 202
Pueblo Revolt: 130
Pye, Harry: 42, 229
Pye (lode): 42
Pyramid Mining and Milling Co.: 170
Pyramid Mountains: 195
Pyramid, N. M.: 170
Pyramid Peak: 170

Quaker City (Union ship): 79
Quarles, George G.: 229
Queen City Copper Co.: 163
Questa, N. M.: 174

Rabenton, N. M.: 172
Ralston (mining district): 195
Ralston (Shakespeare, N. M.): 195
Ralston, William C.: 195
Ransom, Sam: 217
Raton Coal and Coking Co.: 16, 87
Raton Coal and Coke Company Hospital: 87
Raton Country Club: 87
Raton Museum: 118
Raton, N. M.: 16, 21, 34, 50, 63, 87, 117, 129, 166, 182, 200, 202, 220, 234
Rattlesnake (mine): 112
Raventon (Rabenton, N. M.): 172
Ready Pay (mine): 112
Real de Dolores (Dolores, N. M.): 70
Reardon, Jack: 27
Redbird (mine): 104
Red Cross Association: 185, 220
Red River: 73
Red River News (newspaper): 174
Red River, N. M.: 109, 131, 153, 174
Red River Pass: 109
Red River Prospector (newspaper): 174
Red River Record (newspaper): 174
Red River Sun (newspaper): 174
Red Wave (mine): 178
Reekie, Dr. James: 43
Regulators (vigilantes): 139
Reiling, H. J.: 74
Remsberg's Store: 74
Retort (newspaper): 100
Reynolds, Joseph: 170
Rice, John M.: 168
Richardson, J. W. "Jack": 178
Richardson, Mrs. J. W.: 178
Riley, N. M.: 175
Rincon, N. M.: 198
Rinehart, Mary Roberts: 168
Río Bonito: 138
Río Feliz: 138
Río Feliz (ranch): 139
Río Grande: 32, 79, 96, 184, 198
Río Grande Eastern Railroad: 108
Río Grande Press: 98
Río Hondo: 138, 210
Río Hondo Canyon: 7
Río Hondo Placer Co.: 7

Río Pecos: 140
Río Peñasco: 138
Río Puerco: 24, 136
Río Salado: 175
Río Tularosa: 139
Rip Van Winkle (mine): 224
Roberts, Andrew "Buckshot": 139
Roberts, John: 3
Robinson, N. M.: 102, 177
Rock House Ranch (Cerrillos, N. M.): 34
Rocky Mountain News (newspaper): 13
Rocky Mountains: 96
Rogers, Alex: 78
Rogers, Mrs. D. C.: 110
Rogers' Ranch (Engle, N. M.): 78
Rogers Store (Engle, N. M.): 78
Romero, Eugenio: 182
Romero, Vicente: 141
Roosevelt, F. D. (President of the United States): 58
Rose (mine): 12
Rosedale (mine): 178, 184
Rosedale, N. M.: 178
Ross, Miss (identified with Leopold, N. M.): 137
Ross, Mr. (identified with Fleming, N. M.): 84
Roswell, N. M.: 226
Rothschild, Baron: 195
Roughing It (book): 125
Route, John L. (Governor of Colorado): 7
Royal Dye Works (San Marcial, N. M.): 185
Ruidoso, N. M.: 20
Russell, Charles: 229
Russell, Lillian: 125
Russell, Miss Nellie: 102
Ryan, Paddy: 184

Sacramento City, N. M.: 179
Sacramento Valley Irrigation Co.: 179
Sacramento Mountains: 220
Sacramento River: 166
Saint Francis Catholic Church: 155
Saint Jerome (feast day): 183
Saint John Methodist Episcopal Church: 117
Saint Louis (mine): 169
Saint Louis, Rocky Mountain and Pacific Co.: 21, 129, 200, 202, 220
Saint Louis, Rocky Mountain and Pacific Railroad: 50, 87
Saint Paul (feast day): 183
San Antonio Coal Co.: 208
San Antonio Mission: 180
San Antonio, N. M.: 32, 180
San Augustine: 182
Sanchez, Potfitio: 176
Sanda Mountains: 186
San Diego Exposition: 214
Sandoval Co.: 2, 13, 24, 107, 136, 193
Sandoval, Paul: 21
Sands, Lieutenant (identified with Malone, N. M.): 152
Sanford, Henry: 49
San Francisco (church): 100
San Geronimo, N. M.: 182
San Marcial Bee (newspaper): 184

268

San Marcial Land and Improvement Co.: 184

San Marcial, N. M.: 184

San Marcial Reporter (newspaper): 185

San Marcial Skating Rink: 184

San Marcial Standard (newspaper): 185

San Mateo Mountains: 178, 184

San Miguel Co.: 154, 182, 206, 208

San Pedro and Canon del Agua Co.: 186

San Pedro Hotel: 187

San Pedro Land Grant: 186

San Pedro Mining Co.: 100

San Pedro Mountains: 71, 100

San Pedro, N. M.: 39, 186

San Pedro (smelter): 187

San Patricio, N. M.: 140

Sansom, J. W.: 229

Santa Fe Co.: 19, 26, 32, 38, 70, 96, 100, 130, 148, 186, 223

Santa Fe Eating House and Dining Car System (San Marcial, N. M.): 185

Santa Fe Fire Department: 96

Santa Fe Gold and Copper Co.: 187

Santa Fe, N. M.: 19, 24, 26, 27, 38, 70, 73, 96, 130, 148, 207

Santa Fe Railroad (Atchison, Topeka and Santa Fe Railroad): 16, 32, 87, 117, 148, 177, 223

Santa Fe, Raton and Eastern Railroad: 234

Santa Fe Ring: 138

Santa Fe River: 130

Santa Fe, San Juan and Northern Railroad: 136

Santa Fe Trail: 96, 130

Santa Rita Catholic Church: 175

Santa Rita del Cobre (Santa Rita, N. M.): 189

Santa Rita (feast day): 175

Santa Rita Massacre: 189

Santa Rita, N. M.: 188

Santa Rita Presidio: 189

Santa Rita (Riley, N. M.): 176

Santa Rita Steam Laundry: 189

Santa Rita Store (Santa Rita, N. M.): 189

Santa Rosalia Grant: 71

Satisfaction (mine): 91

Savage, Ed (mine boss, Blossburg, N. M.): 16

Sawyer, N. M.: 192

Sayles, J. K. (merchant, Allerton, N. M.): 2

Seal Package (mine): 178

Second Texas Cavalry: 79

Senorito, N. M.: 193

Separ Station, N. M.: 105

Seventh Cavalry: 53

Seven Day Adventist: 34

Shaft (newspaper): 124

Shakespeare Guard: 196

Shakespeare Mining Co.: 195

Shakespeare, N. M.: 195

Shamrock (Valmont, N. M.): 220

Shandon, N. M.: 198

Shannon, P. Carick: 13

Shapley, B. A. (dentist, White Oaks, N. M.): 225

Sheddon, Jack: 124

Sheppard, E. D. and Co.: 234

Sheridan, Mr. (identified with Clairmont, N. M.): 48

Sherwin-Williams Paint Co.: 121

Shoemaker, Charley: 48

Shoshone (mine): 7

Shu, Lee: 30

Shuler, Dr. James: 16

Sibley, General Henry H.: 97

Sierra Co.: 10, 42, 78, 99, 102, 110, 112, 124, 132, 198, 208, 229

Sierra County Advocate (newspaper): 113, 124

Sierra Del Oro (Ortiz Mine): 71

Sierra Grande Co.: 133

Sierra Madres: 189

Silva, Bernardo: 198

Silva Gulch: 198

Silver Bar (mine): 59

Silver Brick (newspaper): 91

Silver Cell (mine): 170

Silver City Enterprise (newspaper): 199, 206

Silver City, N. M.: 12, 56, 84, 91, 102, 137, 155, 163, 169, 171, 188, 206, 213

Silver Creek: 155

Silver Lode Mining Co.: 98

Silver Queen Museum: 155

Sinclair, H. M.: 133

Siqueiros, Mr. (identified with Santa Rita, N. M.): 189

Sixteenth Infantry: 53

Sixth Infantry: 53

Slack, John: 195

Sloan (mine): 107

Sloan, Mr. (identified with Blackhawk, N. M.): 12

Slocum, Colonel Herbert J.: 51

Slough, Colonel John P.: 97

Smelter Saloon (Park City, N. M.): 167

Smith, Dr. (identified with Tererro, N. M.): 207

Smith, Jitney Jack: 79

Smith, Morris: 3

Smith, Paschal R.: 169

Smith's Store (Blossburg, N. M.): 16

Smyth's Mercantile Store (Shakespeare, N. M.): 196

Snake Gulch: 112

Snively, Colonel (identified with Pinos Altos, N. M.): 169

Socorro, Co.: 32, 61, 120, 167, 175, 177, 178, 180, 184, 208

Socorro, N. M.: 32, 120, 167, 180, 184, 208

Solitaire (mine): 124

Sonora, state of: 70

Southern Baptist Assembly: 98

Southern Hotel (Catskill, N. M.): 35

Southern Hotel (La Belle, N. M.): 131

Southern Pacific Railroad: 20, 42, 197, 198, 217

Southern Pacific Sunset Limited: 198

South Homestake (mine): 224

Southwestern Mercantile Co. (Coalora, N. M.): 50

Southwestern Milling and Electric Co.: 185

Southwestern Smelter and Refining Co.: 166

Southwestern Stage Co.: 78, 102

Spaniards (nationality): 38, 172, 189

Spaulding, A. J.: 83

Spear (ranch): 175

Sperry (mine): 234

Springer, N. M.: 10, 50, 74

Springfield (rifle): 52

Stag Canyon (mine): 63

"Steamboat" (Dolores Martinez): 166

Steeple Rock (Carlisle mining district): 30

Stein, Captain (identified with Steins, N. M.): 198

Steins, N. M.: 198

Steins Pass: 198

Stevenson-Bennett (mine): 164, 182

Stephenson, Hugh: 182

Stinson, Joseph: 73

Stitzel, Dave: 112

Stratford Hotel (Shakespeare, N. M.): 196

Stubblefield, Robert: 3

Studebaker, Mr. (identified with Parsons, N. M.): 168

Studebaker (wagons): 168

Sugarite (Chicorica) Canyon: 200, 234

Sugarite, N. M.: 200

Superior Coal Co.: 234

Supreme Court, of New Mexico Territory: 223

Sullivan, John: 12

Sullivan, Mr. (identified with Blackhawk, N. M.): 12

Sullivan, Mr. (identified with Carbonateville, N. M.): 27

Swastika Fuel Co.: 202

Swastika, N. M.: 21, 202

Sweet, Mr. (identified with Santa Rita, N. M.): 189

Swisshelm, John: 169

Sycamore Canyon: 59

Sycamore Creek: 59

Sylvanite Merchantile Store (Sylvanite, N. M.): 204

Sylvanite, N. M.: 204

Talbert, E. H.: 116

Taos, Co.: 7, 96, 131, 174

Taos, N. M.: 7, 73, 96, 174, 210

Taylor, James: 230

Taylor, Mr. (identified with Cooks Peak, N. M.): 56

Taylor, Will E.: 230

Teapot Dome Scandal: 125

Tecolote River: 154

Tecumseh (mine): 206

Telegraph (mining district): 206

Telegraph, N. M.: 206

Tenth Cavalry: 53

Tererro, N. M.: 206

Territorial Court: 27

Texas Cavalry: 97

Thanksgiving Day: 63

Thirteenth Cavalry: 51, 53

Thirty-Fourth Indiana Regiment: 79

Thompson, F. D.: 60

Thompson, Mr. (constable at Carbonateville, N. M.): 27

Thomas, Oliver: 138

Thompson Saloon (Engle, N. M.): 79

Thornton, N. M.: 3

Tierra Blanca, N. M.: 208
Tiffany and Co.: 195
Tijeras, N. M.: 107
Tinan, P. (merchant, Allerton, N. M.): 2
Tokay, N. M.: 208
Tompkins, Major Frank: 53
Tongue Clay Products: 108
Toribio (Apache Indian): 4
Torpedo (mine): 164
"Torreon" (fort): 138
Trementina Creek: 208
Trementina, N. M.: 208
Tres Hermanas Mountains: 110
Tri-Bullion Co.: 121
Trigg, Mrs. Nellie: 39
Trujillo Creek: 208
Trujillo Gulch: 198
Truth or Consequences, N. M.: 42, 78, 79, 102, 110, 112, 113, 198, 229
Tucson Mountains: 222
Tucumcari, N. M.: 63
Tuerto, N. M.: 100
Tularosa, N. M.: 79
Tunstall and McSween Store (Lincoln, N. M.): 139
Tunstall, John H. and Co.: 138
Tunstall, John H.: 138
Turner, District Attorney (identified with Shandon, N. M.): 198
Turner (mine): 234
Turner, Mr. (prospector identified with Cooney, N. M.): 59
Turquesa (Carbonateville, N. M.): 26
Turquoise City (Carbonateville, N. M.): 26, 213
Twain, Mark: 125
Twining, Albert C.: 210
Twining, N. M.: 7, 210
Twomey, Mr. (identified with Blackhawk, N. M.): 12
Tyrone, N. M.: 137, 213
Tyrone Union Church: 214

Una De Gato Arroyo: 107
Uncle Sam (mine): 91
Union Army: 97
Unita Mountains: 195
United Mine Workers: 86
United States Government: 79
Uptegrove, N.: 102
U. S. Army: 32, 73, 186
U. S. Bureau of Mines: 86
U. S. Forest Service: 174
Ute Indian: 10

Vail, Mr. (identified with Fleming, N. M.): 85
Valedon, N. M.: 197, 217
Valencia Co.: 60, 69, 192
Valle, Alexander: 96
Valmont, N. M.: 220

Valverde Copper Co.: 169
Van Hall, Victor: 217
Van Houten, N. M.: 129, 220
Van Houten, S.: 87, 220
Van Patten, Eugene: 198
Van Roush, Mr. (identified with Dawson, N. M.): 65
Vargas, Governor Don Diego de: 130
Varnish, Madam (identified with White Oaks, N. M.): 225
Venus (Viola Mine): 170
Vera Cruz (mine): 222
Vera Cruz, N. M.: 222
Vermejo River: 50, 63
Victorio (Apache Chief): 4, 58, 99, 125, 155
Victorio (Chance City, N. M.): 42
Victorio Hotel (Kingston, N. M.): 125
Victorio Mountains: 42
Victorio Theatre (Valedon, N. M.): 217
Victor Land and Cattle Co.: 49
Villa, Pancho: 51, 53
Villistas: 51
Vincent, William A.: 186
Viola (mine): 170
Virginia City, N. M.: 10, 222
Viscarra, Billy: 164

Waddingham, Wilson: 184
Wagstaff, George: 16
Waldo Gulch: 223
Waldo, Judge Henry L.: 223
Waldo, N. M.: 39, 148, 223
Walker, Charles: 184
Walker, Walton: 52
Wallace, Lew (Governor of New Mexico Territory): 27, 141
Wallace, N. M.: 100
Wall Street (brokerage center): 234
Wardell, M. (Physician, White Oaks, N. M.): 225
Washington, Dr. T. O.: 166
Waterbury Co.: 174
Weames, John: 49
Webb, Colonel R. W.: 100, 186
Weems, John D.: 198
Wells Fargo Express Co.: 39, 50, 110, 180
Wells, George: 112
Western New Mexico Townsite Co.: 51
Western Union Telegraph Co.: 34, 39, 180
Westoby, Ed: 174
Wheeler, Mr. (identified with Cooks Peak, N. M.): 56
White, Bill: 184
White, Mr. (prospector identified with Council Rock, N. M.): 61
White Oaks Avenue (White Oaks, N. M.): 224
White Oaks, N. M.: 32, 180, 224

White Oaks Spring: 224
White Sands Missile Range: 81, 167
White, Scott: 198
Whitewater Canyon: 3, 104
Whitewater Creek: 104
Whitewater (Graham, N. M.): 104
Wicks Gulch: 112
Widenmann, Robert: 139
Wild Bunch (Butch Cassidy's Gang): 4, 104
Wilder, Bill: 34
Wilder (lumber mill): 34
Willcox, Mr. (identified with Alam, N. M.): 4
Williams, Bob: 199
Williams, Captain George: 52
Willow Creek: 10, 73, 222
Willow (Van Houten, N. M.): 220
Wilson, George: 224
Winchesters (rifles): 156
Winslow and Sons Meat Market (Valedon, N. M.): 217
Winston, F. H. and Co.: 102
Winston, Frank H.: 230
Winston, N. M.: 78, 102, 177, 229
Winters, Jack: 224
Women's Christian Temperance Union: 34
Woodbury (Allerton, N. M.): 2
Woodbury (mill): 2
Woodbury, R. W.: 2
Woods, Dr. (Lordsburg physician): 30
Woods, Henry: 2
Woods, John: 85
Woods, Mr. (Sheriff identified with Cooks Peak, N. M.): 56
Woody, W. M.: 96
World War I: 118, 156, 174, 187, 202, 214, 220, 234
World War II: 22, 74, 87, 98, 149, 156, 172, 199, 202, 209, 220
Wortley Hotel (Lincoln, N. M.): 140
Wright, Thomas: 187
W. S. (ranch): 4

Yankee Amusement Hall: 234
Yankee Fuel Co.: 234
Yankee Mercantile Co.: 234
Yankee, N. M.: 234
Yellow Jacket (mine): 196
Yellowstone (whisky): 164
Young, Brigham: 210
Young, Jesse: 210
Yue, Dong: 30

Zamora, Francisco: 141
Zimmerman, Martin: 184
Zuniga, Fray Garcia de Francisco de: 180
Zuni Mountain Railroad: 192
Zuni Mountains: 192